JUREMA'S CHILDREN IN THE
FOREST OF SPIRITS

Dedication

This book is dedicated to:
Adalberto P. Mota, my father,
Pedrito Santana and F. Bruce Lamb
in memoriam;
Francisco Suira, in gratitude;
Silvia Helena, my daughter.

JUREMA'S CHILDREN IN THE FOREST OF SPIRITS

Healing and ritual among two Brazilian indigenous groups

CLARICE NOVAES da MOTA

INTERMEDIATE TECHNOLOGY PUBLICATIONS 1997

Intermediate Technology Publications
103–105 Southampton Row, London WC1B 4HH, UK

A CIP catalogue record for this book is available
from the British Library

ISBN 1 85339 402 5

Typeset by J&L Composition Ltd, Filey, North Yorkshire
Printed in the UK by SRP Exeter

Contents

Acknowledgements

The research that gave origin to this work was funded by: Conselho Nacional de Pesquisas e Tecnologia (CNPq), Brazil; Sally Butler Scholarship, Association of Business and Professional Women, Washington, D.C., USA; and the Graduate School Summer Scholarship, University of Austin at Texas, USA.

My gratitude to these institutions as their financial support enabled me to do fieldwork. The writing was funded by CAPES, Ministry of Education, Brazil, and by CNPq, Brazil. I am indebted to several people who read parts of this work and gave me suggestions, especially Dr. F. Bruce Lamb, of Santa Fe, New Mexico and Dr. Brent Berlin, of the University of California at Berkeley. Their work has always been very inspiring to me: their abundant knowledge of South American flora as well as indigenous medical practices was proof that, with persistence and patience, one can accomplish one's purpose and meaning in life.

Parts of this work appeared in the following publications: Posey, D.A. and Overal, W.L, (eds.) *Ethnobiology: Implications and Applications*, First International Congress of Ethnobiology, Volume 2, MPEG, Belem, Brazil, 1988; Proteus, Columbus Quincentennial, 9:1, Shippensburg U., Pa, 1992.

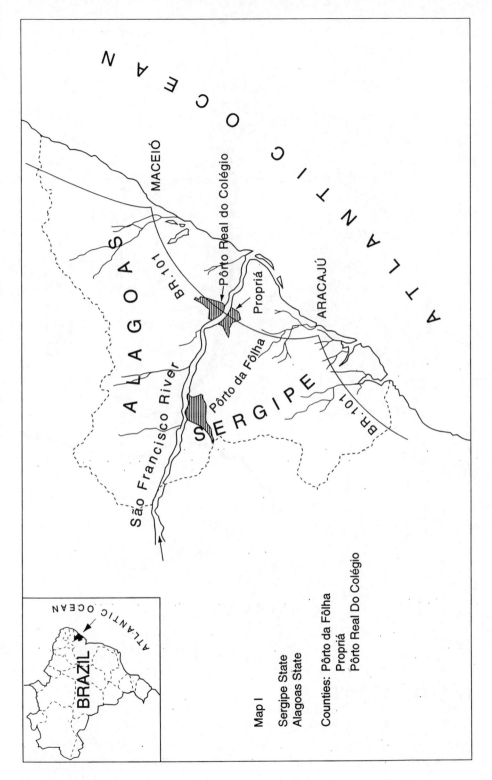

ATLANTIC OCEAN

MACEIÓ

ALAGOAS

BR.101

Pôrto Real do Colégio

Propriá

São Francisco River

Pôrto da Fôlha

SERGIPE

ARACAJÚ

BR.101

ATLANTIC OCEAN

BRAZIL

Map I

Sergipe State
Alagoas State

Counties: Pôrto da Fôlha
Propriá
Pôrto Real Do Colégio

Map 1

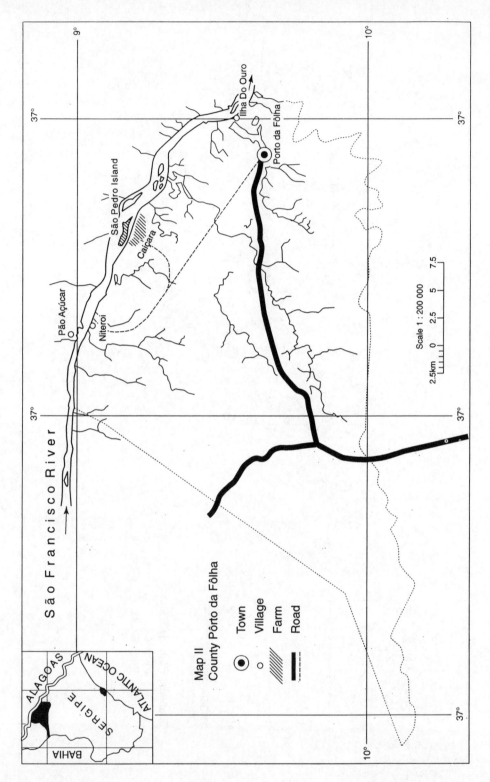

Map 2

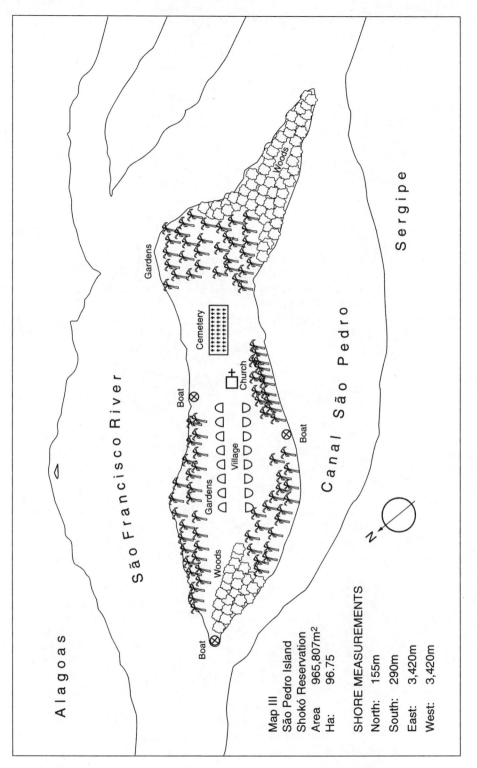

Alagoas

São Francisco River

Boat ⊗

Woods

Gardens

Village

Church

Cemetery

Gardens

Woods

Boat ⊗

Boat ⊗

Canal São Pedro

Sergipe

N

Map III
São Pedro Island
Shokó Reservation
Area   965,807m²
Ha: 96.75

SHORE MEASUREMENTS

North: 155m
South: 290m
East: 3,420m
West: 3,420m

Note: map drawn by author; measurements by FUNAI's agricultural surveyors

Map 3

Introduction

'Hoja para poder hablar
  el habla de las Fuerzas.
Hoja para curar
  alejando el hechizo
Hoja para sentirse
  uno con los otros
Hoja para recordar
  la palabra
que viene con la sangre
  que viene de tan lejos
  y es tan honda.'

'Leaf that enables one to speak
  the discourse of the Powers.
Leaf that heals
  warding off the evil
Leaf to make one feel
  together with the others
Leaf to recall the word
  that comes with our blood
that comes from so far away
  and is so deep.'

Muinane people, Museu del Oro, Colombia (author's translation)

Part 1: Meanings and objectives

WHEN THE SÃO FRANCISCO river turns sharply in the east direction, thus changing its northern destination, it soon becomes the boundary between the *sertões*[1] of Sergipe and Alagoas, the two smallest states of the Northeast region of Brazil. The river has a special significance in the area because of the severe droughts that periodically affect its vegetation. Thus the São Francisco is the solace and hope for the people who live at or near its margins. In the last three decades extensive poverty, partially caused by these inhospitable climatic conditions, has created constant migratory flows of the drought-stricken population to the southern states and urban centres all over Brazil. Thereafter, the Northeast region has been primarily represented in Brazilian popular imagination as the home of small landowners and impoverished sharecroppers, known as *sertanejos nordestinos*[2]. What very few people know, or even imagine, is that among these *sertanejos* there are communities still identified as indigenous tribes, or the descendants of native pre-European Conquest peoples.

Two of these contemporary Brazilian indigenous groups are the Shoko and the Kariri-Shoko, who are the subjects of this book. They live respectively in Sergipe and Alagoas states, both located along the São Francisco river, in areas that, due to the type of vegetation and climate, are known as the *Agreste* or *Zona da Mata*[3].

Their stories are presented mainly because they are the last remnants of the peoples who populated those coastal forests at the time of European invasion in the 16th century. Moreover, due to the patterns of colonization, either past or present, they have demonstrated an indomitable will to remain as 'natives' and thus have struggled continuously and valiantly to retain at least some shreds of their past lifestyle, beliefs, knowledge and traditions.

I met them while doing research for my PhD in anthropology. I have been fortunate in that I actually enjoy what I do: the study of old documents, fieldwork and the analysis of the data collected. Meanwhile I always have a glorious time. The difficulty was in how I was going to impart the experience I had and what I learned in the field to other people who, unlike myself, had not had the good fortune of being in the presence of those selected for my study. Writing the present work is a way to repay not only the time the Shoko and Kariri-Shoko peoples spent with me, but also the knowledge they shared with me, so kindly and generously.

Most writers, especially social scientists, feel indebted to the people they 'study'. And I am, of course, no exception. It cannot be any other way.

Whether you like the experience of field work or hate it, or feel connected to, or alienated from the people you have disturbed for so long with your very presence, you inevitably end up making some sort of alliance with them. Sometimes, or most of the time, such alliances go unbeknown to the interested parties or are not explicitly talked about. But, deep down, whether spoken or not, it is there: waiting for one's innermost revelation, like in a dream, or pouncing upon one's spirit like a burst of sunshine. And then one is irremediably committed, against one's very training and best intentions, fighting whatever is left of one's 'scientific neutrality'. One then becomes – not 'one' – but a multitude, someone who has just gone through the joys and the sadness of living within another mystery also known as humankind or, better yet, human-kindness. All the while, as one tries to show the special nature, the uniqueness of such an experience, one perhaps finds – not too soon and never too late – that what has been shared is too much for spoken or written words.

Therefore, like many others, I owe it to my 'informants' to attempt to speak for them and to tell their stories, as they told them to me and as I understood them.

My intention here is not only to present stories and make an ethnography of their present life-styles. My immediate objective is to identify their relationship to the botanical resources of the area regarding their medical systems. The focus is on how they utilize botanical resources for medicines, thus selecting and recognizing certain species among what is available in the local vegetation. Therefore, the purpose of this study is to compare their systems of ethnobotanical knowledge, as such systems relate to their medical and magical practices, and to the tribes' daily struggles to retain an identity as indigenous peoples. In other words, how cognitive and belief systems – the utilization and cognition of plant species for medicines and medical practices – are related to their systems of ethnic identification. I examine their relationships to land and nature, their daily and ritualistic forms of resource management, and finally the ideologies that underline and justify their actions. In sum, the study focuses on their native skills as managers of the natural environment and producers of plant medicines, which are part of their survival strategies.

To retain their lands and what they consider as their traditional culture, the Kariri-Shoko from Alagoas have developed a unique relationship with a magical and medical ritual complex, utilizing botanical species as mediators. However, in order to survive, both groups have made extensive use of an ideology of ancestry. This is an ethnic ideology producing ethnic categories and classifiers within the context of interethnic relations. It is through this all-embracing ideology of ancestry that each group has constructed a theory of human existence and of the cosmos, claiming their rights as 'Indians'[4]. According to the perception supported by this ideology, they are 'Indians' because they have inherited rituals, performances, knowledge and use of the environment, and medical practices from their native ancestors, the ones who form their 'roots' and 'trunks'.

The Kariri-Shoko perceive plants as symbols of their ancestors, literally the roots and trunks in the 'tree of life,'[5] or their origins. They interpret the natural habitat as if it were a history book, and the forest as a place where their ethnohistory has been imprinted. One has to be 'forest-literate' in Kariri symbolic language in order to decipher sounds and meanings, because plants have been imbued with symbolic meaning. Cultural categories of botanical entities are consistent with biological reality.

However, plants are also categorized in other meaningful ways. Thus plants stand out as symbols that signify differently according to cultural history. As far as the Kariri-Shoko are concerned, plants – more specifically those that are used as medicines (*remédios*) – play a fundamental role in their socially constructed imagery, in a quest for ethnic identity and property rights to the land they have defined as ancestral. Plants, then, are recognized not only as biological organisms, or for what makes them stand out in unique and concrete ways, crying out to be named. They are also culturally meaningful elements that have biological and cultural properties, part of the Kariri–Shoko's resistance to total domination from the colonized frontiers that have plagued their territory since European invasions. As it will be further examined, the indigenous peoples of Alagoas were capable of retaining and maintaining a patch of forest – a mere 200ha – for their use as the sacred territory for their rituals of initiation and ancestor worshipping. In that way, not only did they conserve crucial cultural elements for the continuation of their indigenous life, but also the biological diversity of that area, creating an oasis of forest conservation. In that sacred space, several botanical and even animal species were saved from the onslaught of cattle farming and extensive monopolistic agricultural production that today characterizes the area. The preservation of that sacred grove – the *Ouricuri* territory – is an extremely important historical, cultural and biological event. Although the regional flora of the *sertão* has changed through centuries of land exploitation, certain selected species were preserved in the *Ouricuri*. They provide for a set of signs to these descendents of anterior native populations, standing out as symbols of their lives and realities.

On the other hand, the Shoko of Sergipe have been through a culturally damaging form of integration into the regional society. For a century they were forced to deny and forsake their indigenous ancestry. They had learned to use the environment and natural resources much like other native groups elsewhere (cf. Alcorn, 1984; Berlin, 1992). However, due to the historical process of colonization, they were forced to part with their 'ancestral roots' or mythical grandparents, losing the set of signals of ethnic indentification and the cognition of plants as ancestors imbued with specific symbolic meanings. As their land was controlled by an extensive form of agricultural exploitation, the Shoko became sharecroppers on their own lands, losing control over them. Nothing similar to what happened to the Kariri-Shoko characterized their struggle for survival: they did not maintain their sacred rituals and therefore they did not save any portion of the natural environment for the preservation of cultural and biological life.

In terms of cultural meanings and relationship to the botanical world, the Shoko were not conservationists. In the 1970s, they agitated in order to repossess their old territories. A century after their loss, the indigenous group returned, as owners, to the island of São Pedro in the São Francisco river. Botanical species that still existed there were no longer perceived as culturally significant elements for ethnic identification or as markers of cultural boundaries, although they were constantly utilized as medicines and food sources as well. It is important to point out, then, that biological entities did not necessarily lose their traditionally held forms of utilization, but – as native cultures were modified – plant species lost the cultural significance with which they had been traditionally imbued by anterior generations of indigenous peoples.

Human organizations – especially those composed of people with no political–economic dominance – are nevertheless capable of persisting in their resistance to total domination by political majorities. The action of resistance can take apparently non-political forms. One way is through cultural reconstructions of reality and consequent cultural–political movements. The Kariri and the Shoko are the specific examples I work with, analysing the processes of cultural maintenance, revitalization and communal self-definition, as well as their strategies of survival as individuals and as groups.

The reasons I embarked on this research were embedded in scientific as well as philosophical motives. First I wanted to describe ethnobiological knowledge through the uses of the preserved flora, focusing on native selections related to medicines. As a human being, I felt a personal commitment to reveal the consequences of the gradual vanishing of the beauty of plant life as well as the beauty of native knowledge. In this way, I hope to make a small contribution to some form of preservation of the natural resources, the people and, consequently, to the general knowledge of resources preservation and management.

Presenting the data and telling the story

Native narrative illuminates theoretical perspectives at the emic and etic levels. The presentation of data shifts from native narratives and discourses that were collected throughout the research, to the anthropological analysis and ethnobotanical data organization.

The work is partially composed of tales based on experience and observed social dramas in a literary non-fictional exercise, as a way of introducing the reader to the actual lives of these contemporary 'Indians'. These narratives are subsequently analysed in terms of the symbolic processes of the social organizations, examining meaningful relationships between botanical taxa, rituals and social actors in the two societies studied.

Starting with cross-cultural comparisons and descriptions of their ethnohistory, I discuss the methods and the politics of fieldwork, as political tension and economic constraints put pressure on the people and the author, creating a unique and rewarding triangular relationship. The problems of rituals, language, symbolism and ethnic identity are issues that permeate the stories. Rituals, as analytical categories, occupy a pivotal place, because ritual action gives meaning to the universe, (cf. Kertzer, 1988). As rituals are organized and re-enacted around the ideas and symbols of power and cultural heroes, an entire chapter is devoted to the description and analysis of the main Kariri-Shoko ritual: the *Ouricuri*. As the São Pedro Shoko are more dedicated to Catholic traditions than religious nativism, the absences of the *Ouricuri* and related supernatural beings, like *Jurema*, are examined in order to discover what such absences mean to the Shoko's present struggle and lives. Relations with the botanical world and theories concerning the natural environment, as outcomes of the cognitive structures of both societies, form another topic that will lead to the medical ethnobotanical data collected in both areas. With these data in hand, we can then describe, analyse and compare both medical systems: their health concepts, disease causations and plant manipulation for medicines. Tables detail the folk and scientific nomenclature of plant species, relating to illnesses, and each collected medicinal plant species is presented with a full description of its usefulness and place in the symbolic structure of the social group that has imparted such knowledge.

Part 2: Brief historical antecedents

ALTHOUGH INTEGRATED INTO the enveloping society through the colonization process, these two groups have contrasting stories as native groups from the same region. Thus, their ethnohistory and life styles serve as background to our speculations about cultural maintenance *vis-à-vis* the use of natural resources.

The communities studied are both located on the São Francisco river, a major fluvial artery linking the Northeast and Southeast regions of Brazil. The Kariri remained in an area of Alagoas state that is now the town of Porto Real do Colégio, apparently around the same places where their ancestors came from. Although gradually stripped of most of their original lands, they managed to hold on to certain cultural traits. These have served as important keys to their claims to ethnic identity and to what they consider as their ancestral lands.

The Shoko, however, split into two different bands. One part went down the river, joined the Kariri in Colégio, thus creating the cultural entity known today as Kariri-Shoko. Allegedly so as not to lose their traditional land, a remaining Shoko band stayed in the area in which their ancestors had settled: the island of São Pedro and the surrounding lands in Sergipe state. Due to pressures from regional landholders, they ended up losing their traditional indigenous ethos and the titles to the land anyway. It was not until a full century later that they re-established their identity as a reorganized indigenous group, attempting to reclaim their land and culture. It is a major historical event that this small band of impoverished rural labourers has achieved some recognition in their fight to reacquire their indigenous land and ethnic identity. It is so not only in terms of the general history of the Brazilian class struggles but also with regard to indigenous autonomous movements. Their histories will be told in more depth, as it is necessary to know about the ways in which these two groups got to the verge of destruction and then became once again organized as 'Indians' so that the complexity of history can give us a clue about their present social status, the way they weave the past in order to secure their children's future.

From a misinformed or naïve perspective, these two societies do not visibly differ from the other equally impoverished rural communitites of the North-eastern *caatinga*, the arid hinterlands covered by *opuntias*, thorny small bushes and trees, the 'pale woods' of the ancient Tupi Indians[6]. Language, dress codes, gestures, symbolic systems, even physical types are similar. It is difficult to differentiate an 'Indian' from a 'non-Indian', unless one knows the region and its social composition well. One of the main objectives of this book is to demonstrate the strength of ethnic identity that is based neither on supposedly racial characteristics, nor on the representation of 'generic Indians' idealized in the imagery of various sectors of Brazilian society. Ethnic identity is constructed upon cultural systems and ideologies, having little to do with biological traits. Taking for example what is happening to the descendents of indigenous populations in Brazil today, it can be seen that ethnicity is related to socially constructed symbols and ideologies, rather than biological traits or physical attributes. Concerning indigenous peoples, ethnicity is defined by situations of

political confrontation and also by social relations within the ethnic group itself
(cf. Faulhaber, 1987; de Oliveira, 1983).

The São Pedro Shoko are still going through the struggle of re-establishing
their Shoko-ness or their recognition as an ethnic group, and not just 'peasants',
apparently an unending battle.

Non-native interpretation of native theories
The analytical framework used here emphasizes cultural processes, assuming
that society is a process of symbols and meanings (cf. Turner, 1989). To interpret
native struggle and cultural theory, the approach of symbolic anthropology is
helpful in understanding my theoretical object. I utilize the analytical tools of
ethnobiology in the framework of cross-cultural perspective as well, as I compare the ethnobotanical taxonomies and social categories of the groups. Systems
of ethnobotanical classification and nomenclature, as they relate to the treatment
of categories of illnesses, are presented in Tables 1 to 10 (see Appendix). These
tables show how these groups share information regarding biological reality.
Nevertheless, the question of symbolic structures and cultural constructions is
raised, as, for instance, some species have names in the language still used by the
Kariri during ritual and 'secret' performances.

Part 3: Theories about ethnicity and the structure of native classifications

THE THEORETICAL OBJECTIVE of this book is to examine how ethnobotanical
knowledge and use of plant resources for medical and magical purposes
are related to the process of ethnic identification. The phenomenon of
ethnicity is marked by guiding signals. I show that plants are part of this
set of symbolic markers of ethnic identity, at least as far as the Kariri-
Shoko are concerned.

Both groups have a similar affinity to the natural environment. Medicines of
botanical extract are the same ones, as they share similar environments where
several botanical species with medicinal properties proliferate equally. Concepts
of disease causation and forms of treatment are also remarkably similar. Major
differences appear regarding magical–religious rituals and the use of mind-
altering substances of botanical origin. In both cases the belief systems, ritual
lives and cultural ethos have not only been modified but, first, shattered to be
later reorganized and reinvented. These groups have emerged again in markedly
different ways from the past and from each other. The Kariri, however, deny that
the Shoko were able to maintain the 'spirit', i.e., the culture, although the latter
want to believe they are following traditions passed down by the mythical
grandparents.

In the Kariri-Shoko symbolic system, medical and magical–religious practices, associated with the knowledge of medicinal plants and plants themselves,
are indexical signals. Thus, systems of ethnobotanical knowledge and medical
practices illuminate the composition of cognitive structures and ideologies. The
Kariri-Shoko have systems of representing their social order that are closely
related to their plant taxonomy and nomenclature. These cultural signals are
fully interpretable. It is necessary to decode them in order to understand the
composition of interrelationships within the culture. These signals are organized
around a native theory of the universe: a cultural model that involves ideological
complexes and structure.

Ideologies are fundamental as they have an integral role in society. They rationalize and justify cultural praxis, providing a meaningful framework for concepts of social origins, disease causations, healing agencies and cultural categories. These are part of the cognitive structures of society from which the discernment and native categorization of plants arise. These cognitive structures should not be understood as different from our own. Plant species are simultaneously biological realities and cultural categories. This is so because plants – which people in the hinterland generalize as leaves and 'foot of wood' (*folhas, pé de pau*) – are the metaphors for life and the preservation of culture and society. Plants in themselves and their names are, as words, representations of concrete symbols of a belief system. They are thus part of the essence of a society's world view, as are also time and space. This is a fundamental part of the Kariri-Shoko interpretation of reality, their comprehension of how the cosmos functions and their own role within it. Thus, what is left over of their 'ancestral language' – still a questionable matter – is related to magical–religious practices and botanical taxa. Plant species and words are therefore interrelated in the construction of a complexity of communication systems.

On the other hand, the Shoko of São Pedro island are eager to relearn 'the old culture'. For that purpose they have been busy with the task of retracing symbols and reinterpreting meanings. Their struggle, therefore, has a double dimension: as a class of landless peasants, they struggle against political and economic domination by outsiders; as a group claiming to be recognized as indigenous, it is also a struggle for ethnic identification. To achieve the latter, they are immersed in a reinvention of tradition within an ideology of ancestry.

Hegemonic and counter-hegemonic processes

At this point in history, for the Shoko and Kariri-Shoko to repossess their ancestral lands is for them to redefine what it is to be an 'Indian'. However, in order for this definition to hold true they must possess those lands. The concepts of social class and ethnicity, hegemony and counter-hegemony are useful as analytical tools (cf. Gramsci, 1978; Williams, 1978), so that we can work with the meanings implicit in ethnic and class struggles as the processes of cultural resistance to non-native domination.

Hegemony relates cultural and social processes to the distributions of power and influence, allowing for the possibility that such power and influence do not belong entirely to one class. In this way it is understood that subordinate classes and ethnic groups are not as subordinate to upper-class domination as they appear to be. Lower classes do have control over certain areas of their lives. They are able to develop social practices that escape the control of the dominating classes. At present the Kariri-Shoko have a constituted 'system of meanings and values', whereas the São Pedro Shoko have been striving to reconstitute their own system. The Kariri-Shoko have always been the proud possessors of a 'tribal secret'. This indigenous secret empowers them to continue living within a socially constructed reality that belongs to a world no one can see but themselves. In that way, they have also been able to become 'invisible' at will and, therefore, somewhat invincible. The 'secret' – the *segrêdo do Ouricuri* – is their form of opposition to domination, their counter-hegemonic movement. According to Williams (1978), politically dominated people are capable of creating 'counter-hegemony' or, better yet, an 'alternative hegemony' through the practical connections of different forms of struggle. These struggles include forms that are not easily recognizable as 'political' and 'economic' (*id*: 111). Such struggles are not readily understood or conceived as such, not even by the people who organize them, because they tend to belong to the realm of 'folk manifestations' and myth. These are the struggles lived and experienced by the Kariri-Shoko as they insist on maintaining a particular world view to fall back on. Therefore, a hegemonic process imposed by one group of people over others is never either total or exclusive, allowing room for a counter hegemonic process to take place, even when, by definition, hegemony implies dominance and control.

In sum, the diverse forms of opposition set in motion by the groups studied – through religious rituals, ethnobotanical knowledge, armed political action, medical–magical practices – have taken place not in spite of the hegemonic process, but because of it. The very development of a complex society living its historical moments of constant transformations requires the existence of different forms of resistance by the various sectors of society. Living and reliving old traditions is a form of resistance, part of counter-hegemonic practices. It is by installing and maintaining their own universe of discourse and knowledge that 'Indians' oppose the discourse and the analysis of the dominant society. In this way they are practising heretical thinking, going against the '*doxa*' – that which is taken for granted and cannot be questioned – of the dominant sectors of national society (Bourdieu, 1993).

The São Pedro Shoko have had to construct a society that is simultaneously imaginary and real, based on a post-modern, mythical native Brazil, related to their claims to the island they now live on. Nevertheless, both groups have been able to build what they consider to be a life of their own, in the midst of the power struggles and the land-grabbing situations that the regional political economy have made an everyday event.

1 Ethnohistory and cultural identity

Part 1: Encountering the 'natives'

AN ETERNITY SEEMED to pass as we canoed across the band of the São Francisco river that separates São Pedro island from land. The river is not wide at all at that particular place, but on the other side lay Shoko territory and its new conquering inhabitants. My anxiety to finally meet them made minutes seem like hours. Crossing that short distance was not unlike the remaking of old adventures by all past and present explorers, naturalists, scientists, anthropologists or any other 'non-native' who has dared to get in touch with 'natives' anywhere in the world. The Shoko, however, seemed to be unlike other 'natives' that have been contacted and then described. Many dwellers in the region claimed that the Shoko were not 'Indians' at all. First, because they did not fit into the representation of the generic Indian held by most Brazilians. Second, it was known that the indigenous population of Sergipe had been disbanded and then disappeared more than one century ago.

'The only Indians around here are those that show up during *Carnaval*', someone said, referring to the street balls, like Mardi Gras, when people wear masks, since it is traditional for many Brazilians to masquerade as a generic Indian. At any rate, that was a rather common pronouncement from people in Aracaju, the capital of the state.

Now these 'pretend' Indians were waiting for me, as Fray Enoque (a Catholic priest who worked with the Shoko) and I journeyed in a small canoe across the river canal, from the side that bordered the Caiçara, a farm belonging to their former boss and present arch-enemy. That farm was the land they had left in order to take over the island. It was still considered part of their ancestral territory, though, and they were still fighting for it.

Fifty people or more were watching silently as our canoe approached the small rustic port. Women, men and a flock of children were gathering at the river's edge, broad smiles and intense eyes watching us. Some waved happily. Most just stood there, as though frozen by a time-machine, but more likely due to curiosity than apprehension. They knew about my arrival, of course. In fact, the entire town and municipality of Porto da Folha – where the island is geographically located – knew of my arrival on the island. Against my express wishes, Fray Enoque had brightly announced my presence, over the loudspeaker, to a crowd of faithful who were in the central square of Porto da Folha for Christmas Eve mass.

'She came all the way from Rio de Janeiro to visit the Shoko!', he had shouted happily, pointing at me as I tried to hide behind a street lamp, and describing me as '*aquela galega ali*', (that fair one over there). From then on, I could just forget my plans of interviewing landowners and the local judge, as I was immediately and irrevocably type-cast as being 'with' the Shoko and, therefore – according to the local politics – against the dominant upper classes in the area. I was, but I didn't want them to know . . . yet! I had research to do. Things do not work like that in Brazil, though. Indifferent or uncommitted people do not count. Whoever wants to do anything worth mentioning has some form of political or social alliance or commitment. That is what counts.

It was Christmas Day when I landed in São Pedro, that green paradise amidst the parched dry lands of the *sertão*. Neither in the *sertão*, nor in the island were there the slightest signs of Christmas as we know it in the 'civilized' Western society. No Christmas decorations, trees, gifts, special dinners, and such like, among these very faithful Catholic people. A day like any other, except for our arrival which had the meaning of a holiday for them.

I tried to keep my physical balance while disembarking from the flimsy canoe. However, my thoughts were also in disequilibrium as I stepped out and looked into those faces for the first time. Probably every anthropologist asks him or herself what one is doing there when first approaching an unknown tribe. I vividly remembered Napoleon Chagnon's description of when he first encountered the Yanomami in Venezuela: he had arrived on a day when the already fierce-looking warriors had snuffed the powerful *paricá* powder, a strong natural hallucinogen that the Yanomami used. Consequently, they looked to Chagnon even stranger than he had expected. The men who ran to meet him at the river had thick black catarrh running down their noses and were shouting what were to him at that time incomprehensible words. That was perhaps daring, intensely dramatic as well, or even romantic. Oh for the fear, the thrill, the doubts that might occur to one when faced with such powerful experiences from human encounters!

'My' natives, however, were different precisely because there was nothing in them that connected to our idea of the 'exotic' or even dangerous. Placid, looking peaceful and even joyful, they dressed, looked, talked and acted as any other riverbank villagers from the interior of Sergipe. In no way did they show any visible signs of ancient tribal traditions or similar postures that I had been familiarized with through the classic ethnographic literature. They appeared to me just as a journalist from Aracaju had described them: 'Black Indians'. Dark, knotted curly hair, wide-eyed, broad noses, they were surely more African than Amerindian as far as biotypes were concerned.

But Fray Enoque was clearly their hero. As the canoe docked, lots of people rushed to the shallow water to greet us and help us with the disembarkation. The tall, broad-shouldered priest was hugged, cheered, kissed by almost everyone, men and women alike. Children hung on to him, shouting happy salutations. One of the older women greeted him cheerfully but in a mockingly critical mood:

'Well, you have gained a lot of weight, father. You are FAT!' He replied in the same tone: 'So are you! You have been eating too much!' and then he let out one of his thunderous laughs.

There was definitely a cheerful mood in the air. My welcome was also very warm, although not as much as his, since that was my first time in the village. They were in the initial phase of eyeing me with some suspicion, not knowing exactly what to say or do. Their behaviour that day was a little more cautious than their usual informal and gay demeanour. It was nearly impossible, however, not to take an immediate liking to them, these 'Black Indians'.

They not only longed for visitors but also wanted outsiders to share their history with. It was obvious that they were very proud of having been able to recover the island. At that moment in their history they were beginning to try to reidentify themselves with the Shoko ancestors. There was little left of their cultural memory as it went back only a hundred years or so. Myths and cultural heroes were relatively modern. There was no trace of a native language, not even in songs or prayers, as they were monolingual in Portuguese. However, they were definitely trying to define their 'Shoko-ness'. They thought that I, being an anthropologist (they also thought I was a nun, since I came with Fray Enoque), could help them in this quest. For the same reason, because of my very training, I doubted that I could. I was interested in their knowledge of the flora, use of natural resources, state of health and medicine at that moment. The historical background would be revealed as the study went along, I thought. However, they were interested in discovering the old selves that had been taken away from them along with the land. Among other things, they wanted me to tell the outside world about their plight.

Technically they had already been considered extinct or 'totally integrated'. Historians and anthropologists had confirmed what politicians and landholders had declared back in the 19th century: that there was no longer a tribe named Shoko in Brazil, except for a band that had joined the Kariri in Colégio. None the less, back in 1973, a group of about 35 families had been able to forge their way back as legitimate heirs of the past Shoko. When I arrived at the island in 1983, they were still determined to demonstrate to the world that they were truly heirs of their grandparents, the mythical native ancestors.

Their voyage was a return to the mythical bountiful land and life of centuries ago. My own journey was a plunge into today's ethnic and socio-economic limits and conflicts, with their consequences to health, nutrition and lifestyle in general. I was there to collect medical ethnobotanical data and to do cross-cultural comparisons with data gathered from the Kariri-Shoko down the river. I was very interested in knowing how much use, if any, they made of the *Jurema* drink, a beverage that was ritually important in the region and also among the Afro–Brazilian rites of *Candomblé* and *Umbanda* in big urban centres like Rio de Janeiro and Salvador. That was what I explained to the young Shoko *cacique*-elected José Apolonio. He was then only 21 years old. In folk Brazilian racial classification, he was more of a *mulato*, whose parents had been White and Black, as he definitely had Black features. He spoke softly and his accent was what could be expected from any other *sertanejo* of Sergipe state.

'We are Shoko Indians, you see?' he said, looking me straight in the eye as though challenging me to contradict his affirmation. 'Until recently we didn't know we were Indians, but now we have found out about our past, about our Shoko great-grand-parents, those who lived here before us, and we are now Shoko Indians again.'

His tone of voice was fierce and determined. I had already heard about José Apolonio and the other leaders, like Pedrito Santana, having read their stories in the newspapers at Bishop Dom José's library. Moreover, long before I decided to go to the interior of Sergipe in search of them, my father had sent me newspaper clippings telling about their struggle to regain the land and their identity as Indians. Being a *Sergipano*, my father was trying to lure me into doing research in his homeland, so, in his letters to me, he used to include little notes asking: 'Why go to the Amazon? There are Indians in Sergipe too!' Moreover, I had learned about a report written by Dr Delvair Melatti, a cultural anthropologist the National Indian Foundation (FUNAI) had sent to São Pedro island, although FUNAI never made the report available to me. Her task was to authenticate their claim to the status of 'indigenous' people and, consequently, to be under FUNAI's control and protection. That she did by tracing genealogies going back into the old times and thus proving that the Shoko – at least some of them! – were related to the indigenous bands that had inhabited the lands on the banks of the São Francisco, in a place known then as *Jaciobá*, 'mirror of the moon'.

On the other hand, the Shoko were not supposed to be alone in the world, as they had living 'relatives' in the Sementeira village of the Kariri-Shoko. These relatives had kept their tribal identity and at least part of the cultural memories.

'*Cultura aqui nao tem mais nenhuma!*' ('There is no more culture here!') was the immediate statement from one of the elderly São Pedro Shoko women, known as Mãezinha, when I first interviewed her. 'If you want to see culture (she was indeed using the anthropological concept of culture, perhaps under the influence of Dr Melatti!), you have to go down the river and look for our relatives there. We only have our *torés* that our parents used to dance when they '*fechavam uma lagoa*' (closed a lagoon, meaning when they finished planting rice in a lagoon). Then they would dance in jubilation and we would learn these dances and songs with them. But the words were always in Portuguese, as they had been forbidden to speak in the language of their own grandparents. They could not do the *Ouricuri* either, so we never drank *Jurema*. It is the truth! That was how we lost ourselves and were left out from the *Ouricuris* of our relatives.'

Those *caboclos*[1] showed no traits – neither physical nor cultural – which could be called indigenous. Dr Melatti had based her arguments on genealogies and traces of their ethnohistory collected orally among the Shoko, so as to defend their rights for being declared 'descendants of the Shoko.' There was little or nothing else she could lean on to link them to a tribal ethos and lifestyle. Except for Fray Enoque, there were no ritual experts! I realized that their folk healers were not unlike the other healers I had known in Aracaju or any other place in the Northeast. My reaction was to try to go ahead and get information on the use of medicinal plants, collect botanical specimens and to gather information on what was left of the island's natural environment after many years of cattle grazing. I would collect ethnographic data as well, working from the point of view of cross-cultural comparisons.

The Shoko had mixed feelings regarding my imminent visit to their so-called relatives down the river. They wanted me to be a sort of 'cultural messenger' or 'broker', bringing back to them every detail of what the Kariri-Shoko were up to those days. On the other hand, they were also distrustful of what could be expected from their long-lost relatives. They had already tried to approach them, but had given up on the idea. The story behind their recent caution – not to mention an avoidance syndrome – was that at some point Dom José had tried to set up a meeting between the two groups. According to local sources, a lay Catholic worker for the Indigenist Missionary Council (CIMI) had told the São Pedro Shoko that they should not trust the Kariri-Shoko, so the meeting was shunned by the former, thus creating greater tension and mistrust between the two tribal factions from both sides of the river.

There was also the very pertinent question of what to do if the Shoko from Colégio wanted to return to the island too. After all, they also had rightful claims over the land. But the island was hardly large enough for the 40 families that already lived there. Those thoughts hung heavily on their minds. We all shared an uneasy feeling when, on New Year's Eve, I left the island to go back to Colégio and then on to the Sementeira village, the Kariri-Shoko's homeland.

I had already been in Colégio, when I first went to Propriá, a small town in Sergipe right across from Colégio in the São Francisco river. My reason for going to Propriá was to visit Dom José Brandão de Castro, the Catholic Bishop of the region. He was well known in the area and reportedly beloved by the Indians. I had gone to interview him about the indigenous situation and also to ask him the favour of introducing me to the Kariri-Shoko, who were the primary population in my research. Dom José – a talkative and energetic man in his seventies – had been actively involved with the Shoko in their recent history of conflicts. Right away he wanted me to work with the Shoko, even before I set foot on Kariri-Shoko territory. He was the first one to see in me the person who was going to teach Shoko culture to the Shoko, if that would be at all possible. Therefore, he made his quiet, pleasantly cool library accessible to me, handing me more or less organized files – several newspapers and clippings, very few dates, no chronological order – on recent Shoko history. As Christmas was approaching, and maybe fearing I would give up the idea in order to enjoy the holidays with my family, Dom José immediately made plans for me to go to Porto da Folha, a town much further into the interior of Sergipe, where I was to meet Fray Enoque who would then take me to São Pedro island. Not to be unfair to the other Indians, he also instructed me on how to make contacts in Colégio: 'Just look for a man known as *seu Francisquinho*', the sweet old man said, 'as everybody in town knows him . . . '

Before I went in search of the São Pedro Shoko, as Dom José so fervently wished me to do, I crossed the river gap between Propriá and Colégio to visit the Kariri-Shoko *pajé*, '*seu*' *Francisquinho*.

That short visit was also memorable. Vera Calheiros Mata, a fellow anthropologist who had already worked among the Kariri-Shoko, had advised me to look for a local schoolteacher by the name of Jerusa, who would then take me to the *pajé*. I arrived at Jerusa's house on a Sunday afternoon. She told me that most of the Indians should be at the *Ouricuri*, since it was Sunday. She had seen them coming back from the street market in Propriá carrying new straw mats and going in the direction of the *Ouricuri*. To find out if the Indians were home in the Sementeira village or had already gone off to the *Ouricuri*, Jerusa sent her maid to talk to Dona Madu, an Indian woman who lived in the same street. It was then mid-December, the time for the Kariri to get organized for the larger ritual to take place in January. The young maid came back with the information that most of them had gone away already, but maybe the *pajé* had not gone yet.

Jerusa informed me that his full name was Francisco Queiroz Suíra and that, in that year of 1983, he was about 75 years old, but typically nobody was sure of his age, as most people did not get registered officially in the year of their birth. He was known and addressed as '*seu*' *Francisquinho*, or *Chico Suíra*, or simply as *pajé* and *avô* (grandfather). However, people in Propriá used to refer to the pajé as '*bruxo*', meaning sorcerer, thus presenting a variety of very pre conceived notions to be reckoned with.

I was surprised to find out that he did not live in the Kariri-Shoko village, a walking distance from his house in Colégio, and that he was also receiving local non-Indian clients on a regular basis. But what was I expecting to see? A feather-clad man sitting by smouldering herbs, perhaps?

Before we left the house, Jerusa and one of her brothers, the city's only mailman, talked to me for a long time about the Kariri-Shoko, attempting to convince me that I should give up going to the *Ouricuri*, the indigenous secret ritual and territory, something I had not even expressed any desire to do since I only knew about it from the literature I had been reading. I just wanted to be introduced to the *pajé*, talk to him and then decide what to do or not to do next.

The *pajé* was a calm, quiet, peaceful, warm human being, living in a shabby three-roomed house in Colégio's main street. When we arrived at his doorstep, he was sitting in a decrepit armchair right by the front door. Suíra, a widower, had just married a much younger woman, a half-breed who was not considered an Indian. He smiled knowingly when he saw us and looked at me as if he knew me from before. I realise that this sounds naïve, but that was my interpretation of the moment. Suíra was in the habit of looking at anyone, even at a first meeting, as if the person had been a long-time acquaintance. He never showed surprise, disgust, happiness or fear. Only much later in our friendship did Suíra show something akin to gladness upon any of my arrivals. But it was then on a very hot, dry, lazy Sunday afternoon that I and the *pajé* began to set the pace for all that was going to happen afterwards in my research work.

He received me very amicably. When I told him that I was also going to try to work with the Shoko in São Pedro, he said: 'Oh, yes, go see those poor people who say they are Shoko. They don't have anything and I feel sorry for them. But my relatives here, the Shoko families here, also say they have nothing in common with them. They don't even have a secret, like we do, like the Shoko here do. How can they say they are *caboclos*? But go see them. When you come back, you are welcome to come and talk to me about my medicine, all right, *senhora*?'

On that first visit, he addressed me formally as '*senhora*' which is the Portuguese equivalent to 'madame'. As we gradually became friends, he later used the term '*minha filha*', which, although translated as 'my daughter', is the informal way for any person of any age to address females they are fond of. In reality, the *pajé*, early in our acquaintance, established that I was to be his trainee as well as an honorary relative at the level of a granddaughter.

Later that same day, his wife, Maria, took me to meet her own father, a non-Indian who knew of Indian ways and who was also a healer and a *mateiro*, a man who gathers medicinal herbs. 'Of course, my father doesn't have the same powers as Chico (as she referred to her husband), nobody does!' she was cautious to add. Nevertheless, '*seu*' Neco proved to be one of the most knowledgeable people I was to meet, and he evidently enjoyed a lot of prestige locally. However, he could not participate in the *Ouricuri* ritual since he was not an Indian.

The *Ouricuri* is the secret ceremony and set of rituals only Indians can take part in. Previous ethnographers, like Estevão Pinto, in 1953, had already established that such a secret is at the heart of an ethnic identity which has always been challenged by 'civilized' society (cf. da Mota, 1987, 1990; Mata, 1989). The patch of forest where the *Ouricuri* took place had remained in the hands of the Kariri throughout the encroachment of economic frontiers of past and present. This fact in itself is as mysterious as the actual ritual. Contrary to their suspicions and even expectations I was not intending to 'uncover' their secret and much less reveal it to the outside world. From the start I realized that the secret – *o segrêdo* – was truly embedded in a vital and rich relationship to the vegetal world around them. That web of complex interactions retained the heart of a specific Kariri-Shoko vision of the cosmos and their symbolic systems.

Therefore, when I talked again to young José Apolonio, a man so determined to reacquire his lost indigenous self, I began to understand what Suíra had told me and the importance of his words: 'they don't know the secrets'. The Shoko had their own folk healers, like Nazinha, an old woman who was half-Fulniô, half-Shoko. They also had woods in the island where medicinal plant species could be found. But they didn't have the *Ouricuri* any more: the key to their renewal as 'legitimate Indians'.

I could learn from them what other backwoods people knew of medicinal plants, their concepts of health and healing, and their curing practices. I did not yet know that with them I was also going to learn how they envisioned the act of becoming an Indian, or how to finally obtain the grace of becoming a child of Jurema, to inherit the right to land and life on this earth. I wanted to allow myself to be there, to observe them and to slowly comprehend a new vision being unfolded. Their own vision.

Part 2: Being and becoming an Indian: the remaking of tribal identity

AT FIRST SIGHT, there are two distinct ethnic entities: the Kariri and the Shoko. With the union of the Shoko, in the early 1900s, a third entity was formed, which is neither Shoko, nor Kariri, but Kariri-Shoko: a complex nation of people, at once united and divided.

There are not many past ethnographic accounts dealing specifically with any one of these three groups, although there has been more information about the Kariri alone. It was in the character of colonial ideology to see 'gentiles' or 'pagans' as an undifferentiated block of humanity, so that tribal references were usually confused and confusing as well. The history of confrontations between indigenous groups in Brazil and the Europeans has been written primarily by Catholic priests and missionaries, and other agents from colonial powers. There were attempts to describe some cultural aspects of the lives of the 'pagans', but – except for a few that were rich in details – those accounts failed to present an impartial view of native life and culture. At times, the Shoko appear as belonging to the Kariri branch, even before they moved into Colégio lands. There are also instances in which they are seen as not being related at all until the Shoko came to live with the Kariri in Colégio.

Since the Indians themselves lacked written documents and their vestiges of oral history are mixed with mythical accounts, it is even more difficult for them to truly know from whom they descend. They want to believe that they have 'ancestral roots' and a genealogy that traces back to pre-European times. But who were these grandparents and what language did they really speak? The Kariri found an excellent way of getting around this problem by adopting their *Ouricuri* village and forest complex as the home of these mythical ancestors, who still live today embodied in the existing flora and fauna of the place.

The Shoko only have traces of a genealogical tree and no identity to speak of. In the past, the Shoko received no more attention than a few paragraphs here and there. It is very difficult to retrace their history. Practically, they already were a non-existent group. An attempt to reconstruct the history of native peoples is a difficult task, for several reasons. A fundamental one is the bias presented by European historians and chroniclers. These attempts become even more complex when examining the social perceptions of peoples who did not leave us any written testimony so that we get in touch with their 'history' through the eyes of a foreign minority who, with some exceptions, presented the facts to explain and justify the colonial situation.

After the Portuguese crown transformed the Brazilian territory into colonies, the lives of native peoples who were in contact with the newcomers were dominated, first of all, by missionary priests and only secondarily by the other landholders. According to Shoko oral history and some historical evidence, that was exactly what happened to them. The church only stepped aside when there was no longer a tribal group to take care of. In 1755, the Portuguese Marquis de Pombal stripped missionaries on Brazilian soil – mainly Jesuits – of all temporal or civil control of Indian villages, so that the 'freedom' bestowed upon Indians in the law of 1755 was merely freedom from missionary control (Hemming, 1978: 4). But that was not the case for the Shoko who remained under the rule of Franciscan *Capuchinho* priests until the end of the 19th century.

To better understand the present-day situation and the way each group has confronted the surrounding national society, it will be helpful to contrast the Shoko in Sergipe and the Kariri-Shoko in Alagoas concerning historical and economic circumstances. Differences between the two tribes in terms of attitudes and destiny reflect the forces which led the Brazilian social formation through the stages of primitive accumulation of capital. However, economic–historical processes were fundamentally equivalent in each state, since patterns of land exploitation were the same. Capitalist frontiers originating from the southern states contributed towards the dispersion of the different indigenous groups of Sergipe and Alagoas, which, by the turn of this century, became known by the generic name of Kariri. Essentially different, however, was the fact that the Kariri and other tribal groups in Alagoas were able to survive – precariously, it is true – as 'remnants of Indians', whereas in the states of Sergipe all tribal groups disintegrated and disappeared at the end of the 19th century, including the Shoko who lived in the land now known as *Caiçara* (cf. Dantas and Dallari, 1980; Figueiredo, 1981).

Kariri history: priests and cows on the path to civilization
The Shoko came to join the Kariri between the end of the 19th century and beginning of the 20th. After that, some authors began referring to the indigenous group in Colégio as being only Shoko, instead of the more traditional Kariri. However, the Kariri have been described so far as consisting of two main groups: the Kipeia from the lower São Francisco river, and the Dzubukua, from the river's islands. Kariri have also been mentioned as Kiriri, a group that until today lives in Alagoas and Bahia, as well as the Cariri of Colégio proper. The latter are the ones left over from different village groups of the 18th century and that got mixed together as a result of the advances of the colonizing national society (Mata, 1989).

The various tribal groups known as Kariri only started to have prolonged contact with the colonizers in the 17th century, when missionaries started to divide mission areas among themselves, thus rounding up the tribes in preparation for the advance of the incoming economic frontier. The Jesuits were turning the Indians into what the Jesuits considered a productive labour force for the cattle ranches, at the time led by the powerful *Casa da Tôrre* (House of Tower), in the state of Bahia. In this way the priests were at once setting into motion irreversible changes in tribal social structures.

Missionaries were supposed to administer each indigenous village – a social structure known as *aldeia* (village) – within land that was 'donated' by the colonizers to the Indians. It was within the context of these *aldeias* – also known as *redução* (reduction) – that the merging of different ethnic groups began. The purpose was to erase tribal distinctions, turning 'pagans' into 'Christians', 'Indians' into 'civilized people'. The Jesuitic reduction can thus be understood as submission and literally as a decimation of the Indians in their very own land.

The set of historical events that took place from the 17th century onward was based on fundamental contradictions imposed by the colonizers. Missionaries and landholders were agents of the colonial forces abroad. As such, their common purpose was to establish a new Europeanized social organization in the 'new' land. One of their immediate tasks was to evangelize native populations and thus to control them. For that purpose, a *Junta das Missões* (Union of Missions) was created in 1681. Nevertheless, these partners in mission were not always in agreement as to methods, objectives or even ends. To accomplish the goal of training Indians for the new social order, missions were taking over good portions of arable land, supposedly for the use of the Indians themselves, but actually for the subsistence of the missionaries. In the 18th century, the sanctimonious Jesuits had begun the process of becoming the greatest of the cattle ranchers in the lower São Francisco region. Otherwise, missions were indeed protecting native groups from the assaults by frontier people. That basic contradiction was to lead to the final expulsion of the Jesuits from Brazil in 1822, the year of Brazil's declared independence from Portugal.

Another contradiction lay in the objective of mission work that related to the concept of 'being an Indian' and what such a concept meant for the survival of indigenous groups. As missions did protect and even save Indian lives in many instances, they were also responsible for the perpetration of profound cultural transformations within native culture, gradually undermining indigenous belief systems, languages and entire bodies of knowledge (which were declared as bodies of ignorance, instead). In the first place, it meant that if Indians were becoming civilized they were deemed to have lost their tribal identity. But as Indians lost their ethos and life-style, they also lost the land: tribes were considered 'extinct', as a whole group of people turned from Indians into *caboclos*, and thereafter lost their right to ancient tribal territories.

Indians were doomed either way: if they remained tribalized, they were identified as 'primitives', and considered as 'savages' that had to be exterminated by the 'civilized frontier'. On the other hand, if they submitted to the colonial process they lost their rights to the land that was reserved for 'aborigines'. Apparently, there was no way for them to win the battle against land expropriation and tribal persecution, unless Indian people fell back on their resources in order to survive and hold on to their lands. The work of colonization had an ideological impact, of course. Indians until today think that somehow 'civilization' is an attribute that passes through genetic inheritance. If there was to be an intermarriage with Whites, the offspring would be more 'civilized' because of the 'White blood', an idea that many people worldwide share, that is based on the premise that cultural patterns could result from hereditary transmission.

Be that as it may, in 1850 the central government of the newly independent nation of Brazil declared a *Lei da Terra* (Law of the Land). Brazil then had its first legal instrument concerning land ownership. It established that a bill of sale was the only legitimate means for owning lands that were given as abandoned. That included, 'naturally', former territories of the tribes that had been legally declared 'extinct' by decree. Therefore, the detribalization of *caboclos* became an important political move for taking over indigenous properties. It became useful to deny the existence of indigenous populations through the manipulation of the biological criterion of race, so that somatic aspects were taken as efficient indicators of 'being Indian' and sufficed to expel Indians from the lands they had lived on for centuries, as well as to deny them the right to a differential identity (cf. Mata, 1989).

Throughout the 17th century another contradiction was in process. This time it involved another axis of the colonial take-over: the inter-ethnic confrontation between Indians and the Africans who had been brought to Brazil as slaves, basically to fill in the gaps left by the lack of an indigenous labour force. As Black slaves began to run away and form liberated villages known as *Quilombos*, colonizers were hiring Whites and Indians to destroy them. One of the more important of the *Quilombos* – *Palmares* – was located in Alagoas. In the meantime, mercenary soldiers known as *Bandeirantes* were brought mainly from the state of São Paulo and acquired the status of national heroes for killing Blacks and Indians, as well as for hiring Indians to help them kill Blacks. So it is told that those men brought along with them a group of 'pacified Indians' from the southern states, notably the Kaingang, a tribal group belonging to the Gê linguistic macro-family. The fact that the Kariri of Colégio still think of themselves as descendants from the Gê may well be due to this historical incident.

Since 1715, the Kariri and other tribal groups in the lower São Francisco – *Tupinambá, Karapató, Acorane, Natu* – had been under the control of a Jesuit mission that built a *colégio* (a school) in the area. When the Jesuits were expelled from Brazil, the Union of Missions was replaced by another administrative organ called the General Directory of Indian Affairs, that was, however, short-lived, ceasing in 1872. Afterwards, the indigenous villages that had been under this General Indian Directory were simply declared extinct. Entire villages were pronounced defunct and native lands were turned into 'public lands' that could be acquired by non-Indians.

Thus disbanded, the Kariri and the odd assortments of other local dwindling tribes were somehow able to maintain their identity as native peoples. They kept, as mentioned before, a small parcel of land of about 200ha in size, where they continued to hold their ritual ceremonies, which had by that time been renamed *Ouricuri*. However, the land where they had subsistence farming and houses had fallen out of their hands. As a consequence, the Kariri band was scurried into a corner of the town of Colégio to live in utter poverty, dispossessed of their old means of livelihood, except for the utilitarian pottery for which they became well-known in the region (cf. Mata, op. cit.).

Now, Porto Real do Colégio is the seat of the municipality of the same name, belonging to the micro-region of Penedo, in the state of Alagoas. The Indian population of the municipality today accounts for less than 20 per cent of its urban population and a little more than 5 per cent of its total population. In 1983, the Kariri-Shoko population was 1050 people, then living in a place that had been known as *Sementeira*. With 290ha in total, it is really a small piece of land, if compared to other farms in the area. It had belonged to the Ministry of Agriculture since the beginning of the 20th century, when the indigenous village had been declared 'extinct' and its former inhabitants had been relocated in a street that became known as 'the street of the *caboclos*', as it is still called, in fact.

1978 was the year when the Kariri-Shoko decided to take back what was still considered their ancestral land. Their historical decision was based on two factors: a divination of *Jurema*'s designs for the group and the still bright memory of a visit by the then Emperor Dom Pedro II, when he donated a piece of land, its size two by one league, back to the Kariri in the end of the 19th century. Upon invading the Sementeira to claim their territory, the Kariri were not only representing themselves as 'legitimate Indians' but were also holding on to a system of beliefs that, whether 'original' or not, sustained and symbolized the group as well.

Shoko history: the mirror of fate in Sergipe

The process of land expropriation was fundamentally the same for the Shoko band. But the Shoko in Sergipe had a worse fate than the Kariti, as they lost not only their lands, but also the cultural reference from which they could model and shape their lives.

In the 16th century, Indians in the area now comprising Sergipe state had joined the French colonialists to fight Portuguese domination in the region. European nations were eager to control a commercially desirable wood known as *Pau-Brasil* (*Caesalpina brasiliensis* Linn.) that could be easily transported down the navigable rivers of Sergipe. The monoculture of the area was then sugar cane. Cattle ranching found its way into Sergipe in the 17th century, being brought by the House of Tower from Bahia. As a result, and due to the land scarcity, old tribal rivalries were exacerbated among the various ethnic groups in the area, a situation clearly imposed by the incoming horde of 'civilizers' and their assortment of legionnaires.

In a typical gesture, Dom João VI, King of Portugal, 'donated' a small piece of land to a tribe allegedly known as Urumari which, at the time, went on to comprise one of the formative branches of the present-day Shoko. The land was called *Jaciobá*, a Tupi word meaning 'mirror of the moon'. It was located in the Alagoas state, at the São Francisco river's edge, where today there is a small village of *Pão de Açúcar* ('Sugar Bread'). At the same time, a group of *Ceocozes* had migrated from Ceará and were already living in and around São Pedro island. The latter fought the former, while the Urumari ultimately moved closer to São Pedro, founding another village of Jaciobá, this time just a few miles upriver from São Pedro.

The next step was that the former enemies started to live side by side in and around São Pedro island, away from the missions and the Jesuit control over the other 'pagans' of the area. The Urumari had helped the Portuguese to fight Dutch invasion and, subsequently, the Portuguese wanted to show their gratitude to their native friends. A Portuguese capitain by the name of Pedro Gomes gave a piece of his *capitania*, a gift from the Portuguese crown to the nobility that was colonizing their 'New World' territories, for the Indians to live in. However, soon enough the Indians were also charitably endowed with the presence of a French Capuchin missionary that was supposed to 'take care' of them. It was not so much that the Indians themselves needed protection, but rather that other Portuguese settlers needed to be protected from the lads of the land. From the historical accounts available, it becomes reasonably clear that the missionaries were there to keep the Indians under control and away from any undesirable wish to return to their original tribal territories.

The property known as Caiçara was part of Pedro Gomes' *capitania*, where Indians also lived until Gomes' heirs started to push them to move further down the river. Many Indians followed that path, going to the village of Propriá and establishing another village named Pacatuba. Other groups started to join the Kariri in Colégio, and that was at the same time as the metaphorical and geographical descent of the Shoko and Urumari bands took its fateful course.

By the end of the 18th century, a mission had been firmly established within São Pedro island, being first run by Jesuit and later by Italian Capuchin monks. In 1878, a Capuchin priest by the name of Fray Dorotheo de Loreto took over the São Pedro mission. At the same time, a local farmer named João Fernandes Tavares was appointed as the regional director of the Indian Directory of Sergipe. By the first half of the 19th century, natives living on São Pedro island had already been dispossessed of their basic means of livelihood. Ten years after Fray Dorotheo's arrival on the scene, the lands belonging to the village of São Pedro were parcelled to be rented and then later sold to neighbouring farmers (cf. Dantas and Dallari, 1980). By that time, Indians – whether Urumari or Ceocozes – had been intermarrying with Blacks and Whites in the area, whereas Fray Dorotheo and João Tavares – in some kind of alliance – had been keeping the remnants of the indigenous population within the island. The monk was attempting to protect the Indians from genocide and the farmer was keeping Indians away from the good lands edging the river. According to oral history, indigenous rites and ceremonies were still taking place in the area known as Caiçara, where the natives' 'sacred woods' – their place for the adoration of the natural elements – and traditional burial grounds were situated.

While Fray Dorotheo lived in São Pedro there was an official mission and, therefore, an indigenous population, since missions existed to take care of Indians. However, Fray Dorotheo met an untimely death when, although known as an excellent swimmer, he drowned in the São Francisco river while taking a bath. Right after his mysterious death, the Shoko were declared 'extinct' and their lands were put up for sale, because whenever a tribe was considered extinct, its territory could be sold. The land was declared 'abandoned' even if the native population still lived there. In that way, the new owners would have not only the land, but a cheap labour force with nowhere else to go and, subsequently, a rather submissive labour force too. Accordingly, João Fernandes Britto, who was already renting three parcels of indigenous territory, became the sole owner of more than half of the tribal lands that included Caiçara, Belém and São Pedro island, with Indians still established there.

At the end of the 19th century the amalgamation of the remaining Indians in that area of Sergipe totally lost their tribal rights. Their struggle to repossess the rights to land and a 'native culture' had just begun. For that they had, first of all, to reconstruct their social history.

Part 3: Shoko cultural heroes

BECAUSE MYTH AND HISTORY are two modes of the same social consciousness, they account for a past not only to be cherished but constantly rewritten. The cultural heroes who appear in historical accounts are still alive in the cultural memory of the peoples they belong to and not only in a few pages of the history books. Shoko's cultural heroes that I could identify as such are symbolic of the mixing up of ethnic groups and national histories – Fray Dorotheo, Inocencio Pires and Fray Enoque – but only Inocencio Pires is a *caboclo*.

From the oral history available that the modern Shoko inherited from the old, Fray Dorotheo appears to have been a brilliant planner and administrator for the Portuguese take-over of Indian land and the extermination of Indian culture. The local people believe that his ghost still wanders around the old mission church and that the monk can be seen bathing at the very spot where he drowned over a hundred years ago. I learned more about him, in fact, the night when I was to sleep in the huge room adjacent to the church. I was then kindly warned that the old monks – Fray Dorotheo being the star, of course – were in the habit of visiting that place at night, when they would idly chat among themselves. But – my friends said – I should not be afraid because those were kind souls! Unable to sleep after such a warning, I called upon people to stay with me and so I began to collect bits and pieces of Shoko ethnohistory with the people who kindly volunteered to hang their hammocks close to mine.

Another night, lodging in less ghostly quarters, the centenarian Mãezinha, also unable to sleep much, told me the stories her parents and grandparents used to tell her at bedtime: 'Fray Dorotheo had as much magic as any old Indian *pajé*' she said, 'because priests do have magic. They know how to control spirits and human beings as well. It was because of his magic that Fray Dorotheo destroyed our *Ouricuri*, our *torés*. My old ones told me these stories so that I would know that I was an Indian, but we could not talk about it to anyone else, not even to our neighbours, because we could be killed if we said that we were Indians . . . When Fray Dorotheo lived we were no longer allowed to hold the secret *Ouricuri* of our grandparents, but our grandparents used to hide within the sacred *mata* (forest, woods) and have the *torés* and the songs honouring our *troncos*[2]. This was done in secrecy, of course. No one could find out about it and only Indians were allowed in that place. Our grandparents had sentinels at the entrance of the *Ouricuri* to watch out for whoever might approach the area. They would, from time to time, lie down on the floor and press their ears to the ground in order to hear if somebody was coming from afar. Well, one night Fray Dorotheo used his magic: he was able to arrive and nobody heard his footsteps! So he showed up all of a sudden and caught everyone by surprise. He was very, very angry at the people for holding what he used to call the 'pagan feast'. Screaming, he sent everybody back to the village. There he humiliated the leaders of the celebration, including the venerated *Rainha do Terreiro* (queen of the territory)[3]. He forced all the Indians to recite Catholic prayers aloud out here in the square in front of the Church and be publicly baptized, in order to forswear the devil and the pagan feasts. From then on, he kept an eye on all of the Indians and the *Ouricuri* was never celebrated again in our woods. That was the end of the *Ouricuri* for us! When Dorotheo died and João Britto became the boss, well, there was nothing left of our *festa*. The only thing that Dorotheo allowed was that we danced our *torés*, but like *brincadeiras* (games), never again in adoration of our grandparents. Our grandmothers still danced the *toré* when they finished the rice planting around the lagoons, but that was all . . . Fray Dorotheo could be really mean! We were scared of him!'

I heard more stories from another very old person, *'seu'* João de Deus, a man so bent over by the years he could hardly stand up. He liked to tell his stories in the lazy hours of the hot afternoons, sitting on his tattered hammock.

'When Dom Pedro II was Brazil's emperor, he journeyed up the São Francisco river, and stopped by here', he told me, in his slow story-telling mode, 'then the grandfather of a Shoko woman, who now lives in Porto da Folha, complained to the emperor that Fray Dorotheo was giving our land away to the local farmers. Fray Dorotheo was furious with the accusation and punished his accuser by jailing him for three days in the mission.'

Fray Enoque do Salvador stressed how authoritarian Fray Dorotheo was and analysed his late colleague's actions: 'Fray Dorotheo's vision was that of some-one who could not get deeply into the Indian problem. It was the vision of the colonizer. His creed was that only work and religion can transform people into good folk. He could not perceive that the problem with indigenous lethargy and apparent nonchalance was not to be solved with an energetic and towering director like himself. He did not understand that the indigenous situation was the result of a miserable form of colonialism. The common denominator for his work and that of religious missions in general was the conviction that to evangelize was to inflict the European lifestyle upon their charges. He explained to Dom Pedro that he was "allowing" local farmers to use Indian land because the Shoko themselves did not want to plant or do any work in order to save their own land, so he was doing the "charity" of letting those who want to work, do so.'

Fray Dorotheo's presence among the Indians was filled with the ambiguity that characterized other missionaries' work at that time. On the one hand, Indians living in the mission remained there **as Indians** while he was there, because of the missionary's protection. On the other hand, he speeded up the demise of the very Indians he was protecting, as he repressed the Shoko's cultural manifestations, belief systems and the continuing use of a native language. He was – among the colonizing forces working toward deculturation and detribalization – the one responsible for turning the sacredness of the religious performances into simple dances and songs of leisure – *brincadeiras* – and stripping them of their ancient significance of *trabalho* (work). He also wiped out the sacred space reserved for the *Ouricuri* ceremonies, thus leaving that and other tribal territories wide open for the local farmers' invasion. He was even appointed regional director of the Indian Directory when João Fernandes Tavares died, thus becoming responsible for further 'renting' and 'loaning' of indigenous lands to non-Indians.

It is suspected that he was murdered, but no one wants to speculate by whom, or why, as he was both hated and admired by many people with different interests. When death liberated the Indians from him, they immediately found other jailers and the damage had already been done anyway. There was no saving grace for the impoverished landless Indians left there, who followed the path of other groups before them, becoming '*caboclo* peasants'.

Another folk hero appeared on the scene: the Shoko *cacique* Inocencio Pires. In 1917, this *caboclo* hero and two other Shoko went on foot from Propriá to the city of Salvador, Bahia, to ask for help from the local governor. Their intended final destiny was the city of Rio de Janeiro, then the seat of the federal government, where they were also going to plead their case. On February 2, 1917, the *Jornal do Povo* (People's News), a local newspaper in Salvador, ran this report:

> Cacique Inocencio Pires is for the second time in Salvador, having walked all the way from the city of Propriá. Last time he was in Salvador was in 1890. This time he is being commissioned by the poor people of Porto da Folha, in Sergipe, to ask the Republic's President for the restitution of several parcels of their land, presently occupied by the heirs of a big landowner and industrialist from Sergipe. The place where chief Inocencio and his friends live is devoid of villages, of tribes, although they are descendants from the Aramuru. Their intended land is measured by two square leagues and it has been marked by six pieces of rock that were placed there in 1635 by the first Portuguese and Spanish colonizers.

The six rock landmarkers are still around, the Shoko believe, but no one knows exactly where they are. The story goes that Inocencio and his men were able to arrive in Rio de Janeiro, where they were given the papers that proved that Emperor Dom Pedro II had indeed given them titles to the land, when he came to São Pedro island. But when the men were returning home, their mission accomplished, they received an amazingly 'warm' welcome from João Britto's *capangas* (body guards) who invited them to a night of drinking and carousing in town.

The exact location of where these events took place varies in the different accounts: some say the partying took place in Porto da Folha, others that it was in the Caiçara. The fact was that Inocencio was true to his name and innocently let his enemies' games overcome him, falling into the trap that had been set for them. During the feast, the Shoko men got very drunk and fell sound asleep. Meanwhile, their precious land titles were stolen and lost forever. Somehow, nobody can explain why property titles do not have a copy filed somewhere in Rio de Janeiro, but these details are considered unimportant: the main issue was that the Shoko people had once again been deceived and robbed by the White colonizers. The end result was the demoralization and final detribalization of the remaining Shoko. João de Deus finished the story with these remarks:

'Inocencio Pires tried hard but failed. After that, there was no hope left. We were driven off our land and forced to live in exile. Those who wanted to stay, like we did, had to betray our own grandparents. My grandmother was hunted and caught by a dog like an animal. She and other Shoko were brought to the village *no laço* (tied up), because they were legitimate Indians. We had to die, to kill or to run: those were our options. We here stayed because we wanted to protect our land. We, the old 'trunk', knew that one day we would reclaim our land. We just could not go on like slaves forever.'

Those who stayed did so at the expense of their ethnic identity and even personal freedom. They became a subjugated social class, a group of field hands on someone's land, working under the feudal system of *meia*[4], forbidden to exhibit the slightest traces of their past culture. The newly appointed Shoko *pajé* – Raimundo – summarized their situation:

'We were just *meeiros*, miserable workers. At the end of the season, when we took the harvested rice to be weighed and divided by Britto's employees, we brought along a *cuia* (small wooden bowl) to fill with a little rice for our families. Most of the time we were told we owed some money to Britto's grocery store, that our *cuia* would come back upside down on top of our heads: empty.'

This drama started to change with the arrival of Fray Enoque do Salvador to the parish in Porto da Folha. It is usual in the interior that priests visit the surrounding farms to say mass and attend to parishioners living far from town. It is also usual that wealthy landowners feel that they can exert control over the priests, as supposedly priests are there to serve them by giving them political support. Spiritual guidance is only a detail in such arrangements. After all, priests and landlords had historically been working together at the task of 'taming' Indians and appropriating vast territories for capitalist expansion. The custom was for visiting priests to be comfortably installed at the farmer's large homes, saying Mass either inside the house or in the small farm church. Fray Enoque, however, declined the invitation to be a guest in the Britto's home and always stayed at the sharecroppers' humble little houses by the river. That was probably when Britto and other powerful landlords of the area began to smell trouble. For one thing, it was the 1970s and most of the Brazilian Catholic Church had become integrated into the Latin American Liberation Theology Movement.

At that time, Britto had already torn down the houses in São Pedro island, having transformed the area into an open grazing land for his cattle. When the river was low it was easy for the animals to cross the straight channel. São Pedro island was abandoned, though the old mission church still stood. Mission walls had also been brought down and the church was inhabited by bats – and ghosts. Fray Enoque reopened the church and took his humble brethren to worship there. It was there they started to talk about their past as Shoko Indians. Not at all happy with such arrangements, Britto prohibited his employees from receiving Fray Enoque as a guest in their homes, or else he would take away their rights for renting the *posses*. Many people were scared, as their small parcels of land were the only land they could still work on. But Dolores, José Apolonio's mother, ignored the prohibition. She tells the story:

'I saw Fray Enoque hanging his hammock under the trees to spend the night out in the open. I just could not bear seeing that! I went over and asked him to hang his hammock inside my house. Enoi, my godson, had him for supper at his house and we were all happy. The very next morning, Enoi and I were called to Britto's house. I was scared, my knees were shaking, but I went. I thought: what can he do to me, kill me? That would be all right! I just could not allow a man of God, and one who was so good to us, to sleep outdoors, like an animal, right near my house. When we arrived, Britto was very nice and invited us to drink some wine. I couldn't believe it. Enoi is a big fellow and fears no one, but that time he just stood there, afraid of drinking the wine. He kept thinking of what happened to old Inocencio Pires. I, however, drank it: very strong wine indeed. Then Britto asked me if I knew that he had forbidden us to give hospitality to Fray Enoque. I answered: yes, I know, but I would not let him sleep out in the open, what with bats and mosquitoes, and it could also rain. Besides, it was not a Christian thing to do. He asked if we were not afraid of being punished. I said: no, I am not! He looked at me, amazed. Enoi got very angry and asked: what are you going to do? Are you going to beat us, like slaves? Go ahead and beat us! Britto was impressed and just stared at us. Then he said that, no, he justed wanted to know what we thought of Fray Enoque and we said we liked him very much. Then he told us to go.' But that was not the end of the story, for subsequently Britto decided to turn his rice fields into pastures.

That decision was a way of punishing the disobedient farm hands, for a cattle ranch did not need as many workers. They had to go away and leave their ancestral land behind once and for all. The labourers counteracted by getting themselves organized in order to recover Shoko land. They were basing their acts on the idea that they were descendants of the Shoko. As such, they had fully acquired rights to those fields. The concept of legitimacy coupled to that of ancestry gave them a new vision and a new way for fighting against their economic and political oppression. José Apolonio was an adolescent at the time and had never heard about being an Indian, but the elders who remembered parents and grandparents, and who had also felt the loss of ethnic identity keenly, thought that the fight for returning to their indigenous *status quo* made perfect sense. Local labour unions and other rural labour organizations were also supporting the idea.

On September 9, 1979, 23 families from Caiçara, plus 12 families from the neighbouring farm of Belém, marched on to São Pedro island, where they settled down under the trees with their hammocks and other meagre personal belongings, declaring themselves to be the Shoko 'tribe' again. Situations that seemed ludicrous – like fencing off the island so that Britto's cattle could not cross the low river channel to graze – started to happen, giving the group an exhilarating sense of purpose, motivating them to go on even further ahead for their goals. A legal battle began, that lasted more than a year, just over the issue of that fence. But the reappropriation movement had started and gained momentum. It took 10 years for the battle over the island to be legally won. The Shoko installed themselves around the old mission church, rebuilding their small homes out of the island's wood and clay, ready to fight or die, promising themselves never to run away again.

2 *Ouricuri* ritual, secrets and power

'They know the secret language that is denied
all outsiders and without which life in the forest
is an impossibility.'   (Colin M. Turnbull)

Part 1: Nature versus culture, the old debate

EVEN THOUGH BOTH GROUPS – Shoko and Kariri-Shoko – had gone through a
similar process of detribalization and loss of lands, it is fundamental to point out
that the sacred area of rituals, as well as the rituals themselves, were taken away
from the Shoko. Meanwhile, the Kariri-Shoko maintained the equivalent to the
secret and sacred woods, also known as *Ouricuri*. Therefore, the Kariri were
caboclos, but they had somewhere to keep their ritual ceremonies, sacred plants
and objects. The Shoko were only *caboclos*, the lower step in the Brazilian social
strata of the hinterlands.

Keeping the *Ouricuri* was fundamental for the Kariri's survival as a 'tribe'. At
present, Indian land comprises only 2.75 per cent of the 1 666ha of agricultural
land available in the area of Colégio. Dom Pedro II also visited Colégio where
the 'natives' were brought to him as exhibits. He became another mythical hero
to them, when he donated four square leagues (one square league equals approximately nine square miles) of territory, so that they did not have to be banished to
a corner of the Colégio township. When the Kariri-Shoko invaded the Sementeira, they were just claiming back what had been theirs all along. More important yet, they were obeying orders from their Creator – Sonsé – which had been
received through the ceremonial drinking of Jurema wine during the *Ouricuri*
rites. They did not need a Catholic priest to fight for them, nor to help them to
realize they were Indians with rights to the land. They had known that all along,
as keepers of the secret rituals in the 'enchanted forest'. The Kariri-Shoko
shaman explained,

'The *Ouricuri* was and will always be ours, because the enchanted peoples of
the forest, our ancestors, still live there. They live in the trees, the shrubs, the
leaves and the herbs. We cannot gather any of these sacred beings without asking
their permission to do so. They own the *Ouricuri*, we do not. We are only the
keepers of the land. No one has been able to take that land away from us because
we are protected by the *encantados* and the *encantados*[1] are protected by us as
well.'

Nature – natural resources – is thus a conceptually organized space, filled with
cultural significance. This concept of nature and its power is related to the Kariri-
Shoko struggle for the land and its resources and to the power they envisage
themselves as possessing. For this reason, the Shoko who left Caiçara were in
search of their past, their identity, their reasons for being. They chose, in their
own words, 'culture over the land, for we know that with the culture we had a
chance to regain the land. But if we lose the culture we lose everything.'

When the Kariri-Shoko speak of 'culture' they are using the anthropological
concept in its entirety: they are talking about belief systems, lifestyles and social
action. They thus believe that culture orders social action and vice-versa. The
invasion of the Sementeira, the invasion of São Pedro, were economic and social

necessities. Politically, the movements were equivalent in motivation and objectives. Ideologically, even cognitively, they differed. The Shoko were trying to
reaffirm ethnic identity but also to save the São Pedro church with its Catholic
symbols and icons. The Kariri-Shoko were revalidating their ancestral rights
through the formative yet mystical idea of the ancestors telling them what to do.
They were loyal to a voice and vision that had never let go of them. Although
they are also Catholics, the Kariri-Shoko are bound to their ideology of ancestry
for their daily and their extraordinary actions.

What they have in common is the reconstruction of a mythical nation of native
peoples who have rights to land and their own world view. In that way, the
Kariri-Shoko and the Shoko are able to translate a mythical nation of Indians into
the Brazil of today, at the same time that they bring a mythical Brazil of free,
nature-worshipping Indians into the reality of their quotidian experiences.

Part 2: The environment and economics

BOTH COMMUNITIES LIVE WITHIN the range of an ecosystem known as *caatinga*,
which is characterized by long dry seasons, low plains, xerophytic vegetation
and rocky soil.

The city of Colégio, where the Kariri-Shoko reside, is within the region known
as *agreste*, a phytogeographical subdivision of the *caatinga* that is closer to the
sea and, therefore, experiences a greater amount of humidity than the interior
region. Vegetation is taller and denser than deep in the *sertão*, which is the result
of an association of three plant strata: herbaceous, shrubs and savannah type
trees. The vegetal cover goes from herbs and shrubs one metre high to those that
reach 15 to 20 metres in height. The soil is deeper and more aqueous. The soil at
the Sementeira is of three kinds: rocky, soft and sandy. These soils, when
presenting red-yellow patches, have a good level of fertility. Annual median
rain precipitation is about 80mm. During the rainy season the *agreste* swells up,
becomes almost like a forest with its thick, erect tree trunks, being known as
mata do agreste. The region is endemic for several genera *Leguminosae* and
Mimosae. Periods of drought are very serious indeed, followed by hard rains
which can cause overflowing of the São Francisco river.

The Sementeira village, where the Kariri-Shoko have their residences, has
290ha. Most of their land is used for farming: about 245ha. Outside the Sementeira, the *Ouricuri* territory measures 200ha. There is also a small village known
as Colonia, of about 140ha, located on the road between Sementeira and *Ouricuri*. There were approximately 230 families living in Sementeira and Colonia in
1984. The population had a young profile, as 12.5 per cent fell between the ages
of 14 and 19, whereas 9.8 per cent were between 41 and 60 years of age (FUNAI
Bulletin, 1979). This profile indicated a continuous population growth.

Besides farming their backyard gardens and communal vegetable patches,
most Kariri-Shoko live off fishing from the São Francisco river, this being a
predominantly male activity. A state project for economic development of the
São Francisco lower region, known as CODEVASF, was lending small plots at
the river's edge for rice cultivation. A few privileged Kariri-Shoko families were
able to participate in the project that also loaned seeds and fertilizers. However,
the families at the rice fields complained that not much could be produced at
those plots, as the river banks are not as fertile as they are supposed to be and the
loan repayments were too high for their meagre earnings.

The Shoko of São Pedro are closer to another subdivision of the *caatinga* known as *sertão*, which is characterized by dry and aggressive vegetation and intensely troubled by droughts during several months of the year or even two or more years in sequence. Being surrounded by the São Francisco river, the island's terrains are able to absorb more water. Soils are eutrophic alluvial, generally of great agricultural potential, with medium to high fertility conditions, not as shallow and stony as the sertão's typical soil. However, an irrigation system needs to be installed on the island so that the land can sustain productive agricultural systems. The terrain is flat with altitudes varying from 60 to 80 metres. The climate is dry and semi-arid. The median annual rainfall precipitation is between 500 and 600mm, of which the driest month is October and the most humid is May. When the surrounding mainland areas are so parched and dehydrated that the scenery turns gray and yellow, the island is the only green patch around. However, without a proper irrigation system its inhabitants are not that much better off than those in the intensely hot, dry areas.

The same vegetation that is found around the Kariri-Shoko area is to be found in the São Pedro Island, where more aquatic species are closer at hand for the use of the native population. The island is considerably smaller than the area the Kariri-Shoko have available, as it measures only 96ha. The farm on the adjacent shores that the Shoko claim as their ancestral territory, measures 4500ha. The island's shore measurements are: 155m north, 290m south, 3420m east and 3420m west.

The population of the island was 150 fixed residents until 1985, plus several sporadic additions to the 40 resident families, people who come and go seasonally. There were 10 live births between 1984 and 1985, so that there was a steady population growth.

Basic subsistence activities are fishing and horticulture. Rice cannot be planted on the island, since there are no suitable lagoons for swamp rice fields, the type they are used to and which are appropriate for that riverine region. The main agricultural products of the Shoko are cotton, corn and beans. Other minor agricultural products are watermelons, pumpkins, manioc and a few green vegetables such as okra. There are some hard woods, like *Pau-ferro* (*Caesalpinia ferrea* Mart.) but it was not exploited commercially.

Part 3: The meaning of *Ouricuri* as territory and ritual

THE PATCHES OF FOREST in the *Ouricuri* territory enable the Kariri-Shoko to speak of a 'forest of spirits' where they go in order to forsake their Brazilian identity and turn to their ancestral roots instead. The *Ouricuri* forest refers to a piece of the surrounding woods known by the Kariri-Shoko and other tribal descendants as the 'enchanted forest' (*mata do encanto*) and by the local people as the 'forest of the caboclos' (*mata dos caboclos*). The ritual of the *Ouricuri* takes place during the driest months, usually during the first two weeks in January, depending on a cultural and seasonal calendar.

In that region, the word *caboclo* has two related meanings: it refers to the descendants of local Indians and it also relates to the forest entities, the spiritual beings or the people of past times who lived and died in that environment and continue to 'live' there, guarding, protecting and inspiring their descendants. In the latter sense, the forest is the link with the past, with dead ancestors and, therefore, a link to the future as a nation of tribal origin, based on the premise that they – the living and the dead – are together in the task of guarding the land and the people known as Kariri-Shoko.

This special piece of land has always been known as 'the *Ouricuri*' as it has the name of the ritualistic ceremony the group performs at the beginning of each year. Following a tradition they claim comes from the beginning of time, for two weeks at the beginning of every year, as well as a number of weekends through-out the year, the Kariri-Shoko get together as a 'tribe'[2] to re-enact a complex of magical–religious ceremonies. In the past this complex was known as the feast of *Varakidra* or *Warakidza*, an ancestral Kariri deity.

From the time I first heard about the *Ouricuri* I became intensely interested in what immediately seemed to me as a phenomenon of great social importance, due to the secretiveness and fear that surrounded the tales about that particular forest space. What bewildered me more was that I heard about the *Ouricuri* from the local White people, mainly the school teacher Jerusa and her brother, the mail-man. In a conversation during the siesta time of a lazy hot Sunday after-noon, they spoke of what the *Ouricuri* meant, not only for the Indians but for the regional people who are in daily contact with the Kariri-Shoko. Fear was what they had to show, rather than some form of respectful knowledge, reverence or simple conformity. They did not seem to hold Indians in high regard, but did show apprehension over what they considered as *bruxaria* (witchcraft) allegedly practiced during the *Ouricuri* ritual. Their discourse was one of distaste mixed with consternation:

'They do not allow any White person inside the *Ouricuri*', said Jerusa, 'None of us has ever set foot there. We only know that place from afar. You have to be expressly invited to go in, if you are not invited by one of them and go inside, then you will surely die. We only know they do some dances. Vera (Calheiros Mata) and I went there a few separate times, were allowed to watch some of the dances and then we were told to leave. If you are caught "spying" you are beaten to death.'

Another important fact that the strangers to the ritual revealed was the con-tinuing existence of the tribal secret regarding the *Ouricuri*, as told by the mail-man:

'This secret is kept by all Indians, from the little ones to the adults. Whoever starts to talk about it becomes deranged. They do something there and the person goes crazy. That was what has already happened to a young Indian woman by the name of Dina who told the secret to a non-Indian: she became totally crazy shortly afterwards. The man she revealed the secret to left town and does not dare to talk about it. I think they get people killed at the end of the festival or sacrificed to be eaten. I don't know. But some people never come back from the *Ouricuri* so I guess they must die there!'

While we chatted, a Kariri woman came by to announce that the *pajé* was still home, so we hastened to go there after finishing the delicious lunch that Jerusa and her maid had prepared and invited me to share. On the street, I had the uncanny feeling that everyone was looking at me, deep down from their chairs at their front doors or from the wide-opened windows, turning their eyes in my direction. We were walking down the street that faced the river, in the middle of the afternoon, when the sun had already left everyone exhausted from the intense heat and the main meal of the day was still being digested. Most people just lay in their cotton hammocks, or were in bed or sat on easy chairs at the doorsteps of the front door, dozing or leisurely chatting with neighbours and passers-by. Nobody should be such a fool as to be strolling around as if there was nothing better to do! As we walked, Jerusa kept introducing me to the seemingly relaxed folks on the sidewalks by their doorsteps, making sure that everyone knew who I was and that I was interested in seeing the Indians. She also made sure I knew her opinions regarding the *pajé*.

'The truth is that he is the only one who really knows anything about medicine from the woods. He knows how to heal. The other healers only pray on you and don't use any plant medicine. He has a lot of prestige. Also, he is the only one who can legitimately invite you to go to the *Ouricuri*. Besides, that is where most of their medicine is located. If you want to learn about herbal medicine you have to go to the *Ouricuri*; if you want to go to the *Ouricuri* you have to know the *pajé*.'

And how right she was! Only after I had already visited him a couple of times, did I finally gather the nerve to ask him if he could take me on a visit to the forest and the village known as the *Ouricuri*. It was January then and the feast was about to take place. If I didn't go there before the feast, the place would be off-limits to me until the middle of February.

Francisco Suíra had no doubts in his mind when he said, in his systematically careful way, 'You need to concentrate in order to enter the *Ouricuri*', pronouncing it as though it was a final answer to a question not to be asked in the near future, at least. When I asked what he meant by 'concentrate' he answered: 'You will see.' It seemed to me that he was trying very hard to sound mysterious and thus to attain the status of the enigmatic persona that I thought he was intent to show to the world. His approach toward me indicated he thought that I was a totally naïve and ignorant White person regarding their way of life and beliefs. In fact, he was right. Yet he was also impressed by the fact that I did seem eager to learn. Piecing together parts of his tales and other peoples, together with what I learned from ethnographies, I probably did get some insight into the *Ouricuri*.

Ouricuri history

In the beginning of the pre-colonial era and in the legendary past as well, the *Ouricuri* – *Varakidra/Warakidza* – used to take place during the time when the fruits of a palm tree named *Ouricuri* (*Cocos coronata* M.) were ripening. Considering the belief system of today, it is possible to think that the *Ouricuri* tree was the embodiment of the deity otherwise known as *Warakidza*. At that time, which is still the present in the tribal perception, consultations or divinations took place in a new hut made of fresh leaves.

According to Siqueira (1978) the hut had to be built so that the main deity, *Poditan*, could be manifest. However, the author does not explain how such a manifestation took place, whether it was through a phenomenon of incorporation or the ingestion of substances of botanical extract like *Jurema*, or any other. There were three magic powers: *Warakidza, Bizamu, Bizamye* (Siqueria, *op. cit.*). They were supposed to be unleashed during the rituals, for *Bizamu* is a spiritual being – *encanto* – that is called forth by the shaman through knowledgeable invocation. Moreover, *Bizamu* is the *Iate* (a native language, still spoken by some of the local Indians) word for witch or sorcerer: one who orients the faithful in their work, bringing them the necessary knowledge so that they can go on in their task of surviving in this world. *Bizamu* taught followers to locate the best places for fishing and hunting, also how to win wars. It is easy to see the importance that such rituals had for the group's very existence at the daily level.

As a consequence of the Jesuits' pressure against indigenous religious manifestation, the ceremony known as *Warakidza*, which meant 'companion', was renamed *Ouricuri*, since it would be easier to make it acceptable as a seasonal celebration rather than a religious one. The tree had, after all, an economic significance besides the ceremonial one. As a consequence of environmental shifts, the direction and magnitude of which we have not been able to ascertain yet, the tree lost its commercial impact and, along with that, its supremacy in the Kariri animistic concept of the world. However, the ceremony continued to be known as *Ouricuri*, although to the contemporary Kariri it is also known as *Matekrai*[3].

The designation *Matekrai* is actually very suggestive of the relationships being established between humans and botanical species through the ritual, as well as what the vegetal world means to the Kariri. The word root '*akrai*' means 'root' as well, whereas the prefixes 'ma' and 'to' are related to the idea of ancestry, as 'to' expresses the meaning of 'old one'. The ritual's designation could be interpreted as 'Old ones' roots' or 'Old roots' or even 'Ancestral roots'. This name clearly established a tight bond with the 'old roots', literally taken as such; not a metaphorical title, but one directly related to the beliefs in the vegetal world as being part of one Universe in which plants are the embodiment of deities and ancestors.

Some of the central elements of the rituals stand out as signals of cultural entanglements and complexities. Such elements are the medicinal botanical species known to both groups, but which only hold special significance to the Kariri and the Shoko associated to them. However, reading from the codes built around the plants differs for the São Pedro Shoko and the Kariri-Shoko of Colégio. For the latter, rituals and plants in the *Ouricuri* belong to the realm of the *segredo* (secret) which validates the group's existence as an indigenous one.

The knowledge and use of plants are signals for group identity and represent a systemic complex, dialectically related to the *Ouricuri* and, in fact, tied to its very existence as a ceremonial and ritualistic complex. This complex does not have the same purpose and meaning for the Shoko at São Pedro island, who unfortunately have lost the tribal tradition and set of signals.

Therefore, it is safe to affirm that the *Ouricuri* ritual is a magical–religious process of enculturation in which only truly recognized members of the Kariri-Shoko group can take part. The *Ouricuri* sets boundaries between members and non-members of the Kariri-Shoko tribal family. *Warakidza*, the 'companion', was one of the divine trio. *Bizamu* and *Bizamye* were the powers, but *Badzé* and *Poditão* were the ones who held the power. *Badzé*, or *Padzo*, means 'father', and is still recognized today as the deity of tobacco, and could also be the origin of the term '*pajé*,' which also means father. *Poditan*, *Politão* or *Inhura* meant 'son' but is never mentioned by the Kariri of today. It is unclear whether the trinity composed of 'companion' (perhaps the Holy Spirit?), 'father' and 'son' were influences from the Jesuits' catechism or existed even before colonial times as the originating ancestors. Until today, *Badzé* appears as an important figure, forever embodied in the tobacco plant, who is brought to life at the beginning of the rituals through the communal smoking of the pipes and who is in charge of protecting the group by making it invisible.

These godly presences were bequeathed with a power known as *Bizamu* or 'enchantment': the power to see the future, to divine the problems existing in human affairs, thus helping the group to face adverse forces. Nowadays, the same power helps the Kariri when it is invoked by the shaman as he smokes the sacred pipes and drinks the sacred *Jurema*. Through *Jurema* – who is also

Sonsé, the master/caretaker – *Bizamu* orients the people in their relations with the non-Kariri-Shoko, helping them to take the political steps that are crucial for their survival in a hostile world. Therefore, the feast initiates a time for healing the community, protecting its members from the dangers inherent in the universe. At present, the more readily felt dangers are those coming from the enveloping national society. *Ouricuri* members stand out as 'special people' to be feared because they receive protection from entities such as *Badzé* and *Sonsé*; consequently they also maintain the ritual as an insurance against any type of disaster or misfortune that may accompany their participation in the larger national society. They are disturbing people, a nuisance that is feared and will not go away, and as such they have to continue looking for spiritual protection. Since *Ouricuri* membership is that of a secret society, ritual performances are maintained in strict secrecy as well, so that outsiders cannot observe them. Being an outsider, I was not allowed to observe the main rituals, only the beginning of the feast. I was also allowed to hear some of the *torés* which were not entirely secret. Some were sung in Portuguese, some were only hummed or were monosyllabic. The people who sang the *torés* were careful to point out the parts that were not known to the Shoko in São Pedro, since 'they are not real *caboclos*' and, therefore, do not possess the knowledge of the right procedures for the ritual to develop according to the indigenous 'laws' and 'science'.

According to the contemporary members of the *Ouricuri*, the São Pedro Shoko had not participated in the *Ouricuri* for almost a hundred years, ever since the group split in two. That was one of the reasons for the Kariri-Shoko's hesitation to have any of the Shoko from São Pedro coming over to participate in their rituals. In 1985, they allowed Raimundo Shoko to come over for part of the festivities, while there was a film crew there from the Indian Museum of Rio de Janeiro making a documentary about the two groups, and they filmed the dances 'White people' can observe. The Kariri still believe that the São Pedro branch lost the knowledge of rituals and medicines that are crucial for the performances. The ceremony in fact separates the two groups as a form of cultural/ethnic borderline. This is because the people who can enter the *Ouricuri*'s ideological and geographical territory are within the Kariri-Shoko cultural boundaries. The keeping of the secret as a form of maintaining identity is fundamental as a cultural 'pass-word': the key to unlock hidden treasures.

Part 4: Learning the magic

THE DAY I FIRST ASKED Suíra to take me to the *Ouricuri*, he took me instead to the Sementeira village to visit his son and apprentice, Júlio Suíra. Then suddenly, as if the question had just been asked, he responded to what had been posed to him earlier, stating that 'to concentrate means to be of the *Ouricuri*, that is, to be born of Indians and therefore to belong to the tribal secret'. 'Belonging' was thus equated with 'concentrate', a word that means 'to be in the centre' and is used to signify the beginning of many forms of meditation.

Júlio was sitting in the front room of his small home, near the door, just like his father used to do. His house was one of the former workers' dwellings that were built by the Ministry of Agriculture for the Model Farm Sementeira. When the Kariri-Shoko took over the farm, the workers' houses were occupied by the 'new' owners. These were square brick constructions divided into four rooms on one floor: a front room, a kitchen and two bedrooms. The bathroom was an outhouse at the back. The furniture in Júlio's home was sparse and dilapidated, consisting of the bare minimum, but including a black-and-white television set.

Suíra introduced me to Júlio, describing me like this: 'she is doing research and then she has to write a "representation" for FUNAI. But what she really wants to know is about the forest medicine (*remédios do mato*), to know the woods. You and I are going with her someday to the *Ouricuri* so that she can see how it is.' That was how I got to know that I was going to go to the *Ouricuri* woods with him. Having said that, he turned to me and then introduced Júlio to me in this manner: 'he is the *pajé* here in the Sementeira. Since I live out there (in Colégio), people here come to him more than to me. Since he has my science, it is good for you to know him.'

Naturally Júlio knew about me already and even had his speech ready. He started with a complaint against the federal government because it was failing to send payments to the indigenous workers involved with the 'work fronts'[4]. It was another hot summer day in the Sementeira and no one seemed to be in a hurry to do anything other than lounge around the place. Describing the general lassitude that seemed to hover over the village may sound like another ethnocentric statement about the 'natural laziness of Indians,' and I was painfully aware of every one of my mental reactions to what was happening, but I also felt great languor due to the high humidity and heat. The village known as Sementeira had a peculiar stillness about it that day and I asked Júlio if most people were out at work. He seemed to pick up on my concerns and, in his usual quiet way, responded that people were gathering wood and other necessities in order to get ready to go to the *Ouricuri* the next Sunday. Júlio seemed almost morose to me, so quiet and taciturn was he, but there was also an eagerness there that made him resemble his father. He clearly wanted me to have a good impression of the village and his people, but had not changed anything nor taken any special measures to present the place and its dwellers as any different. I detected a silent pride and much actual hurt in his facial and bodily expressions as he spoke to me. A child cried in the bedroom and he smiled peacefully, saying 'It's my grandson.' His wife went unhurriedly into the room to see the baby, who stopped crying as soon as she picked him up. A bitter-looking man came by on a bicycle and asked for 'seu' Francisquinho, who rose ever so slowly to greet him. The two men then went away from the house without a word, walking toward the fish pond that was located some ten metres from Júlio's house. I observed Júlio's preoccupied eyes following them, so I asked who the man was.

'Oh, someone from Colonia. There's been a lot of trouble there because of a family of Tingui-Botó who just arrived from Pernambuco. I think we'll have to have them expelled but we have to discuss that during the *Ouricuri*.'

Then he was surprised at himself for having answered so candidly and his face brightened with a big smile. 'I guess I can trust you,' he quickly added. 'But can I write about what you have just said?' I asked, trying to be responsible about what their conversations with me could mean to them, rather than to myself. He scratched his head, thinking.

'Well, everybody knows about these problems. They create a lot of nuisance around here.' He seemed to remember why he was being interviewed: he pointed towards a potted plant on top of a shelf that was built high on the wall dividing the room from the kitchen.

'See that? It's called *pinhão roxo* and it's used to protect the house against *ôlho grande, ôlho mau*, bad intentions, that is. We always have it in our house, if it dies it means that someone really wanted to harm us and the plant fought so hard to protect us that it died in the process. Then we have to bring in another sprout from the bush that we keep outside.'

He pointed towards a sick-looking bush outside his house, covered with dust and in dire need of a good shower of rain. 'I'm never afraid of bad people or people I don't know, like you, for instance, because I know no one can really harm me. I'm protected forever, not just because of this little plant here but because of the *Ouricuri*.'

I wanted to ask if they could explain to me why then they were so poor, had so much trouble making ends meet, but first I had to discover what poverty meant to them – lack of resources or material goods, for instance? – before I could dare verbalize my own preconceived notions about how to live.

Júlio shifted his gaze towards the front patio where his father was still engaged in conversation with the apparently unwelcome visitor. As far as I could tell from the little I knew of him, he was worried and slightly uneasy. Those were the sort of moments when I wished I was another type of participant in his world, so that I did not have the acute feeling of being an intruder. He didn't look as sure of himself as his father and therefore it was probably also hard for him to simply say: 'Look, I have other pressing matters . . .' But that was not his style, nor that of his people, I was soon to find out, unless they were inside the *Ouricuri*. The *Ouricuri* was indeed their magical place in which they were transformed from toads into princes, from ordinary into extraordinary people. But the Kariri-Shoko – with venerable exceptions – were never arrogant nor demanding in their relationships with the outsiders, like me, who came willingly to them. Júlio, however, was afflicted with the burden of power that can only belong to the shamans' lineage. He reminded me of some princes who become kings against their will and spend a lifetime suffering their fate. It wasn't a tragedy for him, because he did enjoy the prestige and when we talked about his role, his position within and outside of his closed group, he was splendidly complacent about his duties and privileges. However, he did not possess the same aplomb and confidence that was so typical of his father and other shamans I had met in my life. Júlio once told me that he was a good soccer player, that he wanted simply to be a soccer player even though he had been instructed since childhood into the paths that led a person to become a true shaman. He secretly kept hoping that someone else would be the 'chosen one' but when the *Jurema* told them that he was his father's immediate heir and that he had to serve his people as shaman, he simply had to obey. He trusted *Jurema* enough to believe that was what he had to do in life: it was as simple as that. So he abandoned his career as a soccer player, which would have taken him away from his village and his calling from the universal source of power and secrets that was the holy *Jurema* of his ancestry. Then he spoke, ever so softly, words I really did not expect from him:

'I hear the cries of the desperate people, the Indians who abandoned their villages, who lost themselves in the White people's lands and I know I did the right thing. I hear these cries in my mind, in my dreams and when I walk into the forest. It pains me, this knowledge of these cries, it pains me! So I walk in the forest paths and I look for ways to bring these people back, because we've lost so much and so many. The only way back is through the secrets that we keep within the forest itself, within our hearts.'

It wasn't Júlio's style ever to hold lengthy discourses with explanations about himself and his work. He did not look like a passionate man, a person filled with duty: his eyes were placid, and, even though he was taller than most men in his village, he did not have an imposing demeanor. Yet he was capable of proffering words of great depth. Through them, one could glimpse the seriousness of the problems they had to face as an ethnic group and as individuals within a class society.

Francisco Suíra came back inside the house but he did not look at all happy. 'They continue like this and we will have to take action during the *Ouricuri*', he announced gravely. He talked as though I was not present. Then, remembering a guest's presence, he turned to me and briefly explained about the inner struggles that the group was experiencing in the area known as Colonia, where a few families belonging to the Tingui-Botó descendants were living. Júlio, however, seemingly troubled by his father's externalization of a group problem to a stranger, cut into the conversation and, as a good public relations man, invited me to take a look at the communal fish tanks.

But I could not let go of the idea of learning more about the *Ouricuri* and the sacredness it holds for them. Walking back to the town, Suíra told me that in order to call people forth for a secret meeting he simply lets them know he has spoken the word '*Quetalique*' which means 'Let us go!' To that, the people respond '*Akra-uan*' or 'I am going'. Júlio added, in his clear-cut style: 'The forest of the *Ouricuri* is enchanted. It has a power that cannot be destroyed, as it dominates over everything. The *Ouricuri* is stronger than anything, than any-one's will. The white people just cannot wipe it out, no matter if they try.'

I wanted to know if the *Ouricuri* was a person, a legendary grandparent. Júlio patiently said: 'it is all the people of the forest, all together, all under the orders of *Sonsé*, our *Jurema*.' (*Sousé* is the highest god in the Kariri-Shoko pantheon.) As I probably looked dumbfounded, Suíra smiled and said: 'it is very hard for *them* to understand.' I was one of '*them*,' of course, even if momentarily a trusted one.

Later that week, I was introduced to José, the *cacique*'s son and, at that time, FUNAI's representative in town. José was young and prosperous, an Indian hired by the Brazilian government to supervise his own people. Suíra had assured me they preferred to have one of their own as FUNAI's chief, over a 'foreigner.' José wanted to make sure to me that, even though he received a salary from a government agency of the national society, he was a true Kariri-Shoko, a 'real *caboclo*' who still respected the *Ouricuri*. With that purpose in mind, he told me a story to express how a 'legitimate *caboclo*' cannot become either a *branco* (White), or a rich person, because in any case he or she will have to abandon the *Ouricuri* tradition.

'I'll tell you the story of a *caboclo* who became a rich merchant and who, for that reason, started to forsake the sacred religion of the *Ouricuri*. He was becoming middle-class and was being so affected as to be ashamed of his origins. He built a good house and began to refuse to participate in the *Ouricuri*, giving as an excuse that he did not have the time, as he had to take care of his business. But in the second year that he refused to go to the *Ouricuri*, he suffered a serious accident in which he sustained a leg injury. He was taken to the hospital in Propriá but his leg got worse. The doctors told him they would have to amputate his leg. Desperate, he turned back to his people asking for help. His wife begged the *pajé* to intercede for him. The *pajé* said he would make the man dream and repent, so that the *trabalho* of the *Ouricuri* circle could begin. That same night, the man dreamt that he was in the middle of the ceremony, but about to die. He then begged to join the feast and be saved. At the same time he was dreaming that night, the *pajé* had gathered the tribal elders and the man's wife to make a *mesa* for the man, chanting and praying for him, asking for *Sonsé* to save him. He felt his leg being pulled hard and then he woke up. He was terrified, but when he looked down, he saw his leg cured, with no signs of scars or disorder. The doctors came in to amputate his leg and found him cured. They were totally astonished, of course. We believe that the accident happened so that the man could repent and be saved, going back to his traditions. To this day he is one of the most faithful members of the *Ouricuri* circle.'

To his amazement, I asked if he feared becoming rich. He did not consider himself a rich man, even though he had just remodelled his house in the main street of the city. He was also known to be keeping another wife, a White woman, in another town.

'I am not rich! Absolutely not!' he cried out, 'I'm a Kariri-Shoko! I can never deny my people, I will always be a legitimate *índio*, no matter what! I took this position because there was no one else and we were tired of having White people coming around to tell us what to do, but I give a great part of my salary to the *Ouricuri*. God help me! I will never ever leave my *Ouricuri*!'

A few months later, José was transferred to the São Pedro island, where he could take his younger White wife and new baby, to become FUNAI's chief on the island. He was very disquieted by the fact that the Shoko did not have the *Ouricuri* ceremony. He was delighted when his relatives from Colégio agreed to come by in order to teach the Shoko to dance a 'real *toré*', i.e., one that belonged to the *Ouricuri* tradition. But that was a year later, after my visits to them started, and the Shoko had been kept waiting for the Kariri's visit or an invitation for them to come and take part in the *Ouricuri*. At that time, when the Kariri-Shoko danced *torés* inside the São Pedro school, together with their Shoko relatives of São Pedro for the first time, José honoured me by stopping the dance in front of me and saying: – 'we are in front of a person who has always had interest in us and helped us. She is like the wind that comes and goes. She is called *Manusi*, the wind.' And that was how I was baptized.

As for the Shoko of São Pedro, they had lost not only the knowledge related to the *Ouricuri* cult, but also the physical space where the ceremonies were performed. Their ancient forest clearings had been located in the Caiçara land, which, as we have seen already, they had to abandon. Fray Dorotheo had banished the rituals and so they lost the *Ouricuri* at both its concrete and abstract levels. Moreover they lost its structure and meanings and the related social organization that rules the orientation toward the medicinal and magical use of plants.

'Without the *Ouricuri* we are nothing, we are nobody,' claimed various people from the Colégio group. Who were the Shoko, then?

'The *torés* they sing are for *brincadeira* (games),' explained one of the healing women Suíra introduced to me, when we were talking about the ritual and the dances.

'I know that, because I also lived outside my village and began to forget the magical *torés*. *Sonsé* washes the memory out of your mind if you stay away. It doesn't matter, my daughter, you can try and try to keep the remembrance of the music, of the words, but the *Ouricuri* will not let you remember. It's your punishment for forsaking the religion of the *caboclos*.'

She looked at my cassette player and pointing at it firmly announced that even if someone recorded the songs in a machine, like I was doing, *Sonsé* would make sure that the songs were erased from the tapes: 'there is no "machine made by white people" that will keep these secrets, my daughter. It doesn't matter, see?'

One day while we were once again talking about what was involved in the

Ouricuri, Suíra explained that, 'We have our altars, altars that were handed down to us by our grandparents, our "to", containing the sacred objects. When the Shoko came from Sergipe, a long time ago, they brought their own objects and their altar. We now have two altars, side by side, in the *Ouricuri*, one belongs to the Kariri, the other to the Shoko. But those people in São Pedro don't have an altar anywhere. They don't even know the right *torés* to be sung and danced.'

'What is in the altar?' I asked, naturally filled with both personal and anthropological curiosity. Suíra then smiled one of his mysterious smiles I was beginning to dread. Whenever he smiled that way it inevitably meant he was preparing himself to deny some information to me. That day, Maria was sitting by our side and laughed right out loud.

'She does not know what she is getting into!' – she commented about me and then, in a more mellow mood, advised me to be careful 'because you don't understand how terrible this knowledge can become' (Somehow I think I did). In turn, Suíra looked as enigmatic as ever.

'My daughter, the Shoko in São Pedro don't know the secret not only because they allowed themselves to lose it, but also because the secret chose to leave them. They are no longer prepared to handle the secret of the Jurema cult. If they do that without any preparation, that is, if they fall upon the *Ouricuri* secret without the proper care, the proper respect, without dieting, they will surely die. That is why I have to bring you into part of this knowledge little by little. I cannot hand it to you without preparing you. I'm preparing you now, even though you are not aware of it . . .'

'I think I am aware', I said, without hesitation, because I had glimpsed already that he could not, would not, involve me into what was at the heart of his very reason to live without some degree of preparation.

'Good, then you are more intelligent than the Shoko. They think that only because they took over that stupid island that they have the right to call themselves "Indians" and to have access to the *Ouricuri*, or because they sing and dance a few *torés de brincadeira* that they can come and dance and sing in the *Ouricuri*. No way! No, we will not allow that, not only to protect ourselves but also to protect them, even though they don't understand that. I tell you, my daughter, as the word says it: you are now more prepared than they are. Soon I will take you to the *Ouricuri* . . . just wait, just be patient. If you are patient you will see heavens above and earth below, you will be protected by *Jurema*. You can never become a true child of *Jurema* because unfortunately you were born White, and only Indians, Blacks and Gypsies are ready to know the secrets, if they prepare themselves.'

'But the Shoko in São Pedro are both Black and Indians. Why can't they come and be in the *Ouricuri*?' I asked.

'They are not prepared! They walked away from the secret! *Jurema* left them, don't forget this. Now they have to walk back, they have to dream, to walk back, to become walkers and dreamers again. But it is not so easy.'

The ceremonies involve ancestral worship, initiation rites for the young, rites of passage for adults who are developing from one stage of knowledge to the next, spiritual possession and healing sessions. All members of the *Ouricuri* – practically all the residents of Sementeira, except those who came in from the 'outside' as spouses – had to be present at the main rituals of the beginning of the year, even those who lived far away.

'There are people coming from the Amazon, from Rio de Janeiro and São Paulo, everywhere. When it is time, they have to drop whatever they are doing and come here', explained one of the women in Sementeira, 'if you are doing good business and cannot stop your work, you are just going to go down, because the *Ouricuri* is there to help you.'

Her son, a 17-year-old high school student getting ready to serve in the Brazilian Army, stated emphatically: 'I'd never miss an *Ouricuri*! If the army doesn't allow me to take two weeks vacation to come back here, then I'll drop the army. I love MY *Ouricuri*!' His eyes were shining as he said that, so there was no way that one could doubt his sincerity.

'What makes it so pleasurable?' I asked, again astonished by the whole conversation. Mother and son smiled as enigmatically as ever, the kind of smile all the Kariri-Shoko seemed to have been practising for long years, answering in a vague tone of voice:

'We-e-e-ll, it is hard to explain to an outsider. It is just so GOOD! Well, how can I tell you? . . . '

As I looked at them, perhaps somewhat suspiciously, the youth immediately added that there were no 'hard drugs' involved. That could leave room for whatever was not classified as 'hard drugs', however. But it was becoming obvious to me that no one had to force people to participate. It was not like going to church on Sunday, when children and teenagers are sometimes force-fully dragged there in order to attend Mass. The very punishment for not coming was that people felt 'unprotected' and at the hands of 'evil powers' if they did not attend. Even so, there had to be something else, something really enjoyable at the ritual that made people feel so happy and so willing to be there. What was it that made the *Ouricuri* event a gift rather than a chore?

3 Space and time

'Oô, eu vou vadiar na Aruanda'
('I am going to have fun in Aruanda' – *toré*)

Part I: Sacred and profane

IN 1985, THE HOUSES on São Pedro island formed a rectangle: two main rows faced each other across a main field while on the shorter sides there were only a few houses. There was a single house at the northern end, closer to the island's tip, where 'Dona' Nazinha, the healer, lived. The houses in the southern end made a row beyond the church of São Pedro. Their backyards faced the island's old cemetery. The old church was immediately followed, on the left side, by a stone platform left over from a convent built during the colonial era. It was on this improvised stage that the modern Shoko danced what they knew as their old 'traditional *torés*': the songs and dances of their ancestors. The dances were performed during leisure time, while the men drank *cachaça* – an alcoholic beverage made of sugar cane – and everyone was in a festive mood. At times, the *torés* supplanted the *forrós*, which were dances of the *sertão* and possibly the only entertainment of a people living a life of hard labour and poverty.

At the time I was there, the Shoko were not, economically speaking, in very bad shape, mainly because most men worked at the *frentes de trabalho*, and that allowed them to have some spending money. Moreover, the individual family gardens along the western shores served to supply some basic foods such as beans, tomatoes, corn, onions, watermelons and bananas. But even during the hardest times of economic want, when children were being fed only manioc flour and water, the time for dancing the *torés* were always times of great fun for the Shoko. They really revelled in it, showing their best faces and vibrating with their tuneful, high-pitched voices, singing for all the world to hear that they still danced and sang their old folks' *torés*.

Festivities used to go on until late at night, even though there were no real 'free' days for them. Every day was a day to wake up early and go to work, either in the fields, to fish, or to do any other chore that occupied their time. Fishermen were up long before dawn, throwing their large round nets – named *tarrafas* – in the São Francisco river. In fact, except for very old people and babies, most people were up quite early in order to enjoy the day and work at their many chores before the sun became a source of overwhelming heat from the sky.

I wanted to tape-record their songs, so one night the Shoko were dancing and singing at my request. They had already put on some special performances but this was extra special as they were attempting to emulate the dances of the sacred *torés*. Only the men were dancing in front of Lola's house, which used to be a focal point for meetings, since Apolonio, the young *cacique*, lived there with his mother and his wife.

Gradually, Pedrito Santana, one of the leaders of the Shoko political activities, went into what I deduced was some sort of trance: he was sweating, singing in a hoarse voice and whistling with a fury such as I have never witnessed before, even when dancing. 'Dona' Lola – as Dolores was called sometimes – was smoking her pipe, standing quietly by my side. I asked her what was happening to Pedrito. She said: '*Um encantado encostou nele*' (an enchanted one got into him). That was the first time I saw a form of trance during a *toré* session among the São Pedro Shoko. 'What happens now?' I inquired, puzzled by the phenomenon.

'Nothing,' she said. 'Soon he will go away. The *encantado* came because we were calling him.'

Nobody seemed to be especially moved or impressed by what was happening. Pedrito sang with violent emotion, improvising the lyrics, during which he said that he was dancing in front of Lola's house in the *toré* that he was creating right then. During the day a fisherman, at night an 'instrument' or medium for the incorporation of a dead ancestor, Pedrito was also a politician, a diplomat for his group. (Incorporation is a belief that a human being can, at a given moment, incorporate another spiritual being.) I don't know yet for which one of these reasons Pedrito was shot and eventually killed two years later.

There was no doubt in my mind that he had a message for his group, not only from the political encounters he had in the cities with Sergipe's leaders but also the one then being transmitted by an *encantado*. That was the message that would lead them into the promised land of their ancestors. Inevitably, he was a good target for whoever did not want the Shoko to become 'Indians' again. That particular night, Pedrito did not sing any of the political themes, nor the songs of nostalgia for the lost land of Caiçara, composed by his cousin Paulino Santana, which they used to sing all the time. He was doing something else: as he went into the trance he was asserting their capacity to break with the principles of the Catholic Church and the power of the colonizers, thus bringing back the shamanistic tradition of their ancestral past. 'Seu' Raimundo, the group's appointed *pajé*, never seemed to go into a trance, showing no inclination for that. Curious about this fact, such obvious difference of behaviour between the two *pajés* I knew, I talked to Suíra about his São Pedro 'colleague'. Suíra pondered: 'Well, that's because they don't really know what a *pajé* is all about, the poor creatures . . .'

I also told Suíra about Pedrito and the whistling. He thought about it for a moment: 'Did he sweat?' he inquired. 'Yes, profusely.' He was quiet again for a long moment, smoking his home-made cigarette.

'Well, the *encantados* were there, no doubt! Did they just dance? Did Pedrito say anything?' I explained that he was spontaneously composing verses for the *toré* right there on the spot, but that was all. When the dance was finished, he was smiling a lot but he seemed to be his usual self again. Suíra waved his hand and smiled broadly: 'Well, like the word says it, the *encantado* came and went and then they could do nothing else. It's a shame they don't have a real *pajé* there. The *pajé* could have talked to Pedrito's *encantado* and you, my daughter, would have witnessed a healing, finally. However, like the story says, *encantados* are difficult creatures. They are not easy to deal with and they (the Shoko from São Pedro) don't know how. They may even know about the *encantados*' existence and how they show up. But they don't know how to take care of them . . . Taking care is a business that we learn from infancy, that we bring forth from our ancestors. It isn't something you learn from one day to the next. You don't learn how to talk to an *encantado*, how to *amansar* (to domesticate) an *encantado* in a school! You learn in the *Ouricuri*, you learn watching it, seeing the *encantado* right there and seeing your grandparents talking to him.'

In São Pedro, matters like that did bring some thinking about spiritual matters, but people would talk of ghosts and visions, demons and fairies, entities that lived in the woods, and then they would cross themselves with fear and respect.

They did believe in disembodied souls, in the return of the dead, but these matters filled them with terror and trembling as they had not been brought up to chat with spiritual beings. All they knew was that the *encantados* whistled when they arrived during a *toré*, that the souls of the departed were dancing among them, and that was all right. But there was no exchange of information between the dead and the living, no visionary healing as it happened in the *Ouricuri*, a healing brought about by the visions live people had of the *encantados* and their messages. The dead, in other words, were not an integral part of an anthropomorphic nature. When the dead commune with nature, as in the cosmovision of the native ancestors, then they are not a source of fear or misgiving. Suíra and the other people in Sementeira talked about conversing with the dead naturally, as if it was something to be expected. To die was not viewed as a terrible or perhaps even an embarrassing event, as it is in the Christian view of the world, where one tends to mumble apologetically about someone's death, as though the dead should have avoided death at all costs. The Shoko somehow dreaded death as a punishment, exactly as the 'others': the White people or, better yet, the 'dried heads'.

For the same reasons outlined above, the São Pedro Catholic church was closed for indigenous festivities as no *torés* were to be danced inside it. There was an unspoken but firmly understood demarcation between the profane festivities of the *torés* and the sacred mass. Some island residents were devout Catholics who could not even dream of performing rituals like those of their 'ancestors'. They did not identify themselves as being descended from whatever ancestors the Shoko leadership was talking about. A woman whom I interviewed said she was not a Shoko, she was a Catholic. Obviously, she had not constructed her identity around the *Ouricuri* nor an indigenous iconography. Rather, her social being had been built by the European Catholic mode of thinking. For the 'legitimate Indians', therefore, there could be no separation: the *torés* were religious events, when the ancestors were called and when they accepted the invitation by approaching the dances, singing and dancing along with the living.

The only time I saw the church space being invaded by *toré* dancers was during the week the Meeting of Northeastern Tribes took place at São Pedro island in 1986. At the end of a day of much discussion and resolutions, all the guests – *Patasho*, *Fulniô*, *Pankararu*, *Kariri-Shoko* and some Amazonian representatives – started to dance *torés* around the entire circle of houses on the island. At the end of the western row of houses stood the Catholic church, with its doors wide open because of the festivities, but in a quiet recess. Suddenly a Fulniô man in the front line of the *torés* uttered a loud cry and ran into the church, causing a commotion among the host Shoko, who were then unable to go against the gesture or do anything in protest, but visibly alarmed at seeing the old-fashioned Christian space being filled with songs from the ancestral religion.

However, as all the dancers were inevitably drawn into the church space the dances continued there: it was a form of reclaiming the original space – both material and spiritual – that had been taken by the colonizers and giving it back to the Shoko completely. Until then, the São Pedro Church had been the space of 'São Pedrinho', of other Catholic saints and icons. Until then, the *torés* had been kept to the space of profane celebrations and carousal. The Shoko still thought that, in order to have the *Ouricuri* celebration again, they would have to reclaim the Caiçara lands where the rituals used to take place in the past. Apparently, they had not realized that the Ouricuri space is more symbolic, more idealized than a real physical space. That was exactly the lesson their 'relatives' gave them the night they brought the Shoko to dance inside the church. The message was: the *Ouricuri* is everywhere, it is inside one's minds and hearts, and one does not have to wait for the Caiçara. 'Take the sacred space back now,' the Fulniô were saying, 'as you took back the island! Take it back when dancing the sacred *torés!*' The idea was to return to archaic times through the ritual and not just through geographical landscape.

Part 2: *Ouricuri* space

The *Ouricuri* festival continued to be the mysterious object of my imagination, as the Kariri-Shoko so desired. While I lived among them, neither I nor the people of São Pedro island were allowed to set foot in the *Ouricuri* village while the *festa* was taking place. When *pajé* Raimundo was a special guest for the *Ouricuri*, that was considered a great honour for him. However, he was not allowed to reproduce any of what happened in São Pedro, as the Shoko were not yet considered 'prepared'. He could only start bringing back the messages that he was learning, in order to re-acculturate his relatives to an old way of celebrating life.

The message was that the *Ouricuri* is a feast of obligation (*obrigação*) because the proselytes are committed to venerate their ancestors, as well as to pass the ancestors' knowledge of the world on to the next generation. The *Ouricuri* is a covenant made between the ancestors and their followers. It is the obligation of ancestors and children to make sure that the group is reproduced at all levels: biological, economic and ideological. The ritual involves the rebirth of a nation, a very special commemoration in the circle of life, when death is cast away with the return and blessing of the ancestors. Ideally the celebration should take place under the protection of magic trees, thus being related to the rites and symbols of renewal, no doubt the 'vegetal hierophony' that Mircea Eliade (1973) refers to. It is to be performed within the boundaries of a sacred space. But – and the Shoko had not been able to perceive that yet – it is the ritual that sacralizes the space and not vice-versa. The *Ouricuri* forest is sacred because the ritual of covenant between gods, ancestors and the Kariri takes place there. Such space becomes structured and signified space: it has form and power, being the only 'real' space, or, better still, the only space worth living because without it life would not be possible. Life was already so difficult, so filled with real and imaginary enemies for the indigenous peoples! Admitting there was a symbolic, and in that sense 'real', space for them was what their lives meant, their trajectories in those bitter, parched, impoverished lands of the northeastern *sertão* could continue being a possibility. Only when generations joined together at the appointed time could they have a chance. The *Ouricuri* space was, and continues to be, the centre of the Universe, where all things and creatures gain form and significance.

Suíra summarized the meaning of the *Ouricuri* space when he declared: 'The *Ouricuri* is the Kariri language, which is also a secret language.' All forms of communication and of interpreting the world are encapsulated and preserved within the *Ouricuri*, which provides the participants with a code to interpret daily scripts. Thus they share a language and a universe of meanings.

When Suíra first entered the *Ouricuri* forest, taking me along, he was very silent. I had my notebook and my bag for collecting plants, but the first 20 minutes or so went by in silence as we went around the circle of the forest. He wanted me to 'feel' the forest, he explained, and then added:

'Ah, here I am at peace, I am free, I am myself! Here no one can tell me what to do. Only the *encantados* can talk to me here. Only the *encantados* can tell me what to do.'

For a people whose dreams of equality and dignity in the larger society have become impossible, the *Ouricuri* is indeed a magical space. It is through and within the *Ouricuri* – ideological *Matekrai* and physical forest – that the Kariri-Shoko reclaim their space and time away from the control of their 'bosses' in the 'outside world'. There they are able to re-establish continuous ties with a sacred and magical realm, a place that is ideologically in opposition to the rest of the world. From an etic, or outsider, point of view, other authors have already established the importance of the *Ouricuri* feast for the Kariri-Shoko's tribal survival and continuity as it constitutes one of the strongest elements of social cohesion. (cf. Pinto, 1956).

Suíra took me to the *Ouricuri* village right at the beginning of the festival. I could only watch the first round of dances, performed when the sun was setting. All the families were gathered in their small rooms, crowding together in great anticipation of the feast to come. There was an atmosphere of utmost expectancy. The air was charged with a feeling so intense and so strong that no one could avoid being infected by it. My heart was pounding when the first *toré de búzios* started, as I was filled with just about the same gladness and emotion as the people surrounding the dancers there. Then the dancing of the more 'sacred' *torés* was about to start, accompanied by the stomping of feet and stronger vibration of voices. Later, drinking of *Jurema* wine was to happen, and I was not allowed to stay for that part. I was accompanied to the edge of the village, where the FUNAI agronomist waited for me in his truck. We drove back to his house in Colégio. I was sad because I could not stay, but immensely respectful of their right to deny me – a member of the 'outside society' – some kind of shared vision. If they let me in, something would be broken for them, perhaps their resilience, the determination, the image of complicity in the knowledge of the mysteries from the forest and from the past.

I could only imagine the rest of the dances from descriptions I obtained from my hosts. That is when they began to set themselves apart and away, in a superior position, no longer subjugated to their White colonizers and their plans. Thus they are no longer outcasts of a society that places them in inferior socio-economic categories, that disapproves and discriminates against them.

At *Ouricuri* time, all the Kariri-Shoko leave Sementeira and move to the *Ouricuri* village, taking their pots, hammocks, blankets, sheets, clothes, food, water and whatever else they can. Their personal belongings are bedraggled and humble as always, but there they are masters over their lives. The *Ouricuri* space stands outside the profane world of market relations and the business matters of their lives as rural labourers. In the *Ouricuri* the people re-enter the world of their ancestors like children being re-born, in a mythical time when the *brancos* did not yet exist. Visiting the *Ouricuri* village when it is inhabited and observing the patched clothes, the worn-out aspect of the adults and the over-all dreariness of the shacks contrasts sharply with the native huts of the jungle Indians who are not in constant contact with the national society. One may then wonder how these people can think that they are 'superior' and 'free', when their economic situation is so evidently low and their lifestyle so backward.

The explanation may come out of the medical practices and the concepts of healing of the tribal life, rather than from individual lives. The *Matekrai* ritual re-installs magical consciousness, in which concepts about the world and life are changed, in which the goal of the dances and songs is to affirm the sacredness of life and objects that make life meaningful. At the *Matekrai* the world of *brancos* does not exist. They are at the beginning of time. The very shape of the *Ouricuri* village is an attempt to reproduce the structure of past villages, as well as to eliminate whatever class distinctions there are 'out there'. Tradition is then invented and re-invented. It does not matter that most of the plants that are brought in as embodiment of the ancestors are acclimatized exotics. It does not matter that they do not physically look like their forerunners. The world is being recreated. They are at their recreation time, in the double meaning of originating and pleasure. They become extremely happy indeed, emptied of the anxiety and sourness of life in the 'real world' which is 'the world out there'. However, the *Ouricuri* as a concept of 'magic', of something unreal, is fundamentally a Western construction. For the Kariri-Shoko, the ritual and whatever takes place there has the force and the clarity of what we conceive of as being reality.

There is an implicit opposition to 'sacred' and 'profane' spaces in the social imagery surrounding the *Ouricuri*, but that is not necessarily understood as such by the Kariri-Shoko because the space is being interpenetrated by so-called sacred and profane activities. During the day, the centre of the village is a place to cook, stand about in, chat and play. At night, it is a place to comply with religious obligations, to sing and dance the *torés*. However, the *Ouricuri* is sacred not only because the *encantos naturais* (the enchanted natural beings) live within it, but predominantly because it has always been a truly indigenous territory, occupied by the presence of the Kariri of centuries ago. It is thus the place closer to the country that lies beyond death. Therefore, that space makes it possible for a channel of true communication to take place between the spiritual powers and the people on earth. The earth–sky axis is maintained through the rituals and the performances of obligations. Physical structures are of a symbolic rather than an architectural nature, being qualified as unchanging or fixed in time, transcending temporal measurements and limitations.

Space is, in this sense, a field of values, a transposition of the imaginary into the real, more than a transposition of the real into the imaginary. It is therefore always reorganized and reworded by the imaginary, losing its purely physical characteristic. In terms of societies where the imaginary finds itself strictly related to magic, time and space are dimensions fundamentally different from those postulated by Cartesian logic, in which time and space are linear, thus limited, finite and preferentially homogeneous.

At the *Ouricuri*, all time is **now**: the moment when the ceremony takes place. That is the essence of what we know as 'magic time' (cf. Weinstein, 1981; O'Keefe, 1982). The time of magic is a cyclical conception of time with an extraordinary dimension, where time is not understood as an absolute, therefore has no beginning and no end. There are merely interruptions, as time is infinite and unrestricted, making possible the encounter between ancestors and divinities with the humans who celebrate them. It is thus possible to 'see' the future because the future is now, in the same way that it is possible to 'see' the past, in that its emanations remain close at hand. The aspect of biological time is not ignored, but simply understood as a relative phenomenon. Time passes while it stands still: that is their fixed 'truth' and covenant with the archaic generations.

In circular time, ancestors coexist with present generations. In the festivals devoted to ancestors, the spiritual beings whistle or make their presence known when they 'arrive'. They can then embrace, speak with, or otherwise commun-icate with their descendants and celebrants, thus establishing the axis of sky and earth. This concept of time differs structurally from that in which 'time is money', that is, in which time is a commodity for people who live in societies dominated by the logic of capital.

Eliade (1973) discusses this difference between sacred time – circular – and profane time – linear – stating that 'sacred time' is by its very nature reversible, in the sense that it is, properly speaking, a mythical, primordial time made present. Consequently, every religious festival, all liturgical time, consists of the reactualization of a sacred happening that took place in the mythical past, 'in the beginning' of human life on earth.

Nevertheless, there is a way of counting this infinite time. This is done through astronomical and agricultural cycles, which identify the proper times for feasts, obligations, and religious works, as well as the times to attend to the demands of wage labour – obligatory, quotidian, bought and imposed by the larger national society. This type of work time is opposed to what is actualized in the *Ouricuri*, where work is organized around tasks, making it possible for the constant alternation between work and leisure. Indeed both are pleasurable and not mutually exclusive. The time dedicated to wage labour is done **outside** of the spaces dedicated to the integration with the ancestors and deities.

Timeframe is also essential in understanding the organization of the *Matekrai-Ouricuri* feast. Conceptually speaking, this spatial configuration exists in a special time, for time and space are not only interrelated but interdependent as well, as time-reckoning is related to a relative space. It is in the *Ouricuri* space that ancestors or past generations come back to be with their descendants, transcending the barriers of what is known as 'past' and 'present'. Time is no longer linear, with a beginning, middle and end, with mornings and evenings following each other, even as time is surely organized for the ceremonies to take place. The 'time of the ceremony' starts when the *encantados* arrive and never when the clock says so. When the *encantados* return to be with their people, the world becomes as it was in the beginning and all people are like children, made equal by the circularity of ages. The dead are alive, the living are new-born babies, the shaman flies above the earth, returning to any age, any space, *Sonsé* – the Creator – talks to the people. The chaos in the universe is only momentarily overcome, as order is never found to be inevitable. In fact, one way to understand their misery is the inherent disorder of the universe, with which the Kariri-Shoko have learned to live. The universal infinite time is not well ordered, although it is circular. Events become repetitious because – as these people comprehend events – they are destined to be replayed in the round loops of time.

This contrasts vividly with the concept of time that the Kariri-Shoko are used to following 'out there' in their quotidian lives, because our Western view of time is linear – it has a beginning, middle and end. It does not flow in a subjective continuum but marches along in quantifiable units. It is objectified, as Whorf (1956) has pointed out, and conceived of as a series of things, one after the other, rigidly organized like apples sitting on a shelf. As such, time can be added, subtracted, divided, multiplied, gained, lost, saved, earned, borrowed, squandered, accumulated and allocated. 'If time is understood as finite, then the close of life is an irredeemable tragedy, an irreversible loss'. (Meyerhoff, 1978: 158).

The communal space of the village is as circular as time that goes round and around. Most fundamental is that in the circularity of time and space, death is denied. There are no boundaries between life and death, as dead and alive beings commune together in the space and time of the *Ouricuri*, because the dead become alive, becoming 'real' as they interact with the living. The experience of living on earth is not seen as a non-transferable phenomenon. Death is but an occasional event through which the body disappears from immediate sight and feeling. If the archaic ones can play with the living generations, the physical body is an item to be transformed, as time itself is constantly fluctuating. The world of the *caboclos* is truly and structurally an eternal one. Meanwhile, life – the Kariri-Shoko life and being – is affirmed, standing in opposition to the capitalist commoditization of time and space. Land is not economic neither is time. The self-validation process is re-affirmed. Although these people are poor *caboclos*, they are powerful healers; small-scale landowners but engineers of their own fate. Being a *caboclo* is no longer viewed as belonging to a timeframe in a definite space, but an identity with mythical eras and timeless legends. Time, like life, is forever: infinite, boundless and characteristically chaotic and jolly.

'Nobody can get at me here', explained Suíra, walking through the *Ouricuri* forest. Everyone is protected inside the *Ouricuri*, not only because the Whites fear their capacity for vengeance through magical pursuits but, from an emic point of view, because the *Ouricuri* gives them strength: a spiritual power and a perceptiveness that cannot be achieved outside of the sacred space and time. Taking the '*Jurema* wine,' which was prescribed by *Sonsé* at the beginning of time, and another beverage known as *waluá* – made of fermented manioc – the people are allowed to expand their consciousness. Their terrestrial chains are broken, as they do not worry about what the 'White bosses' are going to do or say. They become capable of 'seeing' what normally, in their daily lives, they cannot see or hear or perceive.

The fundamental act of defiance installed at the *Ouricuri* is that of self-affirmation, for all 'native' societies are being constantly asked to show proof of their 'originality'. In order to reproduce themselves at the social level, old tribal customs have to be unearthed from the depths of history. But in circular time, history is all there: the belief is that the dead ancestors are the live history, the re-creators of the myth. With them there is no fear of error. The war against the dreadful *cabeças secas* is won. Traditional social hierarchies which are either not followed rigidly or else are disobeyed during the daily task of survival are reconstructed in order to re-install magic consciousness or, rather, reality. They become a people in love with their own selves.

The *Ouricuri*, as a specially structured space, only exists – conceptually speaking – in an equally special time, a unique time, a 'time of ritual'. Opening the ritual, the *Ouricuri* is symbolically protected by the 'God of Smoke', *Badzé*. The shaman, ritual assistants, and other men in the group smoke their pipes, the smoke that envelops the entire physical space of the *Ouricuri* and, according to their belief, renders it invisible. Thus, the entire village becomes lost, hidden in time and space, apart from everything, far away from all the evil that 'outsiders' might wish to cause them.

The physical space of the *Ouricuri* seeks to reproduce the structure of ancient villages, separating the living spaces of persons, the 'secret and sacred' spaces, and the 'enchanted forest'. This *Ouricuri* space is conceived of as different from the village where the Kariri-Shoko now live and gain their livelihood. The social hierarchy is not the same as that of the 'outside world'; it is spatially distributed according to the following binary opposites: child/adult, male/female, specialist/non-specialist, initiate/non-initiate. The hierarchical divisions of the class society in which history placed the Indians cease to exist within the *Ouricuri*. The dwellings are not differentiated by size, material, or aesthetics. The *Ouricuri* space is devised to negate the outside world and its class divisions as well.

However, recently some signs of the interference of class consciousness, as well as class division, are apparent at the *Ouricuri* village. For instance, the house of the Kariri woman who has a middle-class job as a school director is better constructed than the other rooms in the village.

None the less, men occupy rooms considered to be 'secret', that is, off limits to women. Within this masculine space, there is another division of space: specialists and initiates can enter any of the rooms, whereas non-initiates are forbidden to enter the spaces considered the most 'secret and sacred'. One of these is the space where one finds the altar, with the secret objects that lend the tribe 'magical power' and reinforce its identity.

The *Ouricuri* space is composed, concretely as well as ideologically, of three concentric circles and three distinct parts, which are totally interdependent:

(1) **the circle of vegetation**, home of the enchanted ones and males: the masculine space, outside of the circle of houses, where the altar, secret objects and the most sacred trees are located;

(2) **the circle of houses**, residence of women and children: a feminine space, where women, young children of both sexes, and girls sleep, and where men and boys come to eat. The houses, in reality, are nothing but small compartments located side by side in a circle, covered by a common tile roof and separated by short brick walls. Each room has three walls; the fourth side, which faces the central plaza, serves as an entrance and is closed off by the curtains of cloth or straw, or wooden planks;

(3) **the circle of rituals** or the central clearing, located in the middle of the plaza, surrounded by the women's houses. The communal hearth, where communal meals are cooked, is located in that central clearing, where the dances (*torés*) and some of the sacred rituals are held.

These concentric circles are surrounded by the forest of the *Ouricuri*, which is inhabited by the living 'enchanted ones' – the plants and animals living there – and by the deceased 'enchanted ones' – the spirits of dead people belonging to the group. The forest space is sacred, uncontaminated, secret, thus standing ideologically apart from the dominant sectors of national society with their constraints and power over native life. On the other hand, the forest space of the Shoko in São Pedro is not seen symbolically as the guardian of the tribal being: it is vital and important as a natural resource but not as a symbolic marker.

The entrance and exit from the three circles are marked by plant species to which protective powers are attributed. They are: the Angico (*Piptadenia sp*) and the Juazeiro (*Ziziphus joazeiro Mart*). The distribution of space reproduces the mythical forms of the Universe. The communal hearth is in the centre of the 'earth', from which comes the sustenance of all living beings; the tall trees mentioned above are the guardians of the sacred space, barring those who do not belong to the tribal tradition. This world can only admit the only living persons worthy of belonging and coming into it: the Kariri themselves and other indigenous groups held in high esteem by them. In the space next to the altar there is said to be a 'sacred *Jurema*' plant, possibly one of the *Mimosa* species, from which pieces of root are taken to make the *Jurema* wine that is to be shared by all the initiates during the rituals. In this spatial and ideological structure, persons considered to have the power that comes from the invisible realm, i.e., the shaman and his helpers, other healers of respect and leaders, are located separate from all the others.

The festivities of the *Matekrai* last from 14 to 21 days, depending on the disposition of the participants or the importance of the events. The first seven days are directed by the Kariri, and the following seven by the Shoko, thus maintaining two traditions that, despite being considered identical, are based on 'secrets' and sacred objects originating from two different localities. One of Júlio's sons explained: 'the words are the same, but the objects are different, thus, their *Ouricuri* is also separated even though we are all participating in it together.'

The informant himself is not 'separated', because he is at once Kariri (from his father's side) and Shoko (from his mother's side). During these rituals, certain formative deities of the group, especially *Jurema*, are then celebrated. Chants and dances, known as *torés*, are performed within the circle in the central clearing. It is relevant to note that the *Ouricuri-Matekrai* always takes place at the beginning of the year, during the dry season, well after planting and before the harvest, a period in which there is no agricultural work; or else during specific periods that are considered sacred, coinciding with the collection of the fruit of the *Ouricuri* palm, from which the festival takes its name; or also during individual or tribal conflicts, when the religious works must be resumed.

'When we are together we are as one,' explained Júlio, 'but there are several problems between the Shoko and the Kariri that have never been resolved, so, in spite of the fact that we live together and make the feast together, we have to stress the fact that we are also apart, that our differences have not been obliterated yet.

'Will these differences ever be erased?' I asked then.

'I don't know,' Júlio answered and his sad eyes looked even sadder. 'You see, my mother belonged to the Shoko trunk, and my father comes from the Kariri, so I am two in one, I, more than anyone, am the one – *o que é dois em um, o um* – (he meant that in every level of the tribal life, no doubt), but yet I cannot stop the fights that arise between people from the different bands. How can there be these differences, you may ask yourself, since we now have children who descend from both trunks. Yet they continue. They also inherit the bitterness, the *antipatias . . .*'

Thus, even though the *Ouricuri* was a feast of renewal, of celebration, it was also a celebration of the contradictions, when the Kariri reminded the Shoko that the latter were indebted to the former for having a home, but also when the Shoko reminded the Kariri that the reason they did not possess the São Pedro island was because they could not count on the Kariri's support.

'Our saints are not the same', was the *pajé*'s explanation for the differences. 'They brought their objects, the sacred ones that are located on their altar in the men's house, and thus they are apart from ours. We have our own things. They have theirs. There can be no confusion! Other than the objects, we have everything else. Even *Jurema* is ours, it is our tree, it belongs to our land, to us. No one can claim *Jurema* here!'

This contradiction can be interpreted as a necessity for the constant affirmation of tribal being, but also as part of a continuum, as the duality that underlines society. Therefore, 'it is not a matter of different cognitive structures, but of an identical cognitive structure articulating wide diversities of cultural experience.' (Turner, 1989: 3).

In their daily life, both the Kariri and the Shoko have to reproduce the structure of the dominant society. Their cohesion is a fundamental strategy in order to keep their status as indigenous groups. Once they were pushed into a single street in the city of Colegio, living miserably. It was precisely during the performance of the *Ouricuri* that they 'heard' the advice from *Jurema* and were able to unite their forces in order to reclaim part of their ancestral lands. But it was also within the *Ouricuri*, however, that the subtleties of their re-invented traditions were allowed to come to the fore, as if magic consciousness liberated that part of the unconscious where the enmities and the duality reigned. At the same time, magic itself is a social mechanism of protection against enmity either inside or outside the group. People I talked to expressed a greater fear of 'insiders' than 'outsiders':

'I know' – said a Kariri woman – 'what any of these praying women (*reza-deiras*) can do, even though they say that they only do charity and are unable to do evil. I know they have the strength, the power for doing a lot of harm to anyone they wished. Why should they be different toward somebody inside the tribe, if they become enemies? The *pajé* himself can harm a person if he so wishes. He can do that better than anyone!'

Social change outside the tribal apparent cohesiveness was dictated mainly by economic pursuits. Families who were able to achieve a status that was close to the local middle-class, surely felt and acted like 'nobility' showing off with consumer goods such as large colour television sets, quality furniture, good beds, good bed linen, good clothes and so forth. Such changes were beginning to be noticeable even inside the *Ouricuri* circle where supposedly a strict degree of economic equality had to be adhered to. Ideally, they strove for equality and for some sort of frozen moment in the supposedly glorious mythical past, that was expressed as an all-encompassing time reckoning, as if there was, inside or outside the idealized constructs of the *Ouricuri*, a lack of interest in the passing of time.

Part 3: *Jurema's* orders

Jurema, the source, the beginning, the infinite, stands inside the *Ouricuri* space, filling it with its presence. Such presence happens to be displayed by trees of the genus *Mimosa*. The name comes from the Tupi *Yu-r-ema*. Several species of the genus *Mimosa* and *Acacia*, of the *Mimosaceae* family, are called *Jurema*. Mainly due to the alleged narcotic effects of the beverage made from the roots of one of the *Jurema* trees (*Mimosa verrucosa Benth*), *Jurema* is popularly known as the 'magical drug' of the Northeastern interior, of the dry savannah regions and the *caatinga*. However, *Jurema* is much more than a botanical specimen: *Jurema* is a special beverage, a drug with hallucinogenic properties, the enchanted one, the creation principle i.e. the mythical place of origin. The cultural phenomenon known as *Jurema* displays many symbolic faces.

The cult of *Jurema* is ancient and traditional to the region the Kariri belong to and has been taken up by rural populations in the Northeast, being part of a religious practice known as *Catimbó*, and the Afro-Brazilian cults that, in the Northeast, are named *Shangô*. It seems that it was originally an indigenous religious practice, but nowadays it is clear that it was greatly influenced by the African traditions and Portuguese religiosity as well (da Mota and de Barros, 1990). *Jurema* represents the *caboclo* in the public imagination, its effigy in the Afro-Brazilian cults being that of a brown-skinned woman with long straight black hair. According to a line from a song in an *Umbanda* liturgical procedure, 'she' is the mother of another indigenous representation in Brazilian folklore: the *caboclo Tupinambá*.

'*Ele veio na linha da Umbanda/ Ele é Tupinambá/ Ele é filho da Jurema/ Ele é neto de Iemanjá*': 'He came in the Umbanda lineage/ He is *Tupinambá*/ He is the son of *Jurema*/ He is the grandson of *Iemanjá*.' In the song, therefore, *Jurema*, an indigenous deity, is said to be the daughter of *Iemanjá*, a goddess from the African tradition, imported to Brazil with the Black slaves.

Among the Kariri-Shoko, however, *Jurema* is of uncertain sex, as the creation principle is not tied either to male or female representation. *Jurema* has traits that are supposed to belong to men **and** women and, even though they speak of *Jurema* with the article 'a' in front of the name, thus signifying a female person, it is never clear that *Jurema* is indeed a woman.

Most of all, *Jurema* is a tree that signifies the creation principle and the beverage that is extracted from its roots brings messages from *Sonsé*, the Creator. According to Suíra's words, *Jurema* is indeed the representation of *Sonsé*, the first ancestor, the one who makes it possible for the Kariri-Shoko to travel to the past and to the future, unifying their generations into one. *Jurema* gives meaning to life.

'The Jurema tree shows us the right way,' explains Suíra's son, 'it shows the bad and the good. We drink the *Jurema* wine at the beginning, middle and end of the *Ouricuri* and become *juremado*,' he added proudly, in his slow way of speaking, 'but only *índios* can become *juremado*, not the others . . . '

'Even the people in the *Catimbó* cannot become *juremado*?' I asked. He hesitated for a while, then firmly said 'no, not even the people in the *Catimbó* cult, not the Blacks in *Umbanda*, only *índios*.'

That meant that the sharing of the indigenous *Jurema* drink created a speech-community, since only *índios* could 'hear' what *Sonsé* was telling them and decode messages that were coming from the highest *encantado* through the drinking of the wine.

'Does *Jurema* speak to you in words, can you hear voices after you drink the wine?' I asked.

As a way of answering this question, Suíra told me their creation myth and the reason for this fathomless secret. 'It was like this, in the beginning, before any one of us was born. A father, a son and a daughter-in-law (who were White people), plus six people of Indian blood were driven into the woods, because of the droughts.'

'Nine people, then,' I interrupted.

'Yes, yes!' He answered, good humouredly, but already eyeing me as though thinking 'here she comes!'

'Why nine?' I asked.

'Why do you **always** ask things like that? They were nine, because there happened to be nine people, in the beginning.'

'Is nine a magical number?'

He laughed out loud, mocking me as usual. 'You are always thinking of magic, my daughter! Nine, nine! It is ten less one, right?' He spread out the fingers of his two hands and then bent one down, for even though he was illiterate, he knew how to count. 'Do I always have to explain things? May *Sonsé* help me against women like you.' That said, he was smiling serenely and continued. 'Well, these **nine** people stayed a long time in the woods, eating game and wild plants until *Tupã*, or *Jurema*, or *Sonsé*, whatever way you like to call the Creator, had pity on them and made the indigenous medicine which they drank and they all got very drunk, sleeping very well. Then one of the Indian women made the medicine of *Jurema* and gave it to her male cousin, to her father-in-law, to a female cousin and to that cousin's father-in-law.' He showed four fingers and it was my turn to smile.

'Two were out,' I noticed. He nodded affirmatively. 'These four people drank the *Jurema* wine and got drunk again. This time they all had sexual intercourse – *eles matrimoniaram* – and – he was very expressive as he said the next sentence – 'the woman who made the wine married her own cousin and they had a boy.' He settled down a bit after pronouncing what should be taken as startling news. 'That was the beginning of all the indigenous tribes. That woman formed the tribes with her cousin, with the *Jurema* that she prepared. But she didn't know how to prepare the *Jurema*, she was not prepared, she was not strong enough, so she couldn't have done it the proper way, so she herself got very drunk and her cousin too, that is why they married!'

'However,' I pointed out, 'when *Sonsé* first made the drink the people also got drunk.'

'Oh, yes, but that is different! You get drunk because you have visions, you get drunk with what you see, what you hear, but you don't just burn out, you don't have sex. The *Jurema* that *Sonsé* has taught us to prepare lets us talk to the old ones, to the dead parents. But she made just one family, that woman. She generated their family in the woods.'

'What happened to the other seven people? Three were White people.'

'The White people never got to drink *Jurema*, only the Indians. The White people went on to form their tribes and the other four Indians each formed all the other Indian tribes. The woman and her cousin are our grandparents. Then the fairies started to come there into the woods, to bring enchantment to the woods and the fairies named the tribes in the old languages. Each tribe went to other places, to one corner and the other of the world. The original family stayed here where it is still our village. Thus began the world.'

The world began with a wondrous beverage and then an incestuous relationship, testifying for its socially undesired disorder. The social categories of 'White' and 'Indian' were separated from the very start as the Whites did not partake of the *Jurema* drink. It is also important to note that the Blacks were not involved in the creation story, even though the Kariri-Shoko are undoubtedly Black as well, due to the migration of African slaves to their area. Somehow Blacks come only later to their stories, mostly through their *toré* songs, as when they refer to their origins in Aruanda, an African town, in a *toré* that claims "*Vou vadiar na Aruanda . . .* " (I am going to play in Aruanda). Blacks also know about the enchantment of *Jurema*, even though they were not even born when *Sonsé* brought the beverage.

'It is because they got *Jurema* from us', both Suíra and his son were eager to explain to me, when I enquired about the *Jurema* that was sung about in the *Umbanda*. *Jurema* was responsible for the creation and the spread of the indigenous tribes, but that did not seem to include the Blacks. Taking *Jurema* together does not involve either Blacks or Whites, only Indians, since it has the scope of a ritual of renewal and social integration. When they drink *Jurema* as a group, the Kariri-Shoko are looking for the purpose of their lives, much as the Huicholes of Mexico who, when they take *peyote*, say 'we want to find our lives, we want to see what is to be a Huichol' (Furst, 1980: 96).

The importance of the moment is signalled by the fact that it is supposed to remain a secret: how they share it, what they do when they share the drink, what they say, what they hear or see, it is all to remain among themselves alone.

Jurema's secrets

The *segrêdo* is the converging symbolic centre of the 'children of Jurema', that pays the price for tribal freedom and indigenous identity. These 'children' speak of the existence of ritual secrets with a mixture of pride and reverence. 'It is the tribal secret,' they mumble when one asks about something they cannot – or will not – talk about. This focal symbol has the double function of guaranteeing the absence of non-indigenous interests from the Ouricuri land, protecting their environment from foreign predators. It is in the tradition that any White person who dares to enter the *Ouricuri* territory without their permission, or during the *festas do Ouricuri*, will meet a mysterious death.

Such threatening of a death penalty is part of the regional everyday life, instilling respect and fear in the Kariri-Shoko and their local 'witches'. It also produces the most diverse legends and stories that are similar to the old indigenous legends that make up a general national folklore. The local people seem, in fact, to make certain remarks to visitors who are ignorant of or who do not care about the 'strength of *Ouricuri*'s secret.' In their statements a certain admiration about the *segrêdo do índio* – indigenous secret – comes through. It is the same sort of reverence of a power, or strength, which is at once known and unknown, as though the secret were part of a regional tourist scenario that carries a touch of originality to all of them, Indians and non-Indians, who are then forever after seen as 'different'. It is the distinctive Kariri-Shoko insignia, which serves as an antidote to the stigma of being *índios*. It does not remove the stigma, however it makes it respectable because it is unfathomable.

This fear implies a superiority through the existence of an indigenous social organization identified with myths and rituals of the predecessors. The organization represents itself in order to have members, so it carves out a distinct identity through both mythic and ritual means. 'Organizations propagate myths regarding their origin and purpose, while members engage in symbolic practices that serve to mark off from non-members. These myths often assert the group's superiority.' (Kertzer, 1988: 18)

It is widely known that many other social groups at every level of their historical process have attempted to establish their brand of social distinction and, for such, have maintained a secret that could only be shared by their own members (cf. Fry and Vogt, 1985). Esotericism, therefore, is a key to open a sort of power, that, being unknown to some, becomes magnificent in everyone's eyes, familiar as well as foreign ones.

One of the stories of the local folklore is that of a farmer who dared to violate the *Ouricuri* sanctuary and ended up dead. In that story class struggles and interethnic conflicts are resolved by the mystery of the *segrêdo tribal*. The story's main point is that the farmer was cutting wood from the *Ouricuri* forest without permission, but the problem was not simply one of private ownership. In the native construction of reality the woods retain a sacred nature, therefore it is unheard of to ravish the forest and its purity. Any wood, be it cut or fallen, belongs only to the 'forest enchantments', spiritual beings, and their temporal owners, in that case the Kariri-Shoko. Live trees cannot be cut down without asking permission of the fairies who reside within the trees – the *encantados*. Only the 'children of *Jurema*' who have been initiated can go into the forest and garner its fruits or whatever else they need from it. José Cícero, the *cacique*, told the story of the farmer who paid no heed to the advice of his friends, considering them superstitious.

'He went on using the *Ouricuri*, getting inside our enchanted forest, the forest of our spirits. And he laughed off the stories about death and vengeance that the local people told him. Soon, however, he started to hear a voice that would whisper to him "*tome veneno*" (take poison) . . . Everyday he would hear that and he told his wife and she told him it was the enchantment of the *Ouricuri*. He laughed again. But one day, he was drinking some *cachaça* that was poisoned. Nobody knew how the wine got poisoned, there was no one guilty. But the people knew that the *encantados* put poison in his drink and ended that man's life, punishing him for breaking into the sacred woods. Another idea is that our *pajé* poisoned the man by making him put poison in his own drink, turning his favourite *cachaça* into poison. It is possible, you know . . . '

It is believed that the *pajé*, known as the *feiticeiro índio*, has the power to punish those who dare to discover the *segrêdo* or who break the *lei indígena* (indigenous law) by forcefully entering the sacred space. The *pajé*'s sacred power has a political significance, although in confrontation with the dominant sectors of the larger society, the Kariri-Shoko are totally deprived of political power. This is tied to another kind of power: that over life and death, not only of the 'children' but also of all the others, mainly those who try to be introduced into tribal life without consent.

Jerusa's brother used to tell me, his eyes shining with an impenetrable aversion mixed with an unconfessed homage: 'it is known that they always kill someone at the *Ouricuri* and it is usually somebody who disobeyed the orders that come from *Jurema*. They cannot tell anyone about the secret or they die!'

Such beliefs reinforce a form of social control, tracing the limits of their ethnicity, or the social boundaries of the group, based on ideology and performance, rather than merely on physical and geographic community (cf. Barth, 1969). They also serve as a barrier against the social conflict that exists among the social categories defined as *índios* and *non-índios*, as long as the latter go on being frightened of the possibility of a magical revenge from the former.

Jurema's riddle
There are many sources and many ways of obtaining a *Jurema* drink and every recipe is supposed to be the right one. There is, in fact, a '*Jurema* complex' composed of various ways of making the beverage known as *Jurema*, from many different botanical species, throughout Brazil, but all of them have a religious motive (da Mota and de Barros, 1990). The *Jurema* drink of the *Umbanda* rituals, for instance, is prepared at a special festival when the spirits of dead *caboclos* are supposed to 'descend' on earth through the human vehicle of the faithful. The *Umbanda*'s *Jurema* is different from that of the Indians, as *umbandistas* use totally different ingredients. However, the way that the Northeastern indigenous groups prepare the *Jurema* is not only a secret, but also a riddle. Why? The beverage is considered sacred because it causes the deity – the *Jurema* – to become alive within the people who drink it. In this case, it has the property of making the user realize the divine presence, as it has been classified as an *entheogenic* plant.[1]

In the past the drink was made from the roots of the *Mimosa hostilis* Benth., which the Fulniô of Pernambuco are still using but the Kariri-Shoko are not. The information I got from the Kariri-Shoko was that nowadays they use the roots of a *Mimosa* which has been classified, from my collection, as *Mimosa verrucosa* Linn. The sacred drink of the past was known to stimulate wonderful visions and, according to ethnographic records, dream-states that were related to 'enchanted rocks, fire birds and other natural wonders.' (Nimuendaju in E. Pinto, 1935: 189). Furst also wrote about the *hostilis* species and the effects it induced, explaining that 'the roots of this small tree or large shrub of the dry scrubby *caatingas* are prepared in a potently hallucinogenic beverage taken by priests, strong young men, warriors, and old women, who kneel with bowed heads to partake of it. The ceremony was formerly performed before battle.' (1972: 29)

On the other hand, Schultes found that there was not much known about the 'hallucinogenic properties of this plant, which was discovered more than 150 years ago. Early chemical studies indicated an active alkaloid given the name nigerine but later shown to be identical with N,N-dimethyltriptamine.' (1976: 84) This alkaloid, DMT, has been known as the entheogenic principle of the *vinho da Jurema*. Gonçalves de Lima, when studying *vinho da Jurema*, was the one able to isolate DMT as a natural product, under the name of nigerine (cited in Ott, 1994).

The problem today is to know which one of the two species is used by the Kariri-Shoko, and if there is another plant also used to make the wine. The *hostilis* species is called locally *Jurema preta* – 'black *Jurema*' – and is said to provoke reactions expected from a psychotropic/entheogenic plant. The *verrucosa* is known as *Jurema mansa* – 'gentle *Jurema*' – because its effects are not the same as those of *Jurema preta*. Apparently, the *mansa* kind is not as effervescent as the *preta*, and does not provide the same kind of effect, or as Suíra explained: '*A Jurema mansa, a Tupã do índio, não endoida.*' (The gentle *Jurema*, the indigenous *Tupã*, does not make one go crazy).

The difference in reactions is explained by the fact that the bark of the *hostilis* species has been found to be narcotic, and the seeds have toxic and inebriating properties, as DMT was identified as a constituent of seeds and pods (Conceição, 1982; Ott, 1994). Another author described the black *Jurema* as a strange beverage that has a miraculous powers, being the favourite material of 'sorcerers' who use it for, according to popular belief, the 'excitement of their clients' senses, provoking in them wonderful dreams and pleasant sensations, letting them in a state of ecstasy and enchantment.' (Cruz, 1982: 408) Sangirardi confirmed the information from the Kariri-Shoko, stating that the *Jurema* (he did not explain which one of the two) was used 'in order to foretell, counsel and cure. The ingestion of *Jurema* allowed the shaman to enter in contact with the invisible world, evoking the ancestral spirits and tribal cultural heroes.' (1983: 204).

Even if we consider that the *Mimosa hostilis* is the one used, there are considerable problems in explaining how the visions that users claim to experience come about. This is so because the active ingredient present in the *hostilis* species – tryptamine – is not active when taken orally unless in the presence of a monoamine oxidase inhibitor. Without the inhibitor, the substance tryptamine is rendered inactive when passing through the digestive system, later being unable to effect the expected neurological changes.

Considering this problem, Schultes suggested that the drink itself must contain ingredients other than those of the *Mimosa hostilis* or that the plant itself must contain an inhibitor in its tissues (1976: 84). Elisabetsky (1986) explained that the use of *ayahuasca* – an entheogenic beverage much used in the Amazon region for shamanic purposes – would have the same problems if users did not mix the extract from the bark of the *Banisteriopsis caapi* with the leaves of the *Psychotria viridis*, which enhance the visionary potency of the *ayahuasca* drink. The *caapi* species contains alkaloids known as carboline, whereas *Psychotria* leaves contain DMT, the entheogenic principle. However, even though *aya-huasca* is ingested orally, there is a pharmacological synergy between the carbolines of *Banisteriopsis* species and the DMT contained in the *Psychotria*. Therefore, the carbolines function not as specific psychotropic constituents but as enzyme inhibitors, to prevent the users of *ayahuasca* from deactivating the DMT contained in the leaves, which is not ordinarily active orally. According to Ott, 'plain Ayahuasca is more of a sedative than a stimulant, and generally speaking, entheogens are stimulants.' (Ott, 1994: 26) The *Jurema* wine that I brought to Rio de Janeiro for pharmacological analysis, was reported to have a tranquilizing effect by UERJ (Unversidade do Estado do Rio de Janeiro) pharmacologist Dr. Ricardo Santos. The *Jurema* wine, therefore, needs to be mixed with a plant containing carbolines. Grunewald (1995) has found that indigenous groups in the state of Pernambuco also use the *Jurema* wine, mixing the roots from the *hostilis* species with the leaves of *Passiflora*, which contain the same alkaloids as those from *Banisteriopsis*. The Kariri-Shoka shaman, however, denies mixing the sacred and divine roots of *Jurema* with anything else, or it would spoil the 'purity' of the wine.

Whatever species of *Mimosa* the Kariri-Shoko still use, or do not use nowadays, the fact is that they do report experiences of changes in perceptions, mood and thoughts. They also are supposed to enter a dream-state where they receive messages through the imagery that appears and which they decode as communications from the spiritual realm that are omens, specifically from *Jurema* or *Sonsé*. In that case, the *Jurema* wine does function as an entheogenic beverage, 'realizing the divine within'. The importance that *Jurema* has in the Kariri-Shoko order is such that the partakers of the *Jurema* drink come around already prepared to have visions and premonitions. The preparation is consumed in a charged-up, intense atmosphere, filled with expectations for messages from a creative force, or the sharing of individual visions and thus of individual worth translated as collective communication channels.

While participants are drinking their portion of the drink, some of the men are rhythmically playing the *maracá*, a hand-held percussion instrument belonging to the *Tupi-Guarani* tradition, and originally known as *mbaracá*. Others dance forming two concentric circles inside the *Ouricuri* central clearing: men dance in the inside circle, women are outside, going in the opposite direction to each other. Whistles are heard, while people chant and stomp their feet on the ground, following the *maracás'* rhythm. The whistling is supposed to come from the ancestral spirits who approach the dancing arena, while the dances become more and more impassioned. Some of the players in this social drama fall into a trance in which they are not incorporating the spiritual ancestors, but simply hearing messages from *Sonsé*. The messages will later be imparted to a very committed audience.

Finally, *Sonsé*'s (or *Jurema*'s) 'body' has been partaken by all. The sense of community and commitment is perhaps even more meaningful than that experienced by these same players when they participate in the Catholic mass on Sundays. The *Ouricuri* ritual is their own inheritance, while the Catholic mass is a celebration ancestral to the colonizers, the very *cabeça seca* who took over their land and lives.

Meanwhile, another drink – *waluaá* – is also distributed. This libation is made of fermented manioc and sometimes it includes pineapples as well. Its function is to protect the group from any evil. Since it also belongs to the Afro-Brazilian tradition, its presence in the *Ouricuri* ritual reflects the connections and interpenetrations between indigenous and African religions (cf. da Mota and de Barros, 1990). The *pajé* and other men smoke big clay pipes filled with tobacco, that represents their other mysterious deity known as Badzé. It seems inevitable that some form of induced visions will take place, that auditory and visual delusions will come about.

Although serious business is going on, there is also much passion and gaiety, as the revellers thoroughly enjoy themselves and their shared identity. Their destiny is unveiled by the orders of *Jurema*, because she/he is believed to be bestowing *força ao espírito* – strength to the spirit – so that the participants may be ready to receive spiritual messages, either in dreams or during their waking hours. The unseen realm, which is understood as being as real as that which is seen, is revealed in all its glory to those who are prepared to be able to 'see'. The carnivalesque aspect of the ceremony may not betray the profound reverence with which the appearance of the *encantados*, the *Jurema* among them, is celebrated as people are truly bursting with exultation, dancing, singing, shouting, totally exhilarated by the satisfaction of being with their 'parents' and having been able to stay together as a group. One has to be prepared physically, ideologically and emotionally.

'We have to do many *trabalhos* (works)' explained Suíra's son, 'to prepare ourselves for the visions. The *Jurema* is known as the main medicine for the tribal illnesses. We don't drink it to relinquish our minds. The *Jurema* doesn't get us intoxicated. But if you don't know how to prepare it, you can become drunk or go mad. When you drink the *Jurema*, you have to concentrate: it is a preparation for our penance.'

'Penance? Why penance? Do you feel guilty of anything when you take the Jurema?' I asked, considering the possibility that the idea of penance came from the Catholic tradition.

He looked somewhat embarrassed, first muttering that I would not really understand it, then explaining that, 'well, nobody is perfect, and, yes, we do many things that take us away from our appointed way, which is to follow *Jurema's* orders. We have to obey only *Sonsé*, through the *Jurema* wine. But we do not always do that. When we drink *Jurema* we are pleading our commitment to *Sonsé*.'

I imagined the Kariri-Shoko filled with remorse for allowing themselves to be colonized! But I also wondered – and still do – what made them 'see' and 'hear' messages if, in fact, they were using the supposedly harmless *Mimosa verrucosa*.

I think, therefore, that the *Jurema* wine acts as an 'active placebo,' a concept put forward by Andrew Weil (1972) to explain the effectiveness behind the practice of smoking marijuana. Weil defined an 'active placebo' as 'a substance whose apparent effects on the mind are actually the placebo effects in response to minimal physiological action,' and that 'all psychoactive drugs are really active placebos since the psychic effects arise from consciousness, elicited by set and setting, in response to physiological cues.' (1972: 96)

The effects produced, among the Kariri-Shoko, by the ingestion of the *Jurema* wine, a fermented beverage whose ingredients are not totally known as yet, are perhaps culturally induced and expected. The 'visions' that come through in the people's active imagination are projections of cultural images. The supernatural voices being heard are auditory hallucinations that also occur among people who use substances that have been scientifically proved to provoke hallucinatory states.

The *Jurema* is not taken for pleasure, even though there is a lot of merriment going on during the ceremony. The *Jurema* is taken both for the expiation of the sin of being a colonized *caboclo* and for the realization of the highest wisdom. People gather together in order to learn what to do next with their lives. *Sonsé* speaks to them, but, according to Suíra, 'not everyone can hear'. Only the *índios juremados* can hear, and only *índios* can become *juremados*. The other term for *índios juremados* is *capangueiros da Jurema*, or '*Jurema's* companion spirits', who are constantly called forth in the chants of *Umbanda* rituals, as in the following:

'*A mata escureceu, a lua clareou,/ Cadê os capangueiros da Jurema que ainda não apareceu?*' (The forest became dark, the moon shone, where are the *Capangueiros da Jurema* who have not appeared yet?)

In the past, the Kariri heard from *Sonsé* about what strategies to take during war. The battles they still have to fight nowadays have to do with their dealing with national society. The *Jurema* told them when to take over the *Sementeira*, their ancestral land which was under the possession of the federal government. *Jurema's* orders were received and shared in the secrecy of their *Ouricuri* meetings, when they decided to invade the *Sementeira*. Outsiders laugh about this story, claiming that 'everyone' knew about the taking over the Sementeira, but from the local and state news of the time, the invasion was a total surprise to the inhabitants of Sementeira, who were forced to flee, and the central government that didn't have any *pratol* or guard for the area. José Cícero summarized what was one of their greatest accomplishments:

'We were gathered in the *Ouricuri* and the *Jurema* comes and tells us that it is high time for us to get our land back. We had to do it now! I was a representative of FUNAI, but, first of all, I was a son of *Jurema*. I could not betray *Jurema*! To betray *Jurema* would mean my death, my downfall, the disgrace of my entire family. What happens inside the *Ouricuri* circle is a secret to anyone who is an outsider to it. So we gathered everyone, men, women and children. The men were armed with sickles, axes, and such like. Very few men had firearms, some had hunting guns only. We were a sorry bunch of losers, ragged, hungry and upset. Until then we were living corralled in a street of the town. We had no land, no place to plant our food, to raise our children. We only had the *Ouricuri*. We went over there in the silence and darkness of the night. The road to the *Sementeira* darkened with our presence. There were Indians all over. When the morning dawned, the *Sementeira* was surrounded. We politely told the people who lived in the *Sementeira* and who worked for the government that they should leave, the land was ours. They were desperate, they called for help, here and there. We were determined. We entered the houses, all over the place and sat down. The women brought their pots and started to cook. The children were playing in the streets. It was a great commotion, the newspapers came, the radio, television, everybody saying: how can you do that? FUNAI came too and we said that we were doing their job. I told FUNAI to help us. Well, in the end the government lost, we won! We did that because *Jurema* told us to do so and *Jurema's* orders are not to be discussed, *Jurema's* orders are to be followed.'

4 Nature's kinfolk

'They cast off one way of life and took on another,
and from the little I saw of their forest life it was as
satisfactory as village life seemed empty and meaningless'
(Turnbull, 1961)

Part I: The plant-human continuum

EVERY HUMAN SOCIETY is, by definition, part of nature and, therefore, has to relate
to the other biological realms. The relationship to the vegetal world is a fundamental one because of the obvious implications for human survival on earth.
Even a completely urbanized society, i.e., one that is devoid of a rural life,
requires vegetation both in its surroundings and as food stuff, so that everyone is
at least subliminally aware of the vegetal world.

For the people who live in greatest contact with the forests and woods, the
vegetal world is a substantial part of life. As such, the awareness of its existence
is filled with meaning at every level of the social experience.

In the case of people like the Kariri-Shoko and the Shoko, vegetation presents
an unsuspected challenge since it is there at their doorsteps. The vegetal world
still compels them to take different views on the nature of things, of life on earth
and their role in the Brazilian nation as a separate entity, as a 'tribe'. Plants
present a range of signals, from being a symbolic representation of the group
itself, to being an assurance against starvation and depletion of food supplies.
Beyond these more immediate considerations for group survival, plants are
highly regarded as healing agents as well as elements from the environment
that participate in the task of keeping the group alive, at both physical and
psychological levels.

In their world view there is no separation of mind from body, so that a malady
– or a socially constructed illness – is a reflection of a disorder in the mind-body
duality, characteristic of the human experience. A headache is never simply a
headache, it could be the result of some sort of spiritual intervention. A neurotic
outburst, or a fit of 'craziness' (*loucura*) is a mental malfunction that can present
physical signs, as in the case of a woman in São Pedro who was epileptic, but
who was diagnosed as being spiritually troubled, even though the diagnostician –
pajé Raimundo – clearly could recognize the epileptic signs and thought she
should continue taking her prescription from the hospital at Pão de Açúcar.

As healing agents, plants have two dimensions which are both responsible for
effecting the cure. The more obvious one – at least for the Western concept – is
the biochemical component or the active principles that act in the human body's
chemistry in order to bring about healing.

'*Toda química vem da floresta*' (all chemistry comes from the forest), 'seu'
Neco used to say, punctuating the fact that he did understand about the nature of
therapeutic properties of the plants he used. He said that when I asked him to
teach me about the healing plants, a statement that gratified as much as it
confused me, so I wanted to know what was it that he meant by 'chemistry'.
He was also a good-humoured man, so he laughed:

'You know what it is! The pharmacists when they make their bottled medicines, they use chemicals, they fabricate chemicals. But this chemistry they use comes from the forest and that is what I mean. That is to say, all is derived from the woods, from the trees, the *pé de paus* (trees) we have here.'

The other dimension of plants as healing agents is that which lies in the mental – or cultural – make-up of users as they actively construct, or imagine, the ingredients being ingested as capable of taking the disease away. This second dimension is intimately related to the social construction of illness or to how the 'dis-ease' is confronted. As will be seen, in their rather traditionalist inventory of diseases, the troubles with the body are part of the malfunctioning of harmony, when the society or the individual within it are thrown out of balance. Such lack of grace with the environment is translated into bodily harm and pain. Plants and their extracts are believed to ease whatever is the disturbance, bringing harmony and health back to the individual sufferer and to the society he or she belongs to. Thus, to be able to use plant extracts as medicines, one must believe in the efficacy of the remedy, in the same way that believers in the efficacy of pharmaceutical products are able to use them without embarrassment. 'Seu' Neco, however, reminded me all the time that the pharmacy we use is the same as that which exists in the forest, except that in the forest 'it does not come bottled and prepared, you have to prepare it.' And that takes lots of knowledge and practice. Therefore, using herbal medicines is not easy. Not one of the people who used to prepare herbal remedies would collect, prepare and use botanical medicines experimentally or just 'to see what happens', because they already believed that 'something' happened! There were clear physical results of some sort, regardless of whether those were the expected results or not. In our conceptualization of science they are categorized as empiricists. All plant material was supposed to be active, alive and therefore able to influence the body. The utilization of botanical extracts was based on a belief system that was pragmatic to its core, imbuing plants with the power to cure humans and animals. It also related to a form of connection between the animal and botanical realms, in which biological organisms were also cultural realities, beings invested with purpose and significance. The way the healers and users visualized these powerful plant substances was related to a structured view of the cosmos, to a web of relationships in which they, as human beings, took part. Therefore, for one to understand such relationships also meant to understand Kariri-Shoko social dramas and actions.

Specifically regarding the Kariri-Shoko's perception of reality, there seemed to be more than just one accepted level: one that was concrete, biological and another that was socially constructed. This socially constructed reality presents itself not as a continuum, but as a series of readily definable chunks that can be perceived and known in terms of the objective methods of the biological field of botany (cf. Berlin, 1992).

The continuum existed at the level of humans versus plants since the latter were intimately related to the former, as they were, in fact, interdependent. To call oneself Kariri-Shoko was to have adopted a social identity which implied the cultural process of internalization of a specific ideology and cosmovision. The continuing search and identification of vegetal species had the effect of keeping some of the primordial aspects of native cosmovision and, therefore, the survival of an identity as *índios* and, consequently, as Kariri-Shoko.

At the level of visible and concrete reality, both the Kariri-Shoko and the Shoko perceived and utilized botanical species in exactly the same ways. The difference in outlook was fundamental and had consequences at the day-to-day level since plants for the Kariri-Shoko made up part of the praxis for physical and ideological reproduction of society. Therefore, conceptual recognition was culturally specific. Culturally known bodies of therapeutic plant species also served as index markers for ethnic boundaries and, therefore, for ethnic identification. Considering these facts, we can say that plants and people belonged to the same conceptual framework, sharing the same structured social organization, because the Kariri-Shoko social hierarchical categories were equivalent to those of plants. In other words, besides the unavoidable reality of the natural plant world, there was a reality of another order that was culturally constructed within the daily experience of growing up as an *índio*.

Knowledge of gathering, using and administering botanical specimens for medicinal purposes has always been a common and accepted practice in the interior of Brazil. People have the capacity to discern, classify and utilize plants in structurally similar ways, as human beings everywhere are constrained in essentially the same ways, in fact, by nature's basic plan, in their conceptual recognition of the biological diversity of their natural environments (cf. Berlin, 1992).

However, certain uses and practices, in the case we are focusing on, are directly related to specific beliefs, implying the development of an initiation process, of becoming a member of a closed social group, an exclusive cultural élite that shared specific details in the manipulation of vegetal species. Thus, much of the knowledge was contained within the secret compartments of the culture, and it had a special status inside and outside the boundaries of the villages.

Even though both groups had selected the same botanical species for the same medicinal purposes, the Shoko from Sergipe showed attitudes and ideological postures regarding the botanical world that differed from those adopted by the Kariri-Shoko, since the latter conceived of plants as cultural realities pregnant with significance.

'Plants are not superior beings, as the other *índios* say, no! They can be very helpful, they can really cure, I've seen miraculous sorts of cures, but they are not like gods' said Lola, when asked about the significance of medicinal plants. 'They have power, yes, but it is not a superior power. The one who has any kind of superior powers is Our Lord Jesus!'

This Christian view of nature is different from the one that emerged as I talked to the *pajé* about the use of botanical medicines. It was clear from his discourse that the traditions that made him famous in the region as a healer and user of 'natural medicine' were based on the belief that plants represent the ancestral forces of the universe. His relationship to the vegetal world was based on a perception of the universe and a system of beliefs that had been passed down to him and that viewed plants as the metaphor for life. Plants are family, familial signs, symbols of a shared perception of the world. Consequently, they are also a tribal symbol. People are descendants from the 'roots' and 'trunks' of past generations. Roots are medicine in two meaningful ways: they bring life and healing, as well as being the origin of everything. The Kariri-Shoko interpret the natural habitat as if it were a history book, and the forest as a place where their ethnohistory was imprinted. One has to be 'forest-literate' in Kariri symbolic language in order to decipher sounds and meanings because plants have been imbued with symbolic meaning. Even though cultural categories of botanical entities are consistent with biological reality, plants are also categorized in other meaningful ways.

Entering the *Ouricuri* woods with Suíra made me more aware of these facts, which for them are simple, everyday beliefs. Every wild plant has its place in the woods, as if they had been planted there by a human hand. The forest is managed not only by humans but also by the fairies that 'naturally' inhabit it. 'When you begin searching for plants, for some special plants like we are doing now,' he instructed me, 'you have to call that plant by its name, its natural name.'

'What is a natural name?' I asked.

'The name given by the plant itself, which was revealed to us when we first came in contact with it.' Then he looked whimsical and continued, in a playful mood, 'people like you would have a terrible time finding plants, because you do not see them. You cannot find them because you don't even see them! You pass by the most important beings and you are not called forth, you don't disturb and are not disturbed, because the plants have not chosen you yet, even though you have chosen them. You are definitely close to that, but do you hear anything?'

I probably looked acutely hurt by the norms he was spelling out of a world I did not recognize as my own at all.

'What should I be hearing? I hear the soft wind on the leaves, I hear the birds, some insects, I hear our footsteps. Should I be hearing something more?'

'Well, not really, because the plants are not calling you. They don't know you and you don't know them. That is why you don't see or hear them yet.'

'What do you mean I don't see them? I surely see them, I just don't know their names.'

'Well, exactly, my daughter. But that is precisely why you don't see them, see?'

We walked around some paths, going deeper into the woods. Suíra was pointing out specimens to me, which I would collect carefully and put inside my pouch, so that later I could place them inside the botanical press. He noticed how careful I was to gather the flowers, when there were any. He made an observation in his typical scrutinizing way: 'See, you have ways of knowing the plants that I don't have. But you may go on doing all these things and still not understand the nature of the plant. You still won't be able to speak to them, nor to hear them speaking to you. You need to be trained for that.'

'Can I be trained?'

'If you walk around with us a great deal, perhaps. But you would also need to learn the secret language of the Kariri and I cannot teach you that. You would have to be a Kariri or a Shoko for that. You would have to be born into the tribe, my dear. Otherwise, there is no way that I can teach you that. *Sonsé* would have to give me permission for that, but I doubt that *Sonsé* would open up for you, even though you are so dear to us.'

Suíra was, as usual, very direct. He never tried to spare me the truth nor to promise me anything he could not do. It was in this vein that he explained why he could not – would not – tell me the Kariri names of the plants he was showing to me.

'Only a few of these names can be revealed. Only the most common plants. There are some secret plant names that I could not tell you, even if I wished to do that. I am the highest authority of the Kariri and of the Shoko but I cannot break the secret of the tribe. I'd be guilty of treason. But I can tell you some of the names.'

As we walked around, he kept pointing out plants. There was one that he was unable to find – *mijo de ovelha* – and therefore I could not have it classified by a taxonomist. He kept saying that we would find some bushes of that plant somewhere around because the *Ouricuri* was filled with it, since it is a very powerful herb, giving protection to whoever wore it inside their clothes. But he was disappointed. Finally he seemed to realize what was happening.

'The "owner" of the plant – the fairy who lives in it – does not wish to be seen by you. So it is hiding from us. I am sure of that, because just the other day I found lots of *mijo de ovelha* right here.'

I was so puzzled by this that I failed to question him, which was all right because he went on, perhaps anticipating what I might be wanting to ask but was too disconcerted to do.

'Yes, plants can become invisible if they so wish. We people have the power to become invisible whenever we want as well. Even you, yes, even you! If you are in a dangerous situation and you don't want to become seen, you become unseen. It is just like that - *trás*! You ask your spiritual guide to protect you, to make you invisible and it happens: nobody can see you! Of course there are plants that help you in this task. You can keep a bunch of these plants in your pocket and when you want to disappear from sight, you hold them in your hand and – *trás*!' He snapped his fingers loudly.

'Do you really disappear, I mean, does your body become immaterial?' I asked, as intrigued as ever.

'My darling, I don't know how to explain that to you, because of course it is very hard for you empty headed White people to understand it. No, your body is still there. You can see yourself, feel yourself, touch yourself. But nobody else can see you. You only appear again when you wish or when your protection is weak and your guide cannot help you any more. If you don't carry out your obligations, for instance, you start to lose many of these capacities.'

That moment was one of the instances when I felt I was being made fun of, as he kept smiling as he uttered those words. I felt extremely uncomfortable, thinking to myself, 'well, who can ever believe in this? Of course sometimes you feel like you are invisible, like when you go to a shop and the shop assistants keep passing you by without making any mention of helping you. Other than that, I could not see how this invisibility can be possible. I believe in atoms, in viruses, in the laws of physics.' I am sure Suíra was aware of my doubts, even though I kept them to myself that time.

'Darling daughter, if you could only drink *Jurema* and become *juremado*, then you would understand! You can't take *Jurema* here in the *Ouricuri* with us, because our law will not allow that, but some day I can make you drink *Jurema* and then maybe, only maybe, you will see things that you never thought you could and you will know that you will have to keep them to yourself forever because no one would understand you, nor would believe you.'

At that point, my tape-recorder was running out of batteries. I was trying to write down what he said, keep track of the plants in my pouch, taking notes not only on the plants but also the characteristics of the soil, surrounding vegetation, etc. While in the *Ouricuri* woods with Suíra, I felt close to being hysterical, my back ached, my legs felt like lead, but the 75-year-old gentleman kept going on, slowly but surely, talking away about his system of thinking and of beliefs. I was getting very thirsty and I didn't want to complain about anything as I became overwhelmed by an incredible sense of insecurity for being an 'empty headed White person.' What did it mean to become *juremado*? I could know intuitively, even sociologically speaking I knew what he meant: the sharing of meanings, the togetherness, the keeping of social bonds and the 'tribal law' surely had to do with what *juremado* meant. But how did it feel deep down in someone's guts?

Was it scary? Was it good? Was it close to ecstasy or **what**? Was it like drinking *ayahuasca*? I would leave those questions for later, for he was promising to have me drink *Jurema* and Suíra never made a promise he didn't intend to keep.

Part 2: Plants, language and power

Inside the *Ouricuri* boundaries, most botanical species have been naturalized and some are native, but still they represent the ancestors, from the *Menthas* to the *Mimosas*. It does not matter: the trees are metaphors of native life, what it means to be an Indian – subverting the social order of discrimination and economic want. Like themselves, the flora have been mixed and naturalized, like foreigners who become 'native ancestors', as dictated by the ideology of ancestry. In the context of shamanic tradition and the traditional knowledge of the *Ouricuri*, trees are healing agents that embody the ancestors.

Nevertheless, surely modernity and the influences of Catholicism have had an impact on the Kariri's systems of values and beliefs. Whatever practice or belief that has not been solidly registered by the rituals taking place in the *Ouricuri* has either vanished from memory or is scarcely ever invoked.

Plants – more specifically those used as medicines – play a fundamental role in their socially constructed imagery, in a quest for ethnic identity and property rights to the land they have defined as ancestral. Plants are recognized not only as biological organisms, or for what makes them stand out in unique and concrete ways. They are also culturally meaningful elements that have biological and cultural properties. They signify, mainly, the land and the people as it was explained by one of Suíra's brothers during an interview: 'The land is US. We are the land! We are the roots and the trunks that exist in the *Ouricuri*.'

As has already been pointed out, plants that are taken as medicines are 'powerful' but the power has to be called forth, has to be unlocked by the people. Julio was the one who made me understand this. When I asked him how I recognized the 'power' in a plant so that it could be used as medicine, he told me again about the bond that existed between them and their plants.

'I am walking through the woods and then I see a plant I don't know yet, you ask'. He was in his habitual pensive mood, 'Well, she (the plant) speaks to me, she calls me, I look at her, and then she tells me how I can use her, she tells me her name, how I should call her from then on. But it is a name in the old language, in the language of my grandparents. It is by that name that she wants to be called and not by the name in Portuguese.'

Sound and meaning are two associated elements, that cannot be separated. Therefore, the sound of a name in the native language holds meaning only to the Kariri and the named plant, demonstrating their kind of relationship, the magic in it. To each plant there is a corresponding *Iate* (the language of the ancestors) word which functions like a prayer. Dona Nazinha, the most knowledgeable healer from São Pedro island, was descended from the Fulniô, so she knew some of these words and explained the relationship with the plants and language in the following way:

'When you enter the woods and prepare yourself to cut the plant you want, you have to say a prayer, that prayer is the name of the plant itself. You pray for the power, you pray for the strength, you ask the spirit of that relative to open up for you, to let you take a sample, to drink from him if he is a male spirit, or from her, if she is a woman.' She sighed deeply. 'But the folk here in São Pedro have forgotten how to do this. They even cut down a *Jurema* the other day. I was horrified when I saw it. We still have a *Jurema* inside these woods and I bless her every day I come here, so that she will not leave us. I bless her by saying her name, but I don't prepare her medicine because I am not a *pajé* and the people here don't take *Jurema* anyway.'

The prayers that Nazinha and the Kariri told me about are, nevertheless, highly secret and could not be revealed. 'Maybe one day, when you are ready, I'll tell you the names,' Suíra promised me. The story of when that day arrived will be told later. First, we need to examine the way the power that is so fundamental for their survival is related to the 'secret language' of the ancestors. According to the Kariri's particular world view, the power residing in the plants could only be tapped through a set of gestures, language, ritual singing and dancing of sacred songs and dances of the *torés*. These were signs of a relationship that could not be reproduced outside the indigenous environment because only native peoples – Blacks and Gypsies were included in this category – could establish and hold such 'real' communication with the unseen powers of nature. Reality was not conceived of as what is material, capable of being seen, touched or heard within the structure of physical six senses. Reality was precisely the opposite and was restricted to a privileged few, like themselves. As they related to plants in a manner that differs from what happened to outsiders, they also envisioned plants as possessing a different – or rather particular – reaction to them, as though plants were capable of understanding them through a common set of signals. The contact with the spiritual being who was taking a plant form was multifarious. It could take place through rubbing, inhaling, sniffing, eating, smoking or bathing in a solution from it. In one of our many conversations, during which I tried to get to the heart of the matter, Suíra said: 'anybody can go into the forest and take the medicine. Anybody can just go there and cut a branch of this, get a root of that, and so on. But when an *índio* takes a plant, when I – *índio legítimo* – get a plant in my hands, then it is different, because I bless the plant by saying the words. I pray for her, I say the plant's sacred name, I talk to the plant's heart and she hears me. She stays with me, she makes me well. If you don't know how to say the words, ah, then it is difficult. I need to ask the plant to take care of you too so that if you get a plant from anywhere, from a road side, from an ignorant *mateiro* in the city, you don't get any reaction, you don't get cured, because the plant does not bless you in return for being blessed. She doesn't know you so she doesn't give her power to you. It's useless. So the people in the city say "ah, plants have no power, plants are useless." And I say they are partially right. Because plants do not have power to show off, to give off to ignorant people. Plants give love in return. The spirits love those who love and respect them. It's like our relatives. Relatives are not really obligated to love us, they love us if we love them. They take care of us if we take care of them.'

'So, it is all a sort of trade off, or exchange?' He seemed to be in doubt, looking at me curiously. I tried to explain my way of thinking: 'Is it like going to the market and paying for something?' He was still in doubt. I figured this form of rationality was not the best way to follow his line of reasoning. He seemed to light up, meanwhile.

'No, it is a secret. Something you don't know. Something other people don't know. All the plant medicines have to have the power. Nobody else knows these words but us, the *índios*. You can't pay this knowledge off. You are not trading anything. You are giving freely. It's the plant's will to give in return. If she doesn't want to give back, there is nothing much else to do. You just wait. Because where there is a secret, there is strength. If the strength – the *força* – is not approached in the right way, it will not open up for you. It is a high secret. It is high power. When there is a secret, it is more positive. If I know something, and you know something, and only we know it, we don't talk about it to anybody else. It stays only between us and *Sonsé*, our God. But if you tell it to someone else, and then this person tells to another . . . then, soon, that which was sacred and secret and powerful, will become valueless. It will be a disorder.'

Suíra was no man to waste words. When he spoke, he made sure that he was being heard and understood as well. He always looked at me or whoever he was talking to at close range with very focused eyes. This was not what I was used to in relation to the others in his 'tribe' who generally avoided much eye contact. He always asked 'do you understand?' very pointedly, like the teacher he was. In that particular conversation, it was obvious to me that he was addressing a very serious matter. He always treated our conversations seriously, though garnished with occasional jocular remarks. Other people who have had experiences with modern tribal shamans had also been impressed by these people's concentration, superior intelligence and ability to teach. Suíra was particularly fond of talking when the tape recorder was on, and enjoyed hearing himself, mainly so that he could correct something or even laugh at himself speaking up.

'Medicine that everybody knows is not so strong because it is not secret, do you understand? A hypothesis: everybody knows about tea of *hortelã da folha miúda* [*Mentha piperita* Linn.], so it is a weak tea, it doesn't have any strength, because any child, any *cabeça seca* knows about it. However, the white powder I gave you, and that you are so eager to know what it is made of, is one of my secret medicines, that's why I cannot tell you more about it. But even if I told you, you wouldn't know how to prepare it . . .'

'Then tell me, tell me!' I interrupted, making him laugh. ' . . . You wouldn't know how to talk to it, it wouldn't make any difference. But I won't tell you, nor anyone else who is not prepared, who doesn't belong to the tribe and is ready for it, I won't tell even to some of the *rezadeiras*, because the heart of the matter is the secret code, the hidden language that cannot be opened to every one. People will not know what to do with it. A *rezadeira*, for instance, has to be a very strong woman, very powerful, like my aunt was in order to know how to work with this stuff.'

The 'hidden language', therefore, secures an ordered, well-balanced world in the midst of chaos, in the dangerous zone of political interests in the interior of Alagoas state, where it is easy to be killed off if one doesn't have the proper political training and protection. To tap the plants' hidden source of power, to receive its full strength and protection, one must have the secret code, which is in the enigmatic language of the Kariri, a language no one knows the origins of anymore, whether it is *Iate* or the vestiges of some other anterior language of the Kariri themselves. Suíra was firm on this subject:

'The language', he affirmed, 'is for our protection, our mutual blessing, for I bless the plant and the plant then blesses me too.' The reciprocity is made explicit here, as the idea of the plant power and the secret language is fundamental to the on-going functioning of the tribe. The power is carried through the words that are spoken by a Kariri specialist. But the words can also be sung in a *toré*, or simply said as in a prayer, a blessing. The very name of the plant thus spoken is, in fact, the blessing, the strength that permits the continuation of the tribe.

One example is the use of a medicine made of a plant known as *Autusse*. The medicine is prepared as an infusion. Its ingestion has a double function, for it functions not only as an analgesic, but it is also supposed to bring visions to the user so that she or he can become a 'walker' (*caminhante, andarilho*). One phenomenon is linked to the other, for as pain leaves one's body, as one experiences relief, one is also restored to health and is therefore allowed to see, or to have visions throughout the walks (*andanças*). Movement and vision that are gained – or restored – belong to a non-ordinary reality which can only become possible through the restoration of health, as health basically means balance or re-equilibrium. Words, meanings, visions and health make up part of a structured system of beliefs and relationships, belonging to social and ideo-logical orders. Vision and visionary healing can only be bestowed upon those in good health. And good health is obtained mainly through the knowledge or the science that has been handed down by the mythical ancestors, forming Kariri epistemology. In order to obtain the good favours of the genie or spiritual being residing in *Autusse*, the person who takes the medicine has to beg for his or her health by pronouncing the words '*Autusse akraí*'. This sentence signals to the plant spirit that this person understands and respects the divine powers concealed within the plant form. What is implied is the mutual bond of trust between the plant and the person for the medicine to be efficient. When I heard these words from Suíra, he was supported by affirmative signs from the Kariri who sur-rounded us while he explained these matters to me.

'The plant has to accept the person, so that this person, this woman or man can become a dreamer (*sonhador*) and a walker (*caminhante*). We have to walk, my daughter, in order to see, but we also have to see so that we can walk.'

Walker and dreamer are thus specific social categories that mark those who have been initiated into tribal knowledge and traditions, away from those who have not been able to enter into this special relationship and are still ignorant. Suíra told me only some of these words, because the more I knew, the more I could understand and he wanted me to understand his world view. However, many words had to remain secret. My interpretation of the secret is that is can be an ingenious way of preserving language against the forces of constant coloniza-tion, as well as the preservation of botanical species against the predatory incursions into their forests and gardens. Otherwise, another idea is that the Kariri want to preserve the concept of a defunct language, or the remnants of an ancient tongue, that can give them legitimacy as 'traditional Indians', a people endowed with cultural memory and a language of their own, even though such language is illusory.

Part 3: Plant classification and the gradient of strength

From what I could deduce, the manipulation and classification of plants is based on a system of binary opposites in which signs of positive and negative become the extreme poles of a gradient of strength. This means that anything in Kariri-Shoko life – things, objects, actions and even people – are classified according to the position that it occupies between the two poles or signs. Plants, medicines and prayers – which are interrelated and interlocked in a conceptual framework of the cosmos – fall into this structured system. This highly abstract, but deeply understood, gradient of strength tells us that everything falls between two extreme points that I have reconstructed this way:

The gradient of strength:

negative ⟵⟶	positive
weak	strong
feminine	masculine
hot	cold
obscure	clear
ill	healthy
profane	sacred
cooked	raw
sweet	bitter
open	hidden
overt	secret
soft	hard
leaves/flowers	roots/trunk
non-Kariri	Kariri (indigenous)

As 'feminine' seemed to be intensely related to 'negative', I was very pre-occupied in trying to understand whether the principle of femaleness was equivalent to that of 'badness'. The common response was that 'negative' does not necessarily mean 'bad' and vice-versa. Menstrual blood, for instance, is 'negative' when it is weak, meaning that the woman is not sick. Menstrual blood is normal and natural, but, like any other human secretion, it is not to be touched during religious rites, due to the fact that it 'opens' one's body to spiritual influences, mainly the bad ones. However, if the flow of menstrual blood is heavy and painful, it becomes 'positive', but the woman is under the influence of 'masculinity' because her blood has become 'too strong', thus indicating that her inner body is 'hot' instead of cold and that can be a harmful or 'bad' event, even a life-threatening situation. These inconsistencies in the system indicate that the opposites put things in a correlation that goes from left to right in our columns, but not always from top to bottom, otherwise the 'positive' blood would not indicate sickness and heat. It should be clear, how-ever, that the concept of negative is not simply that of denial of worth. Some-thing is understood as negative in relation to something else which is categorized as positive; whatever falls in between the two extremes is 'more negative' or 'less positive'.

Following their line of reasoning, what is 'open' is out in the air, for everyone to see. In this way, leaves are the most non-secret parts of a plant and also the softer. The region of the bark being used is the inner core, which is hidden, harder and stronger. But the bark is more vulnerable than the roots that are buried deep in the earth, extracting the moisture, the darkness, the silence and the secrecy of the earth. We have already seen that roots and trunks have been conceptualized as metaphors for the ancestors. A 'strong' medicine has to be made with the roots and the inner bark. In this way, the gradient orients Kariri-Shoko knowledge and manipulation of botanical species for medicinal purposes and is related to Kariri social classification. Some people within the tribe know more, or rather, are allowed to know more than others. But the Kariri-Shoko as a whole are allegedly more knowledgeable than all the rest of the non-Indians who live around them. This is an instance of 'private marking'[1] by means of which the social category 'Kariri-Shoko' is differentiated from all others because of their manipulation of plants as 'indexical signs' of identity.

Plants in themselves do not constitute the indexical signals. It is rather the forms of manipulation and of addressing plants by members of distinct social groups that are the signals. The ethnic identity and social subsystems – *pajés*, *rezadeiras*, *mateiros*, *juremados* – are the entities signalled. The fundamental point here is that there are specific **forms** of manipulation of plant species which are allowed only to a certain sector of society, being prohibited to all others. There is a taboo not on finding and using the plant, but in the form of usage, which involves language, i.e., prayers, actions and singing which is concealed in order to be specific to some restricted sectors of Kariri-Shoko society. We have seen that the social category known as Kariri-Shoko is differentiated from others – and even from their alleged relatives, the São Pedro Shoko – by their use of plants as embodiments of protective spirits. Using indexical signalling systems – wherein there is a spatial-temporal or physical connection between the sign vehicle and entity signalled (Urban 1981: 475) – associated to Kariri-Shoko social categories, we are dealing with a binary system of oppositions, along which the principal subsystems of social categories fall. These are:

○ male/female subsystem;
○ age-grade subsystem (child, initiate, adult);
○ specialist/non-specialist subsystem;
○ Kariri-Shoko/non-Kariri-Shoko subsystem.

The Kariri-Shoko are marked positively, i.e., they know the secret usages of all plants, whereas the others – including the São Pedro Shoko – are marked negatively. Thus the criterion for marking here is the level of access to secret manipulation and knowledge of plants. Non-Kariri people do manipulate whatever plants are available to them, that is, the same ones that belong to the Kariri universe of known species. However, non-Kariri do not know how to manipulate these plants 'properly' because they are not aware of how to relate to plants in the 'right' way, meaning the Kariri mode of usage. People from Afro-Brazilian cults are recognized by the Kariri *pajé* as having a similar relationship to plants, yet they are not supposed to have the same words, in songs and prayers, as we have seen in the case of the Jurema cult.

Suíra, his son and 'Seu' Neco explained that certain plants can only be known for all their properties and occult uses by Kariri male specialists like themselves. Neco is more restricted, however, than the *pajé* and son, because he is merely a *mateiro*, besides being a *mestiço* (of mixed blood). Even within the category of male specialist there are degrees of access to Kariri plant knowledge, even though it is clear that Neco knows practically as much as Suíra. The limit imposed by the culture is that Neco cannot deal with all the plants in the culturally prescribed and appropriate ways and that he looks for the *pajé* in order to handle the more 'secret' and 'strong' plants. Other indigenous descendants, like the Fulniô of Pernambuco, are also knowledgeable about the *Ouricuri*, sharing the same constituted Kariri cosmology.

Consequently, a scale can be built in which a Kariri adult male specialist is the least restricted and, therefore, the higher – or more 'legitimate' – representation of Kariri identity. Males, in fact, are the ones holding more knowledge and power in the Kariri concept of the social universe. Non-Kariri people are the more restricted in this scale, or the ones with no knowledge at all and, therefore, no identity as a Kariri-Shoko. The São Pedro Shoko fall within this lower representation of the self in relation to ethnobotanical and ethnopharmacological knowledge, as they do not know how to use the language deemed appropriate to deal with plants. Moreover, plants are not seen as relatives, plants do not signal a relationship to the divine. Plants do not occupy a special space in their cosmology as they do among the Kariri and in this aspect the Shoko are considered as more ignorant and less capable than the plant specialists of the Afro-Brazilian cults of the *Shangôs* and *Catimbós* of the Northeast. Decoding interpretable signals is based on what Geertz (1978) has called 'a semiotic definition of culture.'

To prove to me that non-Kariri people – even those who have the 'science of plants and medicines' – are incapable of sharing the same universe, Suíra ordered the male specialist of his group to prepare a *Jurema* drink for me. Needless to say, I was thrilled and intensely curious when I arrived at his house in Colégio at the appointed evening for the *Jurema* drink. There was no ceremony for our Jurema drinking session, but nevertheless it was a solemn moment. His wife brought the small clay pot with the dark liquid and two simple glasses. He was very quiet, so I asked if I had to do anything to concentrate. He smiled in his enigmatic way: 'It is good to concentrate, but relax, you don't have to be so tense. Nobody is going to eat you up.'

The beverage was a bitter tea, served at room temperature without sugar or honey. According to Suíra, it was prepared exactly as it is prepared for the Kariri-Shoko during the *Ouricuri* rituals. Nothing is added: only the roots which are boiled slowly for two to three days. We drank slowly. Nothing seemed to happen to me. I experienced no sensation other than a bitter taste. Other people came in and out of the room. Suíra seemed vague and abstract, as though he was already in his dream-state of travelling, having become a wanderer. I felt nothing, absolutely nothing and was disappointed. There was an intense silence, as if a vacuum had just been created. Contrite, I asked him if he could hear me. He looked at me calmly, smiling: 'of course . . . '

'I don't feel anything!' I burst out, abashed. I was sure he was happy to prove his point that I couldn't become *juremado* like the Kariri, that I was an outsider and would die an outsider, no matter what. At the same time, I was strangely relieved that I did not have to write about a 'powerful experience with *Jurema*.'

Suíra said: 'little by little you will see things happen, you will feel something. I can't promise you the stars tonight but you will be sensitive to new things. *Jurema* is good to everyone, it is just that you dried heads cannot see. It is not that *Jurema* does not show you things, but that you don't see what *Jurema* has to teach you. You're not *Jurema's* daughter yet . . . '

This was the time when he told me more about the differences between women healers and male healers, so that I could understand how women are marked differently from men in the Kariri system of medical ethnobotanical knowledge. 'Women are made up spiritually weaker. They are soft, they are the moon-children. They bleed monthly, so they cannot have the same condition as men for handling tough matters. Women are more passionate and then make mistakes.'

'You are talking like a regular macho man of the dried heads,' I complained. He laughed in response.

'I knew you would say that, my daughter. It's true, I'm talking the truth, even if you don't like it. You bleed monthly, if you try not to bleed you die. You need to bleed monthly. Also you need to be bathed by the male's discharge during sex, otherwise you suffer very much.'

He kept pointing at me and I was interpreting his discourse as being directed to all womenfolk, not just me. He realized that. 'I'm talking about all women, but also specifically about you. You are of a more passionate nature than many others. You clearly need to be married. Not all women are like you. It is fine. Not all women seek knowledge like you do. That is why I am giving you *Jurema*, even though you are a White woman. This is an honour for you, but also a burden, because you can never be the same again. *Jurema* will seek you out wherever you go. However, like all other women, you will never be a man. Therefore, you will need a man to bring you *Jurema* even as you need a man to give you children. You won't have a mother, nor a father, nor children without the power of men.'

Right then I did not want to go into a feminist discourse to respond to what I analysed as a male-centred view of the world. I was, in fact feeling very calm and relaxed. That night, heat, mosquitoes and a hard bed couldn't keep me awake. I slept soundly even though *Jurema* had not spoken to me yet.

5 The healing universe

Part I: The healers

WHILE IN SERGIPE, I retreated to my father's sister's home in Aracaju for a respite from fieldwork. One afternoon I was taking a nap at my aunt's house before going to São Pedro, where I was going to participate in the Second Meeting of Northeastern Tribes. I had the impression that I was waking up, in a daze, startled by some remarkable fanfare, as though I could hear the Shoko singing loudly, their shrill voices echoing inside my brain. It felt as though I was there on the island, sleeping in Lola's house and not in Aracaju at my aunt's place. I opened my eyes and clearly saw the island's central clearing in front of me and the houses right across from where I was. However, my vision would become blurred, now and then, as if I was still dreaming, but I was awake at the same time or, at least, thought I was. I could see *pajé* Raimundo's house and the house next to his, which were on the edge of the road leading to the river port and the women's bathing beach. Some people kept singing, now in the distance, and those were the voices I could hear. Then I saw a group of people approaching the houses. That was when a crashing sound reverberated above the singing. I focused my eyes and saw that somebody had fallen and was lying down in front of Raimundo's house. I became very scared, thinking that someone had died. Meanwhile I also became acutely aware of the fact that I was not really 'seeing' the scene, nor really 'hearing' those sounds, because I was struggling to wake up from my nap. My aunt's voice, calling me for something or other, made me realize that I was not in São Pedro, that I was still in Aracaju. I became very scared that someone was sick in São Pedro or was dying there. But how could I know that? How could I have such startling clear visions? The answer would come during the following week.

Sickness pervades all societies. It offends, takes away, repairs, reorders. But above all sickness is as creative as its own cures. The distress a person experiences is known to go away somehow, sometime, with the help of someone. This someone is the specialist, that person – man or woman – who manipulates the social knowledge that has been accumulated and passed along for centuries on how to take care of sending infirmity away.

Medicine was and still is a continuous knot within the philosophic and scientific ethos of the surviving indigenous culture. At times it is confused with religiosity, without loss to its character of medical system. In spite of the secrecy that surrounds most rituals, it is possible to confirm that the healing systems used by these people are mixed with elements of African and European origin, as yet another result of colonization. The different ethnic groups that interconnect in the area studied – the Indians, African, European descendants – have learned, through centuries of contact, to share their medical practices as well as discourses, so that there is a constant stream of clients and practitioners going back and forth among the different types of medical resources available.

However, based on diverse epistemologies and philosophies, the different healers are nowadays able to interact and support each other. The already transformed indigenous medicine is supplied mostly by Suíra, his son, and other healers from the Indian villages. The Shoko in São Pedro are not yet so bold as to call themselves practitioners of a 'native medicine', but they do have a good number of women healers who were informally trained in what can be described as a hinterland medicine or, more to the local taste and rationality, a *caboclo* medicine.

Non-Indians do revert to the practitioners of this *caboclo* and euphemized 'native medicine', even though there are some modern biomedical resources around. Jerusa's brother appraises the utilization of herbal medicine by the *índios*, but in a somewhat typical jealous vein: 'The healers in the Indian village are all Kariri: 'seu' Francisquinho, Maria Peri and Marieta who can only pray. There was Dona Iriá who was also a praying woman, but she died. She treated my toothache. She prayed on the tooth with three branches of *pinhão rosho* (*Jatropa gossypifolis L.*) and said that my tongue would be my prayer. After the prayer I went home and slept well. The next day, the tooth was loose and began to fall off every time I put my tongue over it. What cures is faith. When people are desperate they go looking for *mandingueiros*[1], those who know how to make *garrafadas* and prayers. But the *caboclos* themselves don't look for their healers. People come from Arapiraca, Maceió and Recife looking for the *pajé*, but the Indians go straight to the doctor. Any stomach ache and they go running to the doctor. They are taken by the FUNAI van to Recife to the hospital. The young people don't want to learn the forest medicine. They are more supported than we are, because they have FUNAI to help them.'

This is the White people's version, based on their views of the *caboclos* with whom they have lived for so many centuries. It is a view tempered by prejudice and the many sorrows that are common in a situation of interethnic conflicts, defined by ethnic and political frontiers. 'Seu' Neco has other stories involving *caboclos* and the faith in the power of herbs. From his point of view, the medicine that is still practised by the *pajé* and his trainees is veritably the 'native medicine' that has been forsaken by most people on the edge of the so-called civilization. According to him, Suíra did not invent anything, because Suíra learned from his elders a form of healing that has been passed down through many generations. Neco thinks that it remained virtually untouched by the forces of colonization.

'It is the tradition,' he used to repeat gravely, 'that no one can change. It has power, it has force, it has truth. It is a healing that only the *pajé* can practise, nobody else, unless he teaches it to someone, under orders from *Jurema*.'

It is undisputed that the *pajé* exercises a form of healing that is effective, it is also known that he prescribes herbal preparations as medicines. It is believed that he 'sees' the illness, being considered a *bruxo*, a *mandingueiro* or witch. His medicine, and that of those who surround him, is undoubtedly an inheritance from the traditional Kariri medicine of the past which was described by Ferrari (1957) as intimately tied to exorcisms, blowing, frictions, singing, and so forth. The same author also considered that those practices had been openly prohibited by the missionaries who, on the other hand, tried to introduce new cures in the Kariri cultural context, since many of the religious people also had notions of how to cure sick people. Since Kariri cures were considered by the agents of the colonization process as 'diabolic', native healing also underwent the fate of being persecuted and banished, albeit without much success, since it remained in the practices of the *mesinhas* throughout the hinterlands and the hidden shamanic complex among the remaining tribal descendants like the Kariri-Shoko. Such forms of medical practice have spread throughout the continent, being part of various native medical systems. The *mesa* or *mesinha* – table or small table – consists of a ritual altar where the people in charge of the healing place the objects believed to possess healing powers and where the healers get together in order to perform a healing session. It consists of a cluster of things, dead or alive, that are included in lieu of the *encantados* and that make up a pharmacy, as well as a central place of magical-religious power, considered to be the power that can heal. Supposedly medicines only work because of such power.

The region where the Kariri-Shoko live is abundant in this kind of practice. A *mesa* however can only be set, or fixed, by certain ritual specialists: people endowed with knowledge and power. Such people are known as *mesinheiras/os*. They work within the medical system of the Kariri-Shoko. The *pajé* is the main one, besides being the one who bestows authority on all the others. Some of the healers from São Pedro are also *mesinheiras*, but not as famous as the same women who live entirely outside the borders of the indigenous ethnic identity's realm.

Those who work with *mesa* use several forms of therapy: prayers, chants, prophesying games, remedies of botanic origin, mainly under the guidance of spiritual guides or souls. These guides are generally 'disembodied' beings who belong to the indigenous classifications and must remain secret. Not all the sessions of the *mesa indígena* can be observed by non-initiated people who are not already *filhos da Jurema*. The number of participants of a *mesa secreta* (secret table) must be six: three men and three women. These people are in charge of affirming, as well as of 'firming' the *ciência indígena* (indigenous science), which is considered the indispensable foundation for the well-being and sociability of all the group. Some native religious movements, and also those brought from Africa were persecuted by the missionaries and by the political powers of the dominant sectors of the national society, and forced to become more occult, more esoteric, in order to preserve themselves (de Barros, 1995). That was a way of keeping cultural values and allowing the people to be free agents. The practice of shamanism was an important factor for cultural maintenance, as well as for maintaining biological diversity. Such practice, being based on the preservation of native flora as well as the exotic species brought by Europeans and Africans, was one of the elements behind adequate forest management that would ensure the existence of the medicinal herbs needed for the production and reproduction of remedies and beliefs as well. The preservation of medicinal species is, then, a form of environmental preservation, no matter how limited in scope and time frame.

Part 2: The shamanic complex

The Second Meeting of Northeastern Tribes was going on strongly with several events, which attracted enthusiastic participants. Two of these events marked the pace of the entire workshop, especially for me, as the attitudes surrounding them taught me much about the indigenous societies that were represented there.

The first event happened as I had anticipated in my dream. I was sitting in front of Lola's house, chatting with her neighbours, when a group of people emerged from the road, coming from the river port. Since many people were arriving then, we thought nothing of this, until somebody fell in front of Raimundo's house creating a big commotion. I stood up immediately, while several folks who were surrounding the fallen person started to run about wildly, calling for Raimundo, who was nowhere to be seen. Someone was running to fetch Dona Nazinha, so there had been some kind of accident, no doubt. Lola's neighbour walked across the clearing in order to find out what was going on. I was too disturbed even to speak, as I remembered my dream of just a week before.

The neighbour came back and announced that an old man who had not been with the 'tribe' all his life and had just landed in the island, was probably having a heart attack. I saw Dona Nazinha walking slowly toward the scene. Her pace signified that she did not think she could do much for the man. There was a sudden burst of loud screams of *'Acode! Socorro!'* (Help! Help!) followed by anguished cries of 'He is dead! He is dead!' That was the death that had been announced to me, even though I didn't even know the dead man. Lola and I stayed quietly in front of her house as she smoked her old pipe, glancing at me once in a while, trying to divine what had happened to me. Finally she asked: - 'why are you so quiet? Are you upset about someone dying right here? He was a distant relative of the Shoko, I don't even know him.' Yet I could see a grimace of worry in her face and tears beginning to collect in the corner of her eyes.

I told her about my dream. Her eyes popped wide open and she burst out a very impressed *'Minha Nossa Sinhora!'* (My Our Lady!) and said no more. Leaders of the event, including Lola's son, went over to Raimundo's house, to where the body had been carried, and started to sing the songs I had heard in my dream. I finally dared to walk over to Raimundo's house. The old man had been placed on a wooden table in the front room and a group of women were crying in unison, exclaiming about the death. People were commenting that the poor man had been so thrilled to see 'Shoko land' that his old heart could not take it. The unity of the tribes, to be planned and celebrated during that week, had started with a tragedy and people were very disturbed by what they considered as an omen. Two Karapato Indians from Alagoas and a small group of Patasho from Bahia, whose leader was an impassioned young man all dressed up in feather ornaments, were singing loudly inside the house. *Pajé* Raimundo came in and gravely ordered everyone to be quiet, explaining that silence had to be kept in order to honour the dead man. The Patasho leader was quick to retort: 'You are wrong here, cousin. We honour the dead by singing, not by silencing.' And they went on singing a *toré* for the dead. Raimundo was obviously upset by the apparent threat to his authority and challenge to his knowledge of proper indigenous protocol. But he kept silent, shifting his body and crossing his arms across the chest, indignant and dignified.

The old man's death was to bring back to memory a whole plot not only of dissent, but of how the Shoko had truly distanced themselves from the native perspective on life and death. Fray Enoque was also present at the scene and he agreed to do everything according to whatever indigenous ritual there was to follow, explaining to his Shoko entourage that: 'Now you are within your Indian religion. You are not pagans, you are religious too, and I also want to learn with the people who are here, and who have kept the old principles, what is to be done.'

Suíra's son had not arrived yet when the man died, so he was not there to witness Raimundo's first reaction. I later told Suíra about the whole story, including the fact that I had dreamed about it. His interpretations were, first of all, that *Jurema* had 'taken' me, since I was having premonitory dreams and I should be very proud of that.

'It means that now we can communicate through dreams. But also, second of all, that the Shoko *pajé* is not a *pajé* at all! The poor man doesn't even know we have to sing a *toré* for the dead! He doesn't know anything! How can he call himself a *pajé*? He has lots to learn in order to ever become a true Indian *pajé*.'

When the old man died in São Pedro, even though there were other *pajés* there, the ritual for the dead was not followed. Suíra said it would not be possible, partly because there was another festival going on and, moreover the São Pedro Shoko would not know how to do things. Júlio then explained what he would have told the people to do, if they were in his own village.

'When an Indian dies we have three days of praying and wailing in the "language". The women who are the *pajé*'s assistants are in charge of going from house to house, helping with the official wailing and mourning period. Afterwards Suíra comes and, finally, me. We rest for 30 days, cleansing and preparing ourselves for the *Matekrai* to be done for the dead.'

In São Pedro they could not have done the *Matekrai*, because it means literally 'secret' and there were too many outsiders, who would be able to see what was going on. But at the Sementeira, the *pajé* leads everyone to go into the *Ouricuri* village. They get to the *Ouricuri* in the afternoon and start the preparations. At midnight on that day, the *pajé* goes into the woods by himself and meets the recently deceased person. He then talks to that person, verifies if he or she has any wrongs to undo, tells him or her what to do and then to go away, never to return. A very long time has to pass before the dead one can re-enter the world of the living during a *Matekrai*, because he or she had a *Matekrai* done just for him or her. But if the dead one does not receive the benefit of a feast in his or her honour, then the soul will wander through the woods, the villages, appearing to people and scaring them. The obligation, the *penitencia*, has to be performed so that the dead and the living can share the benefits coming from it.

The second event revolved around an epileptic attack experienced by a woman in her 40s, who was already being treated for an illness she had had since childhood. Even the Shoko had always thought that her disease was the result of an 'evil eye' curse and nobody had been able to cure it. People also put her malady in the same category as a mental disorder. When it became evident to her family that she was having another attack, instead of administering her medicine, they called for Júlio and Fray Enoque, in the hope that they could 'cure' her once and for all. She did not know Júlio, so she was very upset when she saw him, and that made her attack worse. However, when Fray Enoque approached her, he immediately asked for her medication, gave it to her and she started to quieten down in a while. He stroked her head affectionately and she smiled blissfully, as he was someone she trusted and loved very deeply. Comments afterwards were that Fray Enoque was a more powerful 'wizard' than the Kariri-Shoko shaman.

Júlio, no doubt, was aware of this. He was sure to come over and talk to me about it. His explanations of his 'failure' were partially sensible, as he mused about the fact that she did not know him and that made it difficult for him to relate to her effectively. But he also said that her illness had been provoked by someone very powerful from outside the tribe and she had definitely to be 'cured' of that curse. The Shoko who heard his theories agreed with him, but did nothing about it, such as asking him to start curing her. In a silent way, they were putting his power in jeopardy.

'If they had let me blow tobacco smoke on the top of her head, she would be on her way to being cured,' he said to me, rather distraught. I understood the Shoko's reaction to his predications as having a double meaning: 'we don't want you to interfere in our affairs' and 'perhaps the priest's magic is greater than yours, so why should we trust in you?' It also related, of course, to their own ignorance of what a *pajé* is really about and what he is supposed to be able to do for his people.

After those incidents in São Pedro, Francisco Suíra told me in earnest about what it meant to be a Kariri-Shoko *pajé*. He defined himself as *médico, conselheiro e padre* (physician, counsellor and priest). Above all, he was a true scientist, someone who 'owns' the indigenous science of health and illness. The frame of reference for the Kariri-Shoko science is the *'mundo que não se vê'* (unseen world): a realm of culture that remains secret to those who are not members of the tribe. Such a symbolic world, collectively constructed by the social imagination, is the famous *'tradição da tribo'* (tribal tradition): the reason for its existence and reality.

The knowledge of natural resources for medicine, the healing rituals, the manipulation of the environment are the 'trademarks' or the signs of power for the *pajé* and other healing specialists. Science and traditions are, therefore, two interrelated terms. Science signifies knowledge and knowledge signifies power. Within this worldview, what is learned now, no matter how important or positive, does not have the same *fôrça* as that which was learned from the *avós* (grandparents), that is, the *ciência dos antigos* (old ones' science). Such belief becomes clear from the words of the *toré* for Caboclo Lindo, an *'encantado que desce na mesa de índio'* (enchanted one who appears in the indigenous ritual altar).

'Caboclo Lindo, que estás fazendo aqui?' (Caboclo Lindo, what are you doing here?) asks the audience, upon noticing his 'presence'. In the version sung at the *Ouricuri*, the others answer for him: *'eu venho de terra alheia caçando minha ciência.'* (I come from foreign lands hunting for my science).

The *encantado* went to foreign lands searching for a lost science because the tribal tradition is in danger of disappearing. Suíra's son explained: 'tradition is a very old thing that I must take care of. We have to have a tradition so that we can go on living.' Traditional knowledge is not an empty exercise in vanity, but what Suíra and his followers have to hold on to. Suíra's job is to ensure that this continues to happen and that is why he was so concerned with the fact that the São Pedro *pajé* did not seem to know anything about this tradition. He knows because he is what he categorizes as a *'pajé* from the wilderness', because ideally he has to perform the same rituals, say the same words as those of the original *pajé selvagem*, who danced holding a clay pot filled with sacred leaves from the sacred woods.

In terms of the Kariri-Shoko's social structure, the phenomenon known in the anthropological literature as shamanism is a form of thinking about 'power' and that occupies a central place in this structure, allowing the continuous production and reproduction of their society. Wherever shamanism is still encountered today, anywhere in the world, shamans function fundamentally in much the same way and with similar techniques, namely as guardians of the psychic and ecological equilibrium of his group and its members, as intermediaries between the seen and unseen worlds, as masters of spirits and as supernatural curers (cf. Furst, 1972).

The *pajé* translates the same efficacy for his people: he, his helpers and heirs in office have the responsibility of maintaining a set of rituals, practices and symbols defined as the tribal tradition. The role of the *pajé* Kariri-Shoko confirms the thesis that shamanism acts as a central force in the expression of a native world view (cf. Langdon, 1989). This view reclaims the return of *Caboclo*

Lindo, so that he does not have to go on roaming around strange lands in search of a lost science and culture.

The place that the group of healing specialists occupies within the tribal social organization is legitimized through the ceremonies taking place in the *Ouricuri* and by the ideology of ancestry. More than a veneration of the ancestors, this ethnic ideology expresses the necessity of reclaiming the past as real and active, having as cultural praxis the remaking of a tradition that should have survived the colonization process. Unfortunately it was not able to keep all its authenticity. The Indians still carry this guilt, the unbearable guilt of having been too weak to confront the colonizers and their armies. Thus they keep on continuously striving to declare their 'power', their 'strength', the surviving force of their long lost traditions. Francisco Suíra symbolizes this struggle to keep the ancestors within their hearts and minds as he keeps alive what is known as tribal science and tradition.

The Kariri shaman has to belong to a specific family that holds office, but he must also possess a vocation for healing, for leading his tribe in spiritual matters. The same way that the old *Caboclo* Lindo journeys through many lands, the path of the shaman is a long one, embroidered by many fantastic journeys, which start during his childhood. He dances in the wild spaces of his own mind, directed by *Jurema*, before he is finally appointed. As he travels the paths of enlightenment, *Sonsé* bestows knowledge through the roots of the *Jurema* tree, so that he can symbolically go deep into the earth of his forefathers and emerge later as the 'powerful' one. If a man declines *Sonsé's* invitation to the job, or is unaware of it, then he will become so sick that he may die, if not rescued in time by his own understanding of his destiny.

Both Suíra and his son Júlio became seriously ill before they and the others in the tribe were sure of their calling as shamans. That was the beginning of their personal journey, a fundamental ingredient in the making of a Kariri-Shoko shaman. The other fundamental factor is their ability to converse with all aspects of nature, including the dead. That the dead can show up and hold a conversation is totally acceptable, although not expected, if a *Matekrai* was held for that particular dead. But the shaman learns from the trees, in the same way, for instance, that the Conibo of the Upper Amazon do (cf. Harner, 1980). Suíra talks to the trees because he can 'hear' their inner voices, as he enters what Harner (1980) has labelled the 'Shamanic State of Consciousness'. It is through these spiritual journeys that Suíra and Júlio are able to roam the earth, becoming experts in healing physical and psychological ills, as well as taking care of the tribal interests.

'Our work is done so that the village and the people are not destroyed,' said Suíra, 'I counsel, I heal and thus we go on.'

All the love and trust encapsulated within such words and acts come through in the *torés*, 'the songs we sing to our grandparents,' as they explain, in verses that claim: '*Lírio branco, lírio roxo,/ lírio de muita ciência,/ para fazer a paz no mundo há que se ter paciencia.*' (White lily, violet lily, lily of much science, to make peace in the world, one has to have patience).

To heal is to build the peaceful state which allows the tribe to survive in the world. To heal is a free 'gift', bestowed by *Sonsé*, as life and death also are.

Since the *pajé* is believed to have the capacity to heal spiritual, physical and mental ills, he is no longer just a poor *caboclo*, but the folk magician, the witch doctor who instils fear in most people. The *Matekrai* secret transforms him into the noble healer, as he works to transform the drab lives of his people in glorious travels of resplendence and intensity.

Part 3: Women as healers

The little child was crying out loud when Dona Nazinha took her in her strong calloused hands. The healer cooed at the baby patiently, making soft chuckling sounds, while the child still fretted in apparently terrible distress. The child's mother, a young woman who has what is considered to be typical Indian features, was wringing her hands in agony as she spoke: 'I don't know what to do any more, Dona Nazinha, only you can help me! She has been just in such pain, shitting just water.'

Nazinha cradled the child and started to gently stroke her belly, while asking the mother if she had given the tea of camomile flowers the healer had recommended. The answer was positive and Nazinha started to 'pray' the child. As she stroked the child, she mumbled Christians prayers like 'Our Father' and 'Hail Mary'. Then she again started to massage the child's belly and to blow over her head. The baby slowly started to settle down and her screams abated. Finally the baby slept peacefully and Nazinha handed her back to a much relieved mother. I was duly impressed. The mother turned to me and murmured: 'Nazinha has God's power. She can do real miracles . . . '

Nazinha smiled humbly: 'if I had God's powers, we would all be in much better shape. So many children died here last year!'

She was referring to the period of famine that had taken some young children on the island. Dona Nazinha was a worn-out old woman in her 70s when I got to know her. That same year, one of the Indian rights groups of Brazil published a poster bearing her picture, with a Shoko statement underneath: 'we stayed in order to save the land.' Nazinha erroneously always attributed the poster to me, declaring to everyone that I had made her 'famous'. It was not the truth, of course, since, first of all, I had nothing to do with the poster, and anyway she was 'famous' long before I ever appeared on the island. She was the kind of healer who synthesized various healing practices from the cultural traditions that formed the way of living in the backwoods where she had been born and raised. However, she liked to think of herself as a descendant of the Fulniô who still practised her grandmother's healing techniques, which she learned in her younger days.

'My grandmother was hunted down like a dog and brought to civilization', was her recollection of her childhood, 'then she married a White man and only returned to the village when there was no more land around. But the *índios* lost their lands too, there was much disgrace, so she brought her family to Jaciobá and crossed the river. Before they crossed the river, they got me married to a Shoko man, as my mother was alone, my grandmother was alone, and I had to have a man to protect us. Then we joined the Shoko and went to live in the Caiçara. But my husband died young too and we women were alone again. I raised all my children by myself, a Fulniô woman among the Shoko who didn't know they were Shoko. Until the priest (Fray Enoque) came along and told us what to do.'

A light-skinned *cabocla*, Nazinha had turned brown from a lifetime toiling under the sun. She had the fine facial features that are attributed to people of indigenous descent: high cheek bones, slanted eyes, straight nose, but her lips were thin, another sign that indicated her mixed genetic inheritance. She lived alone in a three-room mud house that she kept as clean as possible. In her fenced backyard, from which one could see the westernmost point of the island, she lovingly grew some of her healing herbs and she had a small vegetable garden where she planted beans, manioc and a few ears of corn. Sometimes one of the grandchildren who live on the island slept over with her, so that she did not feel the loneliness of a carefully guarded widowhood so much.

Nazinha was a soft-spoken proud woman, who walked with difficulty and was beginning to bend over as age advanced inexorably, but somehow she managed to tend to her chores all by herself. She presented the rugged appearance of someone who has had to work hard to survive, but it is not trite to state that she is one of the kindest people anyone could ever meet. She has had the upbringing of most *caboclas* in which Christian mores were embroidered with beliefs in ghosts and nature-entities and a 'native' way of living. She belongs to many cultural traditions, but is always affirming her Fulniô descent and, therefore, her affinity with the Shoko.

Nazinha told me to come early in the morning, about six o'clock, to have breakfast with her and then we would go on our plant collecting journey. I was staying at Lola's house at that time, where I slept on a tiny cot in Lola's small room. I got up at a quarter to six and Lola was already up, having made coffee in her backyard kitchen. Her daughter-in-law was feeding the chickens and I watched her slender body moving gracefully around the backyard, while I brushed my teeth by the window. Lola wanted me to have a strong cup of coffee before I went out, arguing that Nazinha did not make good coffee. Lola's coffee was not as weak as that served around the island. Although I was helping with the groceries, she was considered a big squanderer – mockingly, of course – by others, since people tried to save the precious grounds by making a rather weak coffee. Lola was concerned that I was not eating properly, so she was putting in more grounds than usual.

I crossed the large uninhabited portion of land around which the houses were built – the 'square', as it was known – with trees beneath whose shade people used to rest after lunch. Lola's old father, so bent with age that his chin was almost at the same level as his navel, smiled his toothless smile and waved his bony wrinkled hand as he walked very slowly in front of the house. All the houses were open at that time, with people getting busy to go out to work or already coming back from work, like the men who went fishing in the dark hours of the very early morning. Nazinha awaited me with her old tin coffee pot steaming with fresh beverage. Lola was right: Nazinha did make weak sugary coffee. I sipped it obligingly, as she brought out a treat that she had proudly prepared for me: a dish of *cuscus*, a sort of corn porridge eaten like a soup as it is doused with milk. One of her granddaughters came in bringing Pedrito's youngest son hanging from her hip. We chatted amicably for a while.

Grace, the 15 year-old girl who was Nazinha's eldest grandaughter, had a very sad personal story and was healing her emotional wounds in her parents' home. Nazinha asked if she wanted to accompany us, but she declined, saying that she had to help her mother around the house. Pedrito was busy fixing his fishing net, sitting in front of their shack, which was four houses down from Nazinha's. When Pedrito first introduced me to Nazinha, he had asked his mother-in-law to 'take care' of me, but he didn't need to bother, because Nazinha and I had taken an immediate mutual liking to each other and she was always in her best mood when I happened to be around. Nazinha was melancholy by nature, filled with nostalgia for what she used to call 'the good times' at the Caiçara farm. That morning, however, she was very happy to show me her healing plants, both the cultivated as well as the wild ones. My plan was to let her show me what she knew, instead of asking her about specific illnesses or plants for healing the categories of illnesses I was familiar with. That worked fine, since her strategy was to start with her backyard garden, walking out of her house and going through the island until we reached the woods at the other end. She then pointed out the plants for me, as she collected the parts that were used for medicine, the flowers I needed, besides naming all the illnesses or problems that each plant was known to cure or to solve, throwing in a few stories of healing she accomplished by using the plant to hand. She was most content to be able to do this for me, as she was particularly worried about the misuse and misinformation surrounding plants. Her calloused bony hands worked very swiftly as she cut whatever parts she saw fit to collect. She had brought her special knife for the purpose, as well as a heavy straw basket in which she kept her specimens. I saw myself in front of an extremely knowledgeable human being, a genuine ethnobotanist of the hinterlands. Suíra had been a somewhat distracted teacher of the healing herbs, talking in mysterious tones and smiling coyly whenever I pressed him for more information. Nazinha was truly pedagogical as she showed me the plants carefully, giving me all the details she could. At one point, she stopped at a *Mimosa* tree and gravely announced:

'This is the *Jurema preta*. Do you see the colour of the trunk? It is rather dark, huh? It is darker than the trunk of the *Jurema branca* or *mansa*.'

I looked at that tree in disbelief, since I had searched for it throughout the parched lands surrounding the *Ouricuri* only to be laughed at by Suíra and Neco.

'Is it called black Jurema because of the colour of the trunk?' I must have sounded annoyed, and I was, because Suíra had allowed me to arrive at the conclusion that it was called 'black' as a result of its properties for provoking hallucinatory images.

'Well,' she said, shrugging her shoulders, 'some people make a lot of fuss over it, saying that it causes one to have dreams and incredible visions. It is true, though I have not tried it yet.' (That statement really took me by surprise, but she probably did not realize it.) 'However, magic is not a "black" thing, we cannot call a plant "black" because it is magical, we call it black because **it is** black! Also, it has thorns, see here?' She grabbed a branch in her hand and showed me the dangerous thorns, 'so it is also called "thorny *Jurema*" and it is not just because people can get crazy after drinking from its roots!'

There are other women healers among the São Pedro Shoko and the Kariri-Shoko, but none was so highly considered as Nazinha. They specialize in the cure of different minor illnesses, such as headaches and stomach aches that can be quickly cured. There is a specialist for orthopaedics and another for skin problems, for midwifery and gynaecological concerns, although Nazinha can take care of all this as she is the general practitioner.

Each healer considers herself empowered to cure only one specific problem. '*Olho grande*' (evil eye), an illness that encapsulates its own etiology, is generally taken care of by any healer and sometimes simply by an expedient grandmother. Such powers are believed to be of divine origin. Divine entities in charge of granting such powers do belong to the realm of the Catholic belief system, in the case of the Shoko healers. In all the healers' houses there are images of Christian saints and also of '*Padim Cisso*', as they pronounce the name of an illustrious Catholic priest who, after his death, has been venerated as a saint in the hinterlands. But even in São Pedro, female healers do not see themselves as having the same healing powers that a *pajé* manipulates.

'The *pajé* has to follow strict procedures in his training,' explained Marieta, a healer of mixed descent who lived in the Sementeira. 'Women could never go through it. WE have children, we nurse babies, we take care of the old, we run the household. We don't have the time or the strength to curse people, to bless them, or to get sick and dreadfully weak as a *pajé* has to do in order to become a *pajé*.'

In the first half of the 20th century, a Kariri-Shoko woman by the name of Maria Matilde temporarily replaced the shaman, while her nephew, Francisco Suíra, was too young to be in charge of such responsibility. Suíra recalls her fondly as one of his main teachers, as someone so wise and so strong that even he feared her. She was sought after by people from the hinterland who found help for their many ills in her expert hands and who were also careful about never becoming an enemy, as she was famous as a powerful female witch. She is mentioned in the literature by Estevão Pinto (1935) who claims she was a leader of the Kariri of Colégio and the great keeper of the customs and beliefs of Colégio's *caboclos*. I have cousins who live in Propriá and who also mentioned her name, as one of the older ones had had dealing with her and everybody thought he was 'crazy' to do so.

Any Kariri-Shoko would admit that Maria Matilde was a powerful sorcerer, yet the customs and beliefs that she kept for the collective memory implied that women were not as spiritually strong as men. That was one of the reasons for never allowing a woman to take office as the tribe's *pajé*. Matilde herself was only a substitute, for as soon as Suíra was declared a man at the age of 14, having already become extremely ill for not fulfilling his inherited role, he became the shaman. Women, then, can never rise to the same rank as the shaman. They are part of his group of attendants and they are highly respected and sought after, since they also specialize as midwives.

Women healers start practising late in life, usually after they stop menstruating. Blood is life and death, bad and good. Menstrual blood is not necessarily bad, but it does mean death, since it indicates that the mother of the body – the uterus – has become empty of life. Therefore, while women menstruate they should not be in charge of such a dangerous task as healing, lest the blood of an empty uterus affects the healing mission and turns it around. Women of the *Matekrai* are glad when they start menstruating, because they are immediately placed among the adult women, but they are also glad when they stop menstruating, because they are freed to do many things they could not do before. For one thing, a woman should not enter the *Ouricuri* sacred dances while losing menstrual blood. Vital bodily fluids such as blood and semen cannot be lost during the ceremony. There can be no sexual intercourse while the *Matekrai* is being held and menstruating women are kept apart in a special hut. The Matekrai is so demanding, physically as well as spiritually, that any sign of loss of vitality has to be avoided. The only passion that can flow is that for the forest of spirits where the *Jurema* lives. Women are as dedicated to *Jurema* as men, but the same opinion Westerners hold about women being more passionate and emotional than men has also found a comfortable corner in the Kariri world view.

I watched Marieta perform several cures. She is a *cabocla* who lives in the Sementeira with her daughter and grandchildren. Marieta learned her craft from the great Maria Matilde, together with Suíra. However, there were things that the women could not learn, not even the teacher, as men held their secret so removed from women's knowledge. I attempted many times to discover if ignorance of the male secret was a secret only for the non-initiated, but Marieta always seemed genuinely and deadly afraid of even trying to find out what men were planning and arranging in their secret hut in the *Jurema* woods.

Being an experienced healer, she professes not to be able to cure all ills, because some are too 'heavy' for her and require the work of a shaman. She is also bound to obedience to her *pajé*, so that, even if she prepares herbal medicines and potions, she has to ask the *pajé* to bless them, especially if it is a difficult, heavy or strong illness, that is, a category of suffering that demands a 'highly secret' and 'very strong' plant to cure it. Women, therefore, prefer to specialize in the *reza* (prayer) and the *limpeza* (cleansing), giving out recipes for medicinal plants only for what is considered by them as a 'minor illness', or an illness that was not provoked by the work of a powerful wizard. Moreover, Kariri-Shoko women know full well about the sex discrimination that is inherent in the *Ouricuri-Matekrai*. Therefore, they know – and outwardly accept – the fact that they cannot acquire the same power and prestige as a shaman, nor become a shaman. Marieta further explained it in this way:

'I can ask for things from the superior beings, but the *pajé* is the one to make *mesa*, yes, he has the right to make *mesa*. I can open a *mesa*, but I must ask for his permission first. I know how to do everything he does, but I don't want to get involved in his work, because his work is to make medicines and I am lesser than him. I cannot become a *pajé*. I am of the same family as him, but I cannot be a *pajé*, only men can. It is not that a woman cannot do the same things as men, but it is because in the *Ouricuri* a man goes where we cannot enter, and a man learns what we are never allowed to learn.'

That seemed like a contradiction, so I asked her how she could do everything he did. She answered, rather simply, that she was only sure of a few things she had learned well. 'My grandmother and my mother taught me a lot of things. Maria Matilde was my aunt too and she also taught me many things about healing. But they were women too, see? I believe that if we were given the opportunity to learn what men learn, we would be able to do everything they do, but the fact is that the *Ouricuri* and *Jurema* do not let us do what men do in the secrecy of their altar, in the middle of the woods, where they stay by themselves. WE CAN DO IT! But we cannot LEARN it! There is a separation in the *Ouricuri*. When we enter the *Ouricuri*, the men go to their place, where there is a *Jurema* or *pé de Jurema*, the holiest of all places. The women stay apart . . . *Posso morrer se eu bulir com coisa de homem*' (I can die if I mess with men's things) 'because I don't have their strength: I've lost too much blood during my lifetime.'

I reasoned with her that men had also lost a lot of semen during their lifetime. That was a dreadful strategy on my part. She was extremely withdrawn after what I had said. Since I had been introduced to her by Suíra himself, I found out from Suíra's wife that Marieta checked me out with him, and he had told her I was all right. She must also have thought a lot about my question, because when she next spoke to me it was to tell me that menstrual blood is much more powerful than the male fluid. However, she warned me, I should never admit that to anyone. Women know that, men know that, but *Jurema* has appointed men as shamans because women have to dedicate a great part of their lifetime to taking care of children. Men lose semen but they do not carry children in their stomachs, so there it was! After I declared myself thoroughly delighted with her explanations and lessons, she was very happy to demonstrate her healing talents to me.

She went to the front yard of her home which faces the São Francisco river, and took three small branches of a *Leguminosae* (a *Parkinsonia aculeata* Linn.) that provided nice shade for the house. She then proceeded to cure a daughter with whom she lived and who was suffering from a bad headache and chronic fatigue. This daughter had given birth to twins two months before, was nursing them, taking care of her other two small children, working on her pottery and doing housework. The postpartum 'diet' – which includes a leave of absence from household chores – was regretfully over. It was not surprising that the woman should be experiencing recurrent and severe bouts of fatigue and migraines.

While the twins were sleeping peacefully, Marieta started to work on the exhausted mother. Grasping the three small branches, she progressed in her work by motioning her hands as though she was 'sweeping' her daughter's body, but without actually touching her with the leaves. She started at the top of the patient's head and worked all the way through to her toes. Her daughter was sitting down, a posture that Marieta prefers, since other healers ask the patients who will be 'cleansed' to stand up. At the same time that she was 'sweeping', she was reciting a sequence of Catholic prayers, starting with Hail Mary and Our Father, ending with a sort of 'dialogue' between Jesus and a disciple, in which Jesus commands all the enemies of the affected person to leave him or her alone. The recitation is said in a low, monotonous tone of voice, following a rhythm during which certain notes have a higher pitch, immediately followed by a kind of inhaling sound. The way the praying is recited, therefore, should induce a lowering of the tensions and a semi-hypnotic state of consciousness. The patient is not asked to close the eyes, although that can happen. On the occasions when I observed Marieta performing a praying/healing, her patients seemed to be awake, their eyes were semi-closed and they seemed to be perfectly conscious of what was happening. They also seemed to relax immensely, as their breathing usually got to be easier and calmer. That was what transpired when she was 'praying' over her overwrought daughter. The patient had a tense expression when the healing began but started to ease her facial lines, and her worry wrinkles were smoothed out as the praying went on and on. It took Marieta approximately 30 minutes to do her work. After that, she gently stroked the patient's body on the chest and on the back with her open right hand. The daughter seemed slightly startled when she was thus touched and smiled sweetly but rather awkwardly, as though she was coming out of a trance state. In fact, she looked cheerful, in total contrast with her sullen disposition before the praying. She got up and went to the backyard to take care of the rest of her chores, as if she had just awakened from a refreshing nap.

On another occasion, I watched Marieta perform a healing of a man who stopped by while I was there visiting. The man, however, wanted his dried tobacco leaves to be healed, rather than himself. He usually sold the tobacco he harvested in the open fair. Lately he was being rather unlucky in the tobacco business. He suspected that some envious competitor had 'cured' him so that he would not be able to sell his merchandise, and this was also conceived as being a cure. She had him sit with his bag of tobacco on his lap, sat in front of him and started to pray in exactly the same way as she had done with other people, except that the leaves in her hand were being brushed around the bag of tobacco and not the man. It was the actual tobacco that had been 'enchanted' or 'cured,' not him!

His commodity had been taken care of in the cash value system inherent in commodities. Marieta charged the man for her work and he left, looking pleased and more confident about his luck.

Part 4: The price of healing

When Suíra takes care of non-Kariri-Shoko people he also charges a small fee for his services as a wizard. In fact, by exacting economic capital fron non-Indian clients, these healers are able to add to their very reduced income as sharecroppers in somebody else's land or as small farmers.

However, shamanic healing should not be a commodity, nor something to be paid for with money. People support the shaman and his family with work and with goods. The money he receives comes from outside the tribe, when he takes care of the 'others', the non-members of the tribe. Paper money as a form of exchange, or recompense for work performed, is prestigious only in the setting outside of the *Matekrai* context where prestige and honour are not paid for or even acknowledged with money. In the *Ouricuri*, participants bring food that is shared among everybody. Water is deposited in a common reservoir and wealth is that originated from the status attributed to knowledge and closeness to the shaman. His immediate aides are more honoured, but nevertheless they live in similar shacks and eat the same food as everyone else. When the *maracás* are played and *torés* sung in beautiful harmony, filling the forest with now wistful, now playful sounds, people are all alike. They sing to their *Ouricuri*, and the *Ouricuri*, in return, takes care of all of them.

Wealth accumulation of any sort should not be possible, nor acceptable, in such a setting. I was curious, however, to find a little brick house that a Kariri woman had built at the edge of the circular row of rooms in the *Ouricuri* village, shining as a symbol of prosperity. The woman is the director of the local elementary school in Colégio, filling a position of dubious prestige in the 'out-side world', but she has no special status in the ritual complex. The Ouricuri proves to be an opportunity to establish an 'anti-structure' to the national class society. The school director, however, brought the class differences from the colonized reality into the *Matekrai*.

Suíra, however, continues to affirm that power within the *Ouricuri* context is the power to heal, to 'see' and to 'walk'. At the Ouricuri, his journey is one of liberation, a flight toward the human possibilities that transcend a harsh reality of meagre economic means. When he treats the 'others', in his Colégio home, he receives cash for his work, although it is never much, since his clients come mostly from the lower classes, anyway. When the roof of his Colégio home collapsed, he asked me to lend him money in order to rebuild it: '*me acuda, minha filha*, (help me, my daughter), we all work so hard, but we don't have any money.'

Paradoxically, of all the male and female healers among the two groups, Nazinha is the one who usually refuses to be paid in national currency. She is tied to the function of healing as a source of self-preservation and affirmation of her own self, apparently much more deeply than the Kariri-Shoko healers. Knowledgeable and serious as Nazinha is, she could never have been a *pajé* within the traditions of the Northeastern tribes. But under her mother's guidance, she was able to retain a conceptual link to the primordial elements of native beliefs and values. She continually conceptualizes natural elements, like plants and celestial bodies, as sacred beings that help humans in their daily actions. She relates to medicinal plants in a visionary way that is not unlike the way the Kariri-Shoko shamans do. However, in contrast to them, she does not ever charge for her services. People may give her food items or some other gift, but she will not take cash as she feels it would dishonour her. 'God is the one who heals, not me. God's words cannot be paid for with money', is her expression of deepest belief.

Nazinha is not bound to obedience to a shaman, nor does she have to ask permission to do a healing session. However, that is due to the fact that there isn't a 'real' shaman in São Pedro island and she doesn't even know Seu Francisco. The healer named Nazinha is a link that could bind the chains that tie the two groups together. However, she is not sought by the Kariri-Shoko as a shaman, due to her gender. Although she suffers with the incapacity of her own people to keep native beliefs and past traditions, without the authority that is conferred on shamans she can do little to help the Shoko in their return to the indigenous way of thinking and living.

'They don't understand the value of this tree', she declared, very sadly, when she found the stump of a *Jurema* tree someone had just cut down, 'They never learned what good it can do for them.'

'Without *Jurema* there is no tribe', the *pajés* say. The Shoko had not heard that affirmation yet. Too bent in their Catholic beliefs, they sought refuge in the Church for their spiritual woes and looked to Nazinha, as well as the small towns' doctors, to heal their illnesses. The tree of life had left them barren, or, rather, it was they who had left it lifeless instead.

6 'Materia medica' and sets of health conditions

'There's rosemary, that's for remembrance;
pray, love, remember.' (Shakespeare, Hamlet IV.v)

Part 1: Native concepts of disease and health conditions

THE ROUTINE OF DAILY LIFE of the Kariri-Shoko and the Shoko followed rather similar paths, as they experienced extraordinarily similar socio-economic and political circumstances that characterize the Northeastern *sertão*. However, since the Kariri-Shoko are closer to two towns, Colégio and Propriá, they have always had easier access to certain facilities of an urban environment, such as super-markets, pharmacies, hospitals and health clinics.

Regarding medical care one could think of the Kariri-Shoko as being better attended: in Colégio there is a health clinic belonging to the state – SESC – offering primary health care, and Propriá has a government-funded hospital. However, these facilities are poorly staffed and maintained, being notorious for poor sanitary standards.

Due to the rather discouraging situation in the supply of modern medical care, coupled with the widespread knowledge of a native medicine, one could think that health clinic, pharmacy and hospital would not attract the people belonging to indigenous groups. The truth, however, is that both Shoko and Kariri-Shoko travel miles and wait for long hours to be able to see a 'modern doctor', spending their meagre earnings on industrialized pharmaceutical products. The simultan-eous use of both 'modern' and 'traditional' folk medicine and remedies is, in fact, a quotidian experience to all the inhabitants of the hinterlands. They visit their familiar non-Western healer as much as they do the detached modern medical doctor. Patients' expectations differ as to the kind of healing to be dispensed. Healers also differ regarding their concepts and views about the human body and sick conditions, as well as, of course, in their very philosophy of life or orientation towards the concepts of health and illness. 'Traditional' folk healers see matters concerning sickness as being closely related to the invisible world of ghosts and forest entities, and to the 'enchantment' springing from the spiritual side of life. There is a marked tendency for *sertanejos* to look for the services of these traditional healers when they believe that spiritual entities caused the sickness. They will not hesitate to go to the 'modern' doctor as well. This is particularly true of indigenous descendants.

Regarding the use of medicinal plants, I found that both groups have a similar affinity to the natural environment. Medicines of botanical extract are the same, as the Kariri-Shoko and the Shoko live in similar habitats, where several botan-ical species with alleged medicinal properties proliferate equally. In both groups the exploitation of medicinal plants follows the same profile for illness cate-gories, based on a belief of spiritual causation, regardless of religious orienta-tion. Followers of *Jurema* among the Kariri-Shoko have a greater affinity for forest entities, and practise shamanic forms of healing that are no longer part of the Shoko experience. However, pragmatic and experimental knowledge of the effects of botanical extracts and remedies in general is very much alike, if not equal.

From a sample of 125 plants that are most commonly used in both communities, it has been found that a great percentage of plants are used for the most common illness categories. The uses and forms for prescribing remedies of botanical extract reflect not only the health conditions of that rural area, but also the categories of illness, as there is emphasis on certain health conditions over others. 'Fever', for instance, is highly rated because it relates to 'internal' and 'external' heat, being the appellation for other illnesses as well, such as diarrhoea, blennorrhea, influenza, and so forth. There are more plants known for abortion than for contraception, perhaps because abortion is considered to be a major method of family planning.

People from rural areas in Brazil have developed remarkably similar ways of dealing with diseases that are based on rather similar concepts of diseases and their etiology. Thus, most illnesses have as ultimate cause a lack of equilibrium at the spiritual level which is reflected in the patient's body, causing an imbalance that becomes physically apparent. The role of the plant is to absorb the 'spirit' of the illness. Fever is a cause of much concern because it is supposed to be the most common symptom of such imbalance, occurring right at the onset of the disturbance. Therefore, plants that can cure fever are very well known and highly appraised.

The greatest contrasts among the different medical systems occur mostly regarding the form of treatment, or how, where and when the medical and/or magical rituals take place. Major differences stand out regarding magical-religious rituals – which also have healing as their final objective – and the use of mind-altering substances of botanical origin. The literature dealing with psychoactive substances as being used by indigenous groups employ the term 'entheogenic' to describe such substances, meaning literally 'realizing the divine within' (Ott, 1994). That is an accurate way of describing the belief that the Kariri-Shoko have regarding the utilization of *Jurema*, for instance, as the 'divine' properties of the plant become actualized within the body of the person taking the medicine.

However, in the case of our indigenous groups here, it is certain that there have been some changes in their belief systems, ritual lives and cultural ethos. First, these have been shattered and later re-organized and re-invented. Thus ritual modes have re-emerged in markedly different ways from what they used to be in the remote past of the worshipped ancestors.

To arrive at an understanding of the place and value of herbal medicines and their uses, it is necessary also to understand Kariri-Shoko and Shoko perceptions concerning the body, its functions, dysfunctions or illnesses, symptoms and causes of such illnesses. Such perceptions are embedded in a system of symbolism that is part of the binary opposites used to classify plants as remedies. I have classified the indigenous or native perceptions as being oriented by the binary opposites that order their world view and which are, in their turn, related to the etiology of illnesses. Health is at one point of equilibrium between these two opposite poles of interrelated conditions or categories, which seem to be, as I have attempted to interpret them:

o open/closed (body) – as it pertains to the supernatural and ultimate causation of illnesses;
o hot/cold;
o thin/thick (blood);
o weak/strong (organ);
o internal/external.

Heat and cold can be internal or external to the body. An 'internal heat' – *quentura por dentro* – can be related to a 'weak' or 'strong' organ, to 'thin' or 'thick' blood. Blood can be 'hot' or 'cold' and 'hot blood' is equated to 'internal heat.' I do not know which one came first: if the internal heat caused the blood to become hot and thin, weakening the organ that is showing signs of distress. However, the ultimate cause of every disease is related to the general idea of 'enchantment' and 'spiritual strength': a person becomes ill due to lack of spiritual strength, when an 'enchantment' was sent to him or her that made him or her sick.

A person with an 'open body' will be more likely to be affected by the illness that was sent in his or her direction, more like an arrow or an invisible dart aimed at someone's vital organs. A person who has a 'closed body' is magically protected and will be more capable of warding off the disease. Nevertheless, the body can become 'open' and be attacked by all sorts of 'enchantments' that will permit, for instance, spoiled food to 'attack' a 'weak' stomach, raising the internal temperature so that the person will suffer from diarrhoea.

A more immediate cause is a foreign invader, a situation that is a consequence of the presence of bacteria or virus (*bicho*), rotten food, snake bite or an accident. But perhaps the most immediate cause is the body condition which makes it possible for the foreign object or invader to get settled and finally cause the person to become ill. A condition known as 'internal heat' is responsible for various symptoms such as diarrhoea, skin rashes, vomiting, heavy menstrual flux and menopause. It is understood that the body is trying to get rid of the foreign objects or invaders that came in through the air, water, food and, above all, 'enchantment', also interpreted as 'bewitchment' and loss of 'vital energy.'

Any part of the body can be affected by 'heat', whether the body is 'weak' or 'strong.' A herbal medicine will have to perform two interrelated actions: to transform the body's temperature and, by doing so, to 'weaken' or 'strengthen' the affected organ or part. In this conceptualization of illness and medicine, any medication attempts to take care of the whole person, based on the idea that each organ or bodily part will be affected by these imbalances and, therefore, will be systematically treated according to what was the perceived immediate cause(s).

Based on these assumptions, I questioned how they organize medicines: around the different sets of causes or the symptoms? A diarrhoea is a symptom that has different causes: it could have been caused by 'internal heat', 'weak' stomach, a combination of both or 'thick' blood that needs to be purged of poison. A strong menstrual flow can result from 'internal heat', 'weak' uterus, 'thick' blood, all of these combined or an aborted fetus. Blood in the stools is a symptom of intestinal haemorrhage, due to intense 'internal' heat and 'thick' blood that allowed for a massive infestation of the intestines and the rectum by foreign invaders, usually after a prolonged bout of diarrhoea that was not properly healed.

'External heat' is manifested by 'fever', and that can have a number of different causes. A 'fever' generally opposes 'internal cold' that affects a particular organ, which was 'weak'. An 'internal cold' can cause the person to become sluggish and fatigued, bringing about symptoms such as headache, runny nose, sore throat, indigestion, constipation, 'weak' menstrual flux or absence of menstruation. The body is keeping the toxins inside, instead of getting rid of them, and the organs are not functioning adequately. Medicines will have to lower the external heat while raising the internal heat.

On the other hand, the afflicted person may have 'thin' or 'thick' blood as well. 'Thin' blood is responsible for anaemia, fatigue, colds, fevers, dizziness, 'weak' menstrual flow, sleepiness, female infertility and male impotence. 'Thick' blood is associated with nervousness, anxiety, insomnia, heavy menstrual flux, high blood pressure, kidney and liver problems, diabetes, migraines, heart troubles, varicose veins.

In view of all this, how can the 'materia medica' collected be useful to us? Around the sets of causes and conditions, the symptoms, or the affected organ/body part? At the moment, I find it more helpful first to group the data around the organs and body parts, then the symptoms, all the while specifying the perceived causes, for example:

1. Organ: stomach; symptom: stomach pains; indigestion;
2. Intestines: diarrhoea, constipation, etc.

Treatment aims, first, at the body part or the organ, so that the illness is thus named after the affected organ, followed by the perceived causation. I have arranged the data according to the native categories of body parts, organs or conditions (such as menstruation, for example) and the problems that affect each one of these. 'Pain' comes from the affected organ as a symptom, combined with the locally perceived origin of the pain. 'Body pain' (*dor no corpo*) is a problematic illness because it has several causations, being presented in rather vague terms, but with such persistency that it is impossible to by-pass it.

Health conditions are taken care of by specific medicines, but it is important to know how these medicines are prepared, what parts of the plant are used, if they are mixed with other plants, or with substances like sugar, honey, powdered rock, etc. Forms of herbal preparation are thus included, as there are the following types:

- tea (*chá*): the part being used is put in cold water and then boiled. The cooking time depends on the part, as a root, bark, or inner wood (harder parts) will take much longer than the soft and smaller ones such as leaves, flowers and seeds.
- infusion (*infusão*): the part is put in hot water and soaked. A note will be made if it is to be put in cold water and then soaked. Sometimes it has to soak overnight (*serenar*).
- honey/syrup (*mel/lambedor*): when it is *mel* the medicine is prepared 'on the spot', cooked in water mixed with sugar for a shorter period of time than for a *lambedor* (syrup), when the medicine is cooked for a long time and preserved in special bottles, for various uses.
- *garrafada*: the parts of the plant are soaked in *cachaça*, but they mention the alcoholic beverage as being 'wine' (*vinho*), and then put in a bottle (*garrafa*). When real wine is used then it is red wine and people call it 'Moscatel', which is a brand name. Sometimes, the *garrafada* is buried for three or more days so that the medicine becomes stronger (*apurado*).
- poultice (*compressa*): fresh parts of the plant are enveloped in a piece of cloth and placed over the part being treated, but sometimes the plant is cooked, or simply heated. If the leaves are large, they may be warmed up and placed directly over the affected area.
- baths (*banhos*): these are usually sitting baths, and the plant is soaked in hot water or boiled in water and then mixed in more water for the bath. If the bath is for the whole body, the mixture is put in a bucket, from which the person is washed.

○ powder (*pó*): usually to be inhaled, if not soaked in water or made into a tea.
○ cigarette (*cigarro*): the herb is dried and rolled into a dried corn leaf to be smoked.
○ tonic (*tônico*): prepared in a way very similar to the syrup, but generally with the objective of increasing the person's 'strength' or, in our language, to boost the immune system.
○ juice (*suco/ponche*): fresh parts of the plant are crushed, soaked in water and drained.

Part 2: Illnesses and corresponding medicines

The charts for medicines that I present in the Appendix are developed from the point of view of the concepts of 'body parts', and according to native perception.

Besides the main categories of illness, there are other maladies that are not shown in these charts, not because they are unimportant, but mainly because they relate more to spiritual causations, or else the ultimate cause of the illness is interpreted as coming from spiritual powers. These problems are known to revert to physical symptoms of disease, which will then be treated with the appropriate medicines.

One illness in particular is usually not treated with any substances, but is instead taken care of with a sort of massage: *espinhela caída*, translated quite literally as 'fallen spinal chord.' Such an illness is not readily visible to the untrained eye, nor diagnosed by a formal medical doctor, as it does not present any readily identifiable physical symptoms. Only a trained folk – and therefore 'true' – healer can detect a case of *espinhela caída*. 'Seu' Neco explained how it is detected: first, the healer ascertains that the person is having diffuse and sporadic symptoms such as occasional headaches, irritation, watery eyes, bad temper, pain in the neck area. The person is also afflicted with a period of bad luck in several areas of life and feels generally depressed. The healer, taking a piece of cloth, measures the distance from one shoulder to the other and then, keeping that measurement, compares it with the length of the person's arms. If the measurements of the arms differ from the shoulders, the person has *espinhela caída* and has to be given a special treatment. The treatment consists of the healer embracing the client from the back, as he or she puts her or his arms under the client's armpits, drawing the client's body toward the healer's, striving to push the client up and backward, so that the client's spine stretches and arches backwards. The client should 'hang' awhile in the healer's embrace, the feet should not be touching the floor. The healer has to have enough strength to hold this person up. Then the client is put down and the neck is massaged, until sounds of an adjustment of the neck vertebrae can be heard. Another measurement is taken after the treatment and they should be the same. If not, another massage will be given until the measurements come out equal. Then the client is sent home to relax and should be feeling sufficiently restored to be able to enjoy an untroubled sleep for at least a few hours. There are no prescriptions for medicines nor for a special diet.

Part 3: Who is sick after all?

In the worldview accepted by the Kariri-Shoko healers, to be healed or to be 'whole' is much more that just being free of physical ailments. Actually, people can be considered healthy, even when they show symptoms of what is usually considered to be an illness. On the other hand, you can be apparently well, but really 'sick' or even 'cured', since 'to be cured' has two intertwined and apparently conflicting meanings: one can be 'cured' to be either healthy or ill, depending on the intention of who committed the act of bringing either good or bad health to another. Sickness can result not just from the wishes of a god, or as a natural occurrence, the result of specific material causes, but from the wish that a person casts upon another. The fear of witchcraft, very common in other societies described in many ethnographic accounts, is an overbearing presence, a weight to be considered when one definitely feels bad about somebody else. Fights and unpleasantness are dealt with in a definitive manner: you either find a way toward a peaceful agreement or you try to 'cure' the person through magical ways, except if one of the parties happens to be pre-disposed to practise murder.

I had an inkling about the importance of witchcraft when I witnessed the *pajés* visit to a terribly sick young woman. We were walking past the *Rua dos Caboclos*, where a few village people still have their old homes, when a woman came running out of her house and begged that *Seu Francisquinho* come in the house to see a sick person. We went into the very sparsely furnished house and into the bedroom, where the young woman lay on a mattress on the bare dirt floor. She was obviously very ill, yellowish and misshapen, clutching her bed clothes over her bony chest. Her eyes were closed but she did not look serene. *Seu Francisquinho* knelt by her side and took her pulse, then swept his hand over her forehead rather briskly. He never said a word. He got up as silently as before and walked to the front room, followed immediately be the anxious relative who had summoned him. He turned to her very gravely and announced that he was unable to take care of that case, suggesting that they should take the sick one to the hospital in Propriá immediately.

'They'll know how to help her in this case,' was his opinion.

The woman was apparently as thunderstruck by that announcement as I certainly was, but she did not protest. She whispered a 'thank you' as we left the house. The *pajé* went on walking as though nothing had happened. I asked why he felt he could not help her.

'Because, my daughter, I cannot interfere.'

'Interfere in what?' I was obviously rather puzzled.

'She was "cured" by a woman from the tribe, a woman she is a rival to, since she is the lover of that woman's husband. The woman from the tribe has to be respected. I cannot overturn her work, may God help me! I could not go against the wishes of a sorcerer, see? Moreover, this sick woman does not belong to the tribe and then she allows herself to become involved with an Indian man who is married. She is on the wrong path! I can only refer her to the hospital. If they heal her, that will be good, if they don't, I cannot do anything either.'

I was appalled. Ethnic ethics went above human solidarity to the sick. It didn't sound like the kind of care that Suíra was used to dispense toward everyone surrounding him.

'What is her problem?' I asked, 'and how did the "sorcerer" cause it?' I said "sorcerer" in a cold, sarcastic tone, which, I am sure, he picked up because he smiled faintly.

'She is paralysed from the waist down and I don't know what the sorcerer did because that is her own secret and even I don't own her secret. That means that even if I wished it would be hard to undo her job, since I don't know what she did. But she did wish it and that is what really matters. She wished her rival to become sick and thus be unable to make love to her husband.'

'Will the people at the hospital know how to heal her?'

'Those dumb people at the hospital?' he laughed quietly. 'Maybe yes, maybe not. They don't have the slightest clue as to what caused the illness, so they won't have too many clues as to what to do to take her out of her trouble.'

'Do you think that is fair?' I was aware of somehow crossing the line of the necessarily 'objective' researcher, to become an outraged human being.

'Listen, daughter, I may not agree with my colleague over there. I certainly don't do these things. I don't do negative healing (that was the first time he had used that concept), but I can't stop people from doing so. Besides, this sick girl did ask for trouble. She knew her lover's wife was a sorcerer and she went ahead and lay down with him anyway. She knew what her chances were, so there, what can I do against people's foolishness? You reap what you sow, even the Bible says that, I know.'

I later found out that the woman was diagnosed as having a 'hysterical paralysis' and was referred to the hospital in Maceió, the capital of Alagoas, but her family could not afford to take her there. Instead, they consulted praying women from other nearby hamlets and eventually were able to have her cured. Her lover also left her, and I have come to believe that she was cured because of the power of that act alone, rather than because of the praying work.

What that incident taught me was that even the *pajé* chooses his patients and that his choices are determined by his belief system, above all other things. He told me later that he could have cured that poor woman in the *Rua dos Caboclos* if he had so wished, that he could take care of any type of illness that had been caused by any kind of sorcery or enchantment. However, he had chosen not to, in that particular case, because of ethical considerations. He could not go against his own 'kind'. The sick woman was a White woman, not related to the Indians, except for her love affair with the Indian man. That qualified her as being 'sick' even before she was 'cured' by the sorcerer. When she looked healthy still she was 'sick' and when she became paralysed she was only demonstrating what was wrong with her soul and her heart, not just her body. The secret is to know who is sick, who is healthy, and who deserves to be safe from suffering.

7 Conclusions: ethnicity, cognition and survival

'*Estava na beira do rio sem poder atravessar, chamei pelo caboclo, caboclo Tupinambá, chamei, chamei, e tornei a chamar.*' (I was at the river's edge, unable to cross, I called the *caboclo, caboclo Tupinambá*, I called, called and called again.)[1]

Part 1: The story of Pedrito Santana or a tale of interethnic afflictions.

It is a memory that will not fade away. The vision of a skinny fisherman standing by the river's edge, securely holding the fishnet by his one lonely front tooth, while throwing the rest of the *tarrafa* – his large handmade net – at the calm waters of the river, in the darkness of the night. The river just flowed by steadily, unaware of our troubles. I sat on a stone staring at the darkness, waiting to hear the sound of the motor boat that would take me down to Propriá just before dawn. I loved that island and that river, but the hour had arrived for the long expected moment of departure. Pedrito had come by at 3 a.m. to Lola's house to wake me up so I could be waiting at the river's edge whenever the boat showed up. He and others assured me that, 'if all went right,' – and this could mean many things – the boat making the bi-weekly trip from the village of Pão de Açúcar to Propriá was to pass by the island around 4 a.m., a dreadfully early hour for me. While we waited, Pedrito took the opportunity to fish: his profession and his pleasure. But the boat never came by and we never even knew why not. That was how life was, before the Shoko were allowed the luxury of having their own motor boat, through FUNAI's generous but overdue donation.

Pedrito would have been a fabulously handsome man if he had had an easier and healthier lifestyle. He was lean but strongly built, his ebony eyes shone with love for life and his thick dark hair framed a gracious face that was always showing a ready smile. Married to a particularly hard, bitter, but nevertheless attractive woman who happened to be one of Nazinha's daughters, they had beautiful children: four boys and only one girl.

His daugher's 'civilized' name was perfect for her: Grace. Helping her mother with the household's chores, taking care of the baby brother everyone adored, she used to swan elegantly around the island as though she had come straight from some enchanted fairyland to adorn the earth. Her father was obviously very close to and careful with her, his 'little Grace' – *Gracinha*, as she was better known.

She was 15 when I arrived at the island and already a virtual prisoner at home. Her confinement was not due to the will of her family. It was a direct outcome of her destiny within the context of interethnic battles, mixed with the chronic and fateful misunderstanding and hatred that sometimes afflict young people's lives and loves.

At 13 years of age she had fallen madly in love, as adolescents are prone to do, with a boy only one year older than herself. The Shoko lived in Caiçara still and the boy was related to a non-Shoko family of neighbours who were also *posseiros*. When the Shoko decided to invade the island, some of the people who were their neighbours but not direct descendants from any native group decided to follow them too, including the relatives of Gracinha's captivated heart. Afraid of the long conflict lying ahead, the young man convinced her to marry him in a hurry, so that she would not have to go to São Pedro island with the others. Both youngsters' families were against the hasty marriage. The boy was still in high school in Porto da Folha, where his parents lived; she was hardly more than a little girl. Moreover, he was supposedly of a 'better' economic status, living in town and being prepared to move away from the hard physical labouring life of *posseiros*. Against all odds, like Romeo and Juliet, he came for her in the middle of the night and off they went to get married. That was how Grace abandoned the struggle of her relatives in the retaking of their lost lands and joined the 'White' family of her beloved.

Unfortunately, in total opposition to the name that had been given her, disgrace haunted her. Whenever the young husband was in school and the other adults were out of the house, Gracinha stayed in charge of the household children, who were many. One day, a six year old boy of the family decided to play with a shotgun, probably in imitation of the television cowboy movies they were accustomed to watch while living in the city. She tells that she took the gun away from him, before he could harm himself or somebody else, and, in an attempt to prevent any further problems, proceeded – inexperienced as she was – to take the bullets out of the gun; instead she fired it. As the boy had not given up getting the gun back, the bullet struck him at close range and he was killed instantly. Terrified, Grace ran out of the house wildly screaming for help. When the family's adults finally came, they did not want to believe it had been an accident. Grief no doubt overcame them and she was taken to jail, charged with murder.

As soon as news of the tragic event reached him, Fray Enoque went immediately to rescue her. His eyes always grieve when he tells about what he saw: a scared young girl, in complete shock, unable even to speak, huddled in the corner of a dirty jail cell. He told the sheriff that she could not be in jail for two simple reasons: she was both a minor and an Indian. Brazilian Indians are not subject to national common law because of their status as *tutelados*, i.e., the state treats them as virtual minors, under its legal protection.

But what was really killing Gracinha was not the tragedy in itself, the boy's death, her in-laws' suspicions and threats to her life. What destroyed her was the fact that her beloved never came forward in her defence. Too young perhaps, himself too terrified, he chose to obey his parents and never did anything to protect her nor to show whatever love he held for her. She was taken back to the island by the hands of the only protectors she ever truly had: her father and Fray Enoque.

The story that circulated in town, among the non-Indians, was that she was bitter with her new family because she was not 'White' and so had killed one of the young ones out of spite. The victim's family swore vengeance: 'an eye for an eye.' One of the dead boy's aunts lived in the island with the Shoko. She sided with her relatives in the city, having once declared:

'It was not a little bird she killed, you know, it was one of our dear children! How can we forget and forgive?'

From then on, Gracinha could not leave her house in the island under any circumstances. A prisoner in her own home, she led an uneventful life, dreamy-eyed and solemn as a dethroned queen, doing things mechanically and without joy, such as learning pottery with her mother and neighbours. Nothing else seemed to bother her but the safety of her parents, for she was aware that if her sworn enemies could not take her life, the life of her closest relatives were in danger. Pedrito, however, went on with his life as usual. Every Monday morning he helped his wife load her many pieces of pottery on the boat, going to the *feira* – street fair – of Pão de Açucar, where she and other Shoko women used to sell their basic clay kitchenware. Pedrito was naturally aware of the dangers he was facing every time he stepped off the island, not only because of the threats to his daughter's life but also due to his leadership in the Shoko takeover of the island. As usual, he was not the kind of person to be thwarted by fear. It was not that he was boastful of bravery, like the young *cacique* José, but that he conducted his life according to what he thought was the right way to live. He was joyful and playful most of the time, loving to dance, to sing, to throw conversation around and to tell jokes. A man who was able to be proud and humble at the same time, Pedrito was also immensely concerned with his family's welfare.

His wife, embittered by the hard life they all led and shared, complained a lot about him, as if he was particularly responsible for their low socio-economic state. Gracinha was also seen by her mother as another burden, because of the preoccupation she shared about the girl's safety. The woman wanted Pedrito to take Gracinha out of the island and into some 'safe' place, but he would not, mostly because there was nowhere to go. FUNAI was not able to help in any way and their friends at the Catholic Church did not agree that she should leave São Pedro.

And so it was that Pedrito was bequeathed with Grace's fate in her stead. When several people from the island were going to a public party in the nearby hamlet of Mocambo, Pedrito was ambushed and shot in the back, falling instantly at his wife's feet. In the midst of the confusion the gunman escaped, but many people were able to recognize the person: one of the uncles of the boy Grace had accidentally shot and killed.

Pedrito did not die immediately from his physical wound, but from the far deeper injury to his soul and character that finally became unbearable. His enemy's bullet had lodged in his back and he became paralysed from the waist down. The hospital in Propriá was not able to care for him, so he was taken to Maceió, the capital of Alagoas, in an agonizing condition. Pedrito lingered on at the hospital, until a FUNAI representative in Maceió arranged for him to be flown to *Casa do Indio*[2] in São Paulo, where he would convalesce.

That was where I went to see him. Before my visit, I had been to São Pedro, where I tape-recorded messages from his friends and family for him, including a melody that Grace sang for him in her beautiful soprano voice, dedicating it to her 'adored father'. Although Grace never once spoke to me of her many pains, I could see that she was aware that her father had given his life for her, in the same manner that he had surrendered it for the advocacy of indigenous rights.

I sat by his side in the shabby room he shared with other sick Indians, as Pedrito heard his daughter's voice coming through that small box, as if by magic. His body began to shake violently and he was visibly embarrassed to be showing his emotions, so I had to leave the room. Later, he asked me to prevail with FUNAI to let him go home, to be taken care by his family.

'I know I am going to die, so I want to die in São Pedro,' he said, calmly but strongly.

'You are paralysed, but you are not going to die from these wounds', I said, once again overstepping my supposed role as an anthropologist.

'No, I am dead already! I cannot fish, I cannot tend the fields. I might as well be dead.'

He went home and lived one more year of what I could only interpret as a life of misery and sorrow. His wife still seemed to blame him for all the tragedies that hit their lives, even the fact that he had become paralysed.

'I have a husband at home and no husband at all.' She used to say, even though he struggled to do everything possible to care for her. The person who stood by his side and truly cared for him was Grace. She saw him die, alone by his side. She never said a word of reproach nor sorrow. She just let it all be, aware of what was still awaiting her in a world divided, where she was not just simply a person, but an Indian girl who had killed a White boy, even if accidently.

Part 2: The ideology of class and ethnicity

Pedrito Santana's personal saga allows us to plunge deeper into thinking about the many dilemmas facing the socially 'integrated' indigenous descendants in Brazil today, who continue to be seen as outcasts. Is it worthwhile to be an Indian or to redefine oneself as such? Was it the best way for the people who, until 20 years ago, did not even want to be known as *caboclos*? We may say that what happened to Grace and her father would have happened anyway, whether they were considered as Indians or not. However, if she were not a Shoko, would she be allowed the haven of an island with an identity? Would she be considered guilty before proven innocent by her husband's family?

Maybe her tragedy would have taken place even under different socio-cultural circumstances. The class differentiation would still persist, as it still does, even after the takeover of São Pedro island and of the indigenous identification.

Furthermore, would their knowledge about themselves and their place in the world have modified Grace's fate? Becoming bicultural is part of this fate; being an Indian, and not just a poor girl of the Sergipe *sertão*, establishes not only Grace's place in this story, but why she was barely spared, while her father perished. For Pedrito had much more at stake at the moment of his death than she could even recognize. He had the ancestral spirits to back him up, the way he took part in the *torés* with his singing, with his voice speaking up for his people, the way he asserted the fate, not only of his daughter, but of an entire group. He was looking for a *persona* to wear as a mask against the adversities of a *sertanejo's* life, so that they could fight for their rights, equipped not only with their class consciousness, but an awareness of an ethnic background.

Grace and her family were persecuted not just as people who had hurt another family, but as members of a socio-economic class considered inferior and of an ethnic group that should be abolished by 'civilization'. It all reinforced a 'defective' social status. Pedrito died for his daughter's sins, including her sin of loving a boy from another social class. He also died for wanting to be himself, to belong to a category known as 'civilized Indian'.

He and the others, Shoko and Kariri-Shoko, are still caught up in the dilemma and contradictions of being 'civilized Indians'. A situation in which biculturalism works as a tangible reality alongside the idea of a magic realm that will 'save' them all. Biculturalism is a formal reality, as being conscious of one's ethnicity co-exists alongside a class consciousness. The Kariri-Shoko claim that 'White' people – the 'empty heads' – do not have the same extraordinary, or non-ordinary, visionary powers that they do. In that way, and only in the way of the 'vision', they are invulnerable, and they shall not perish in the same way as the São Pedro Shoko almost did.

According to this vision, the only 'salvation' for the Shoko in São Pedro is to follow the path of the *Ouricuri*, a hidden reality that awaits them amongst the bushes and the dreams. In the year of 1994, José Apolonio returned to the island, having been away for two years. He became the Shoko *cacique* once again and re-established himself with a large party on the island, to which state politicians, journalists and other distinguished guests were invited. At the party, the Shoko presented their *torés* and, according to what one of the guests present revealed publicly, shared the *Jurema* wine with all the people who were present. At that time, José declared that the beverage was 'traditional' for them, but could be taken by all. If that is true, and if he was really preparing the *Jurema*, I have no way of knowing for sure, since I was not there and I did not take a sample of the drink. If he did so, he broke with the tradition that the Kariri-Shoko have taken so much pride and care to keep as a secret. If he did so, and according to the principles shared by the two Kariri *pajés*, he has committed the mistake that will fatally lead them all to their destruction as *caminhantes* or 'dreamers'. They will no longer be able to define themselves as a people apart from the blameworthy 'others', those who think they can have power over the true 'children of *Jurema*', for they have dared to share the secret of the forest with untrained non-Indians.

When the Kariri shaman announces he is going to use the *Kraunan* (a magical plant), people follow him in silence, because the *Kraunan* is believed to allow people to become a *caminhante*: a person with the extraordinary powers to walk all over the earth and 'see'. What is important to consider is that they believe 'White' people cannot become seers, and are therefore unable to share the non-ordinary reality they have constructed as their own. However, both groups are split with conflicts pertaining to class status and worldly possessions. The dreamers have become entangled with the magic of consumerism.

As a few Kariri-Shoko, through their jobs outside the group boundaries, rise to middle class positions, acquiring some economic wealth, another conflict arises inside the group. For example, the director of Colégio's high school is a Kariri woman who is married to a non-Kariri man. They live in a comfortable home in Colégio, but she also built a house inside the *Ouricuri* village. Her house in the *Ouricuri* differs from the quarters of all the other members of the group: it has four brick walls, wooden doors and windows. Such architecture goes against the homogeneity of the *Ouricuri* village, thus introducing class differences and privileges into a situation where economic egalitarianism is practically mandatory if the tribal ritual is to retain its full significance. The school director introduced secular matters into sacred territory, creating a rift that found voice inside the *Ouricuri* practices. People resent the fact that she locks her doors and windows inside the *Ouricuri* village. The enclosure of her home means that she stands away from and above the rest of the group, blocking access to the other members, thus establishing a form of separation wholly offensive to the social setting.

Conflict stemming from class differences also appeared among the Shoko when Zé Heleno, a Kariri-Shoko from Colégio, was appointed *Chefe de Posto* by FUNAI in São Pedro, earning a salary that contrasted rather sharply with what the others were living with. It became hard for the island people, living at poverty level, to watch Zé Heleno coming home loaded with market goods.

The clashes between ethnic and class forms of consciousness becomes comprehensible: there is a space in people's lives and heads where the confluences of past, present and future become sharper and harder to take. The relationship to medical resources is put into focus too, because the question is not only of traditions to be kept, but of traditions that do not depend so heavily upon economic means. On the other hand, the market economy does exert a fascination that is difficult not to take into account.

Does loyalty to traditions prevent the use of whatever technology is at hand? There are cases of cultural groups that have been able to live in the midst of high technology, but refuse to make use of at least part of it, like the Amish of North America. In the popular imaginary complex of the Americas, 'Indians' should remain completely absorbed in their 'traditions'. Paradoxically at the same time, national societies continuously stupefy these historically marginalized populations with commodities, tempting them to plunge into the quest for the mystical twentieth century pleasantries of modernity.

When Jacques Cousteau filmed the Amazon region recently, his team came across the rich medicinal lore of the Jivaro-Shuar Indians of the Amazon jungle. Impressed by that kind of knowledge, they interviewed Nicole Maxwell, a woman who has been researching the medicinal plants of the Amazon for several years (cf. Maxwell, 1961). In the interview, Maxwell talked rather nostalgically of the gradual disappearance of an ancestral form of knowledge, blaming it on the introduction of Western pharmaceuticals among the jungle populations. Among her statements, Maxwell said that the younger generations are 'ashamed' of even learning about the jungle medicinal lore, because what they really want is the packaged merchandise that comes from the urban areas.

Citing people who have come upon the Amazon riches, as well as documenting them, I want to mention Fritz Trupp. In his book of photographs about South American heritage (1981), Trupp presents several tribal peoples of the Amazon region. Among others, there is an image of an old Auca woman of the Equatorial forest: she is wearing only torn underwear over her frail, and otherwise nude, body, while holding a package of Bayer aspirins. Trupp writes that 'aspirin is the general panacea here.' (id: 244/5).

Such a statement would naturally have been futile in an urban setting. Since the woman is a forest inhabitant and, on top of that, an Indian, then it is seen as an oddity at best that she should be using aspirin to cure her ailments, instead of some wild plants. But what is not analysed is that her ills took another momentum when clothes, among several other civilized ensembles, were introduced into her life, whether she wanted them or not, but not necessarily as comfort, but rather as clutter.

It is fundamental here that these problems be brought to focus. This can be done through the concept of ideology. It is from the framework of ideology, the world of ideas relating dialectically with the economic base, that the different representations of these forest-urban peoples become clearer, if not at least partially understood.

The Kariri-Shoko and the Shoko are ethnic groups that stand out as such within the rural working class to which they have belonged for a long time. What differentiates them from the other labourers is not exactly their way of life and not at all their biotype, even though they may think so. They are differentiated by the way they have constructed themselves as subjects of their own history, through their ritual life, the expressions of their cognitive systems and their organized struggle to keep what is considered as 'ancestral, traditional territory'. Even as José Apolonio breaks with tradition by sharing *Jurema* with outsiders, he is doing so with the precise purpose of showing how 'different' they are from the 'Whites' to whom they still have something to teach. It does not even matter if it was the 'real' *Jurema* beverage or not!

In a review of Althusser's study of ideologies, Laclau (1977) frames the analysis of ideology and the construction of an ethnic identity from the point of view of a cognitive domain. He makes it clear that the basic function of ideology is that of constituting and interpellating individuals as subjects, pointing out that even individuals, who are simply bearers of structures, are transformed by ideology into **subjects**. Thus they are able to live the relation with their real conditions of existence as if they themselves determined that relation. The mechanism that assures the existence of this characteristic inversion is interpellation. What then constitutes the unifying principle of an ideological discourse is the 'subject' being interpellated and thus constituted through his own discourse. Members of differentiated indigenous groups become clearly identifiable to themselves and others through such ideological processes, through their own specific constitution, as they named their world and themselves, labelling themselves and nature over and beyond national identity.

'These trees have their own secret names that only we can know', they affirm. Their identity is with a familial name which serves as a unifying principle for thought and action, which shapes their own cognitive systems and is, in turn, shaped by them. Such systems are then differentiated from the system acquired through participation in the national society, which they have also internalized.

However, no ideology is either 'pure' or devoid of elements from different social classes and ethnic groups. It is a superfluous and unnecessary task to look for 'authenticity' in ideological disclosures and discourses. Kariri-Shoko ideological framework maintains aspects of regional constructions. Along with those there are elements perceived by the group as being derived from their past generations. Indices of cultural practices such as plant lore, ritual movements, language survivals, are hereby isolated as being part of an ethnic identity, of becoming 'someone'. In this way, it can be seen that the São Pedro Shoko relate to their ancestral origins and ethnic roots in a way that differs from the Kariri-Shoko in Colégio. For the latter, medicine is part of a magic realm, medicine is life itself. Through magic, life is made possible in a situation of class domination and subjugation to class interests. Magic relates to the mastery of social forces through the mastery of the self. The social self is being constantly reinforced through spiritual cleansing and purification baths, mediated by the plant world. The medical-magical complex reflects their world-view and social structure.

These allegations are sustained by the contrasting figures of the *pajé* in each group. The São Pedro *pajé* was 'elected' by the group and not by *Jurema*. From the conceptual point of view of the Indians who congregated on São Pedro island for their indigenous meetings, that was a fundamental error.

'He is *pajé* by name only,' said Júlio, under the approving nods of the Karapato and Patasho colleagues around him, 'he does not have any movement. He is blind to the things that we have to see in order to sustain power. He does not have the *Ouricuri*, that's it.'

What they meant by having movement is being able to move at will and not necessarily within one's physical body, with the spiritual body under the guidance of a disembodied being. This is what it means to 'have and sustain power', the kind of power that *pajé* Raimundo himself was willing to agree not owning or even knowing about.

When he was the Shoko *cacique* for the first time, José Apolonio declared once that it was not necessary for them to know about magical or medicinal plants, or about magical rituals, since what protects them are the guns or the prestige they can attain among the regional populations and the state politicians. A young Kariri-Shoko retorted that without his magical plant, without securing his *mijo de ovelha*, and therefore his spiritual protection, he could not do anything in the world. He needed his magic, his *Ouricuri*, in order to go on. This is so because the *Ouricuri-Matekrai* set of procedures permits the masks of the self as Kariri-Shoko, the masks pertaining to the ideology of ancestry, to be the predominant ones in the making of the *persona*. And this is also what explains Suíra's words when he entered the *Ouricuri*:

'Here I am myself, I am at peace, I am strong. Without our *Ouricuri* we could not be *índios*, we could not be ourselves.'

Although ethnicity can serve as the cultural marker we have been talking about, it is a double-edged sword in terms of the group being thus marked. Ethnicity can also serve the purpose of aiding the dominant society in keeping a group defined as 'ethnic' submissive to its demands. This usually happens when the idea of being 'ethnic' is used to hide the essential relation of economic domination and political subordination. The class problem is at the root of the ethnic situation. Since ethnic identity does not exist in a vacuum, it is contingent on a confrontation with another group in which the structure 'we-they' is created. If there wasn't a 'they' group to oppose a 'we' group, and if the domination of one class by another did not constitute part of this opposition, there probably would be no need for the rise of an ethnic identity.

The Kariri-Shoko and the Shoko are bicultural and binational in their social constitution. They are both 'we' and 'they', as they have a dual perception of themselves in their social relations and in the universe. Their structured modes of utilization of natural resources also reflect the state of biculturalism, presenting elements from indigenous, national and regional folklore. It is thus very hard to measure how much of the 'self' and the 'other' is present in these dual personalities and performances of bicultural communities. Marks for multiple *personae* are worn practically all the time, even in daily life. The Ouricuri provides them with a refuge from such confrontation, a haven that is slowly being assailed by the realities of market economy and capitalist class society.

Both groups have merged into the national society as members of an underprivileged class: the rural proletariat. The question then arises of whether class consciousness has not overridden ethnic boundaries and consciousness itself. Not all members of an ethnic group belong to the same class, and vice-versa. Furthermore, what we have established here is that ethnic consciousness has been used to oppose class statuses. The concept of class exploitation masks and eludes the question of the differentiation: ethnicities and/or classes. We lose sight of the cultural factor when we incorporate the Indians into the theoretical mark of capitalist exploitation. In fact, culture and cultural differentiation permit us to establish the difference between ethnicity and the class concept which is manipulated by Western science/consciousness. Thus, 'Ethnic consciousness is the notion of belonging to a group identified from the starting point of participation in a common cultural code. In this case, political consciousness is the consciousness of being exploited for belonging to the exploited group' (Bartolomé & Robinson, 1984: 182). It is clearly understood by these authors that the struggle of ethnic minorities for their liberation, both in cultural as well as in economic-political terms, advances through the reaffirmation of their own identity, in opposition to the models imposed by the dominant standards of Western society.

It seems that the São Pedro Shoko, in their recent past, have been more motivated by their class rather than by their ethnic consciousness. The phenomenon of reacquiring and re-establishing ethnic consciousness, or uncovering it from its hiding place, came about partially as a result of their participation in a class struggle for lands and rights of rural labourers. The Shoko had always participated in an oppositional rural workers' union that was backed up by the liberationist Catholic diocese of Propriá. The union stood in opposition to the official governmental rural workers' union. Thus the Shoko people became totally integrated in the class struggle. It was during the course of that struggle that they found the alternative way to demand land and govermental support: by rediscovering their ancestral rights and claiming their ethnic background. It was then that ethnicity became part of the class struggle. It was as *índios* that they returned to their former lands, in the same way that the Kariri-Shoko did in relation to the Sementeira farm. The anterior indigenous way of life had not been entirely eliminated from their collective memory. It remained in the memories of their elders and in their oral traditions, although they had laboured to keep this knowledge from their own descendants. The memories were fading slowly away, being preserved mostly in the songs and dances that the women performed at the end of a day of planting rice around a lagoon – when they 'closed a lagoon' (*fechavam uma lagoa*). These sacred performances of the *torés* were transformed into profane dances, mixed with the rhythms and the language of the dominant society.

Then the Shoko reentered the domain of an ideology of ancestral identity, which is based on the belief of a common ancestry, into the boundaries of an ethnic community. As such, they claimed to be a political minority, with the specific rights attached to such a claim. They reorganized themselves around the idea of being *índios*, even though few of them knew what that was really all about. The Catholic nuns from Porto da Folha, in an effort to help them in this quest, used to bring necklaces and feather ornaments from other Brazilian indigenous groups that they were able to purchase in other places. The new Shoko adorn themselves with these foreign objects, claiming as their own a tradition that belonged somewhere else, dressing up according to the representation they had created, along with the national society, of what 'real *índios*' should look like. They are thus trying to recreate an ethnic style, to reinvent a tradition that had been mercilessly lost. The picture of José Apolonio in his reinstatement as a *cacique inidígena* in 1994 shows him wearing a Kayapó feather headdress and a Panamanian embroidered belt that I gave him years ago. He uses these artifacts emblematically, to prove that he is loyal to his indigenous roots, no matter from what tribes, nor from where, these articles have come.

Ethnicity is a category of ascription, of an identification which is primarily obtained through the interaction among social agents, depending on the subjective perspective of the agents themselves. Listening to what people say when they tell their own history, interpreting one another as Shoko or Kariri, ethnic identity assumes the category of a status. It is one more identity assumed by those individuals, one that permits them to place themselves in the national social order, just as gender and rank do. Ethnic labels entail a style of life, a dominant style. The boundaries of the ethnic group are thus primarily ideological. The idea of community comes tied to that of ethnicity, for a dispersed or weakened community is of no consequence to the larger society, least of all as an opposing force. The individual becomes an integrated subject only within a community that expresses itself through its ideological constructions and systems of representation.

However, the emergence of an ethnic identity can be a positive as well as a negative event, depending on the context of inter-ethnic relations that prevail. For the Shoko, a century ago it was highly negative to be categorized as an *índio*. In the 1980s, the surrounding national society itself allowed more positive than negative signs to be attached to the category. Ethnic identity is, in the end, a particular case of social identity, in itself a form of collective representation and, therefore, an ideology as well (cf. Cardoso de Oliveira, 1983). As an ideology, ethnic identity has an integrated, systemic nature which contains forms of knowledge, an epistemological orientation towards other groups as well as to one's own group.

It is this knowledge, derived from a system of belief and values, that the São Pedro have been striving to regain. They have gone through the cycle of death and are now entering the stage of rebirth. This is the path symbolically taken in the circularity of the Ouricuri-Matekrai ritual. This is also the path towards self-valorization within a class struggle. When the old man died in São Pedro, during the Meeting of Northeastern Tribes, the Patasho cacique stated that his death was a real rebirth:

'His body is now the fertilizer for this earth. Through his death, we can go back to life, to the *Ouricuri*. How can we fight the landlords if we don't dance, if we don't know our own name?'

Earth is the symbol, the icon that represents the power of the community, the naming of the community. So it is with the *Ouricuri*: without it, as they say, there is no indigenous group, there is no power and, therefore, no life. How can they struggle, if they are dead? And how can they live, if they don't have a 'name'?

Part 3: Epilogue: science and domination

At all times, *pajé* Suíra knew I was collecting data for a work I had to present to my 'elders'. He clearly understood the concept of working to prepare for some kind of ritual. At the times when we talked about it, he always wanted to know what the things were that I had to do for what he called my 'obligation', their synonym for initiation. And it was, after all, an initiation I was going to go through when I defended a dissertation. I told him we just had to collect data, as I was doing, read, think a lot about it and then write. He used to laugh his short, low laughter.

'Just that? You don't have dreams? Well, of course, you do. But *cabeças secas* never know what their dreams are about. They think they do, but they really do not.'

I remember arguing that dreams would not help me with my 'initiation.'

'We just talk a lot. I talk to my elders, they ask me questions. In fact, they will ask me a lot of questions about my work here with you.'

'But, of course, you will know all the answers, whereas they won't even know what to ask. They have not known about our science. You know at least some now. You don't know all of our secrets, though, but we have taught you a few things about us.'

Although I could see the logic of his argument, I was still worried, since I was doing my work in another country, away from my 'elders' and, consequently, unable to exchange views with them directly. I felt relaxed enough about Suíra that I could express most of my feelings to him. After all, he kept saying I was his granddaughter and there was a good understanding between the two of us. He was a good listener, the first sign, to me, of a good healer. So, after listening to my complaints about the test I was going to go through shortly, he said, in his best of solemn ways of speaking:

'Don't worry, daughter, I will come to your help.'

It was my turn to laugh.

'Well, that will not be possible: I will be miles away from you. You would have to take an aeroplane to come to my rescue!'

'Now I begin to think you haven't really learned anything from me . . . '

And then he was silent. I was not in a mood to take him too seriously at that moment, and I did not even take notes about that conversation. Nevertheless, his words stuck in my mind, coming right back afterwards, when I did dream of him. The night before my dissertation defence, I went to bed all tensed up, as only people who have gone through this kind of initiation can understand. That was when I dreamt of Suíra, something that had never happened before, at least that I could remember, and so vividly.

In my dream, the two of us were walking through the *Ouricuri* woods, as we had done so many times before. He was showing the 'sacred trees' to me as he had already done, but there was a remarkable difference: this time he was telling me the secret names of each tree. Every time he said a name, he would also say: 'This I am only telling to you so that you will know us as nobody else does.' At the end of his lesson, he clearly said these words: 'This is what you are going to tell your elders: that this people, the Kariri-Shoko, have a science of their own and that you have had the opportunity to learn about it. You know about something they do not. You are of a higher status now because you own a knowledge they never will, unless you want to share it with them: **you know our names**.'

That was absolutely the end of the dream as I remember it. When I woke up I could 'see' all the images, almost all the trees and what he had said to me. What had been erased from my memory were the names of the trees and I regretted inwardly that I did not take my pencil and notebook to my dream-states as I did in my waking journeys. Of course I did not repeat what I heard in my dreams to my dissertation committee, lest they thought that the effort had done ineradicable damage to my poor brain. But I felt unusually peaceful and in control of myself throughout the academic ordeal.

My 'initiation' went well and my 'elders' agreed to grant me the title I was seeking after six years of work.

Suíra had come to my rescue as he had promised, after all, and without an aeroplane. He had reminded me that for them knowledge or science is the stuff that makes up their daily life and the ritual life that feeds the daily life. Their science is obtained through participation in the 'naming' of the tribe and its secrets, the highest of all forms of knowledge or the only knowledge that a person has to have in order to survive: that of his or her own identity, the core of the self or the core of the culture. 'This is what we know and who we are.'

The versions of the *toré* about Caboclo Lindo express this vision. In the São Pedro version Caboclo Lindo sings:

'*Eu ando por terra alheia procurando o que perdi.*' (I walk through foreign lands searching for what I have lost.)

Non-religious in character, this *toré* speaks of the loss of a culture for the Shoko. But in Colégio, Caboclo Lindo answers in a slightly different manner:

'*Eu ando por terra alheia caçando minha ciencia.*' (I walk through foreign lands hunting for my science.) In this song, in this *toré de índio*, danced and sung for religious and magical purposes, science is acknowledged as a vital part of their cognitive system, their orientation to the world. It includes knowledge of medicinal plants and their use for healing physical and psychological disorders, for bringing harmony and maintaining social homeostasis within the Universe.

The story of Caboclo Lindo is a metaphor for the contrasting ways in which the São Pedro Shoko and the Kariri-Shoko see themselves and their relationships with those considered as 'others'. Knowledge is secret, as it protects them from the domination of the outside world. Knowledge can be shared only with the trusted ones, those who, in one way or another, 'belong'. The new generations of Shoko and Kariri-Shoko know only of their ties to the 'ancestral' spirits that live in their songs and dances, as well as in the vegetation surrounding them. These are the signals of their sign system.

If ancestral native trees were to be once again lost to the rapacious actions of colonizers, the new generations of trees and people are not going to be lost as well. Caboclo Lindo will go on searching for their science and their lives forever, or perhaps while they sing and plead for his presence.

So it may happen that the *índios* are here to stay, in the eternal circle of life.

Notes

INTRODUCTION
1. The hinterland of Brazil in general, but most specifically the desolate and arid areas of the Northeast.
2. The people in the Northeast who live in the hinterlands.
3. A type of semi-arid climate and a corresponding vegetation that characterizes that area, as a transition between the seashore dry zone and the tropical forest of the north.
4. The category of 'Indian' is another unfortunate result of Columbus' error when he thought he had arrived in India, when instead he had reached the Caribbean islands. Historically it has always held a derogatory connotation. Recently, however, the term has been appropriated by indigenous movements in Brazil to signify their oneness and authenticity. Moreover, it has acted as a symbol of an 'anti-structure' that is opposed to the relations of subjection and domination, so characteristic of the colonization of the Americas by Europeans.
5. 'Tree of life' is an allegory originated in ancient cultures worldwide, representing both a real tree that is a metaphor for all life on earth, and also the genealogy of a people.
6. *Caatinga* is a word of Tupian origin, formed by *caá*, which means plants or woods, and *tinga*, which means white or pale. Indeed, most of the vegetation in the *caatinga* is subdued in colour, unlike the bright and luxuriant vegetation of the tropics.

CHAPTER ONE
1. The social–racial category of *caboclo* has its own history: at first, it meant Indians in mission villages, known as *aldeias*, then it began to be used as a form of negating the existence of Indians, since they were of mixed blood and not 'pure'. Presently, it is used exactly to designate 'true or legitimate Indians.' Galvão (1955) used the term as a generic designation for any rural inhabitant in the Amazon area.
2. *Troncos* (trunks) is the term used to refer to tribal ancestors, whether real or mythical. This metaphorical use of botanical terms to refer to genealogies and ethnic origin is probably related to the native concept of an animated vegetal world that possesses or embodies the spirits of the ancestors.
3. The *Rainha do Terreiro* was a female in charge of the ceremony, who would start the dances.
4. *Meia*, meaning half, refers to the sharecropping system in which the worker supposedly retains half of the crops as payment for services and the other half belongs to the landlord. A *meeiro* rents the piece of land, known as *posse* (possession), for planting the crop.

CHAPTER TWO
1. *Encantado* (enchanted one) is a European conceptualization of spiritual beings that appear either as ghosts or live within other live beings. The natives appropriated this European element and mixed it with their own concept of spirits or souls that inhabit the forest and animate the inanimate world.
2. The Kariri-Shoko conceptualize themselves as forming a 'tribe', this being the way they refer to the group. When I mention them as being a 'tribe' I am using their own category.
3. The information was given to me by my informants in that area. Other contemporary researchers who have studied nearby groups that also perform the *Ouricuri* did not register this appellation.
4. The work fronts – *frentes de trabalho* – were labour brigades established by the state

government in order to ease the local problems with unemployment. However, for the Kariri, *trabalho* is work of the spiritual kind.

CHAPTER THREE

1 A group of scientists, convened by R. Gordon Wasson in 1978, decided to use the term *entheogenic* to describe plants used as 'shamanic inebriants' and that are considered, by the people who use them, as 'sacraments, plant-teachers', (Ott, 1994).

CHAPTER FOUR

1 'Private marking' was defined by Trubetzkoy as a 'binary contrast distinguishing phonemes by means of the presence (+) versus absence (−) of some feature' (Urban, 1981: 477). The private opposition thus designates any opposition in which the signifying aspect of a term is characterized by the presence of a significative element of mark, which is lacking in the signifying aspect of the other term. The opposition which is set is between marked/non-marked (Barthes, 1964).

CHAPTER FIVE

1 People who perform *mandingas*, witchcraft, that can do harm as well as good.

CHAPTER SEVEN

1 Umbanda's sacred song, to evoke the spiritual entity known as *caboclo Tupinambá*.
2 There are many *Casa do Indio* spread throughout the national territory, where Indians receive the health attention they cannot get at the village, but the most important ones are in São Paulo, Rio de Janeiro and Brasília.

Appendix

Illness and remedies charts

A. INTERNAL ORGANS:

1. STOMACH (*estômago*): conditions are:
   1.1. Stomach pain (*dor de estômago, dor de barriga*)
   1.2. Colic (*cólica*): pain with cramps, followed by gases, constipation or diarrhoea.
   1.3. Indigestion/acidity (*indigestão/azia*): feeling bloated, heavy, needing to burp constantly.
   1.4. Swollen abdomen (*barriga inchada*): when the stomach area is extended but not due to worms. When the abdomen is touched, it sounds like an empty drum.

1. STOMACH PAIN

Plant nomenclature				Forms of use	
Scientific		*Folk*			
Family	*Species*	*Port./Kariri*	*Parts*	*Preparation*	*Dosage/ Condition*
Aristolo- chiaceae	Aristolochia odore	Jarrinha	root	tea	3 cups daily
Bromeli- aceae	Bromelia kantes	Gravatá	fruit	raw	as pain lasts
Cyperaceae	Kylling odorata	Capim santo	leaf	tea (unsweetened)	1 cup in the morning
Lamiaceae	Mentha piperita	Hortelã da folha miúda	leaf	tea	as desired
Liliaceae	Aloe vera	Babosa	leaf	infusion	as desired
	Smilax japicanga	Japicanga	roots leaves	pounded together	3 spoons daily as tonic
Mimosaceae	Mimosa pigra	Calumbi	bark	tea	3 cups daily
Solanaceae	Physalis angulata	Camapum	leaves	pounded as juice	1 cup in the morning
Piperaceae	Piperomia sp.	Milone	leaves	warm up poultice	over the pain area

1.2 COLIC

Plant nomenclature			Forms of Use		
Scientific		*Folk*			
Family	*Species*	*Port./Kariri*	*Parts*	*Preparation*	*Dosage/ Condition*
Asteraceae	Grangea prostata	Macela	flowers	infusion	1 cup n times
Malvaceae	Hibiscus sp.	Algodão preto/ENDJI	seeds leaves	tea of 3 leaves + seeds	paediatric: 1 spoon 3 × day

1.3 INDIGESTION/ACIDITY

Plant nomenclature			Forms of use		
Scientific		*Folk*			
Family	*Species*	*Port.Kariri*	*Parts*	*Preparation*	*Dosage/ Condition*
Euphorbiaceae	Croton hieronymii	Velande, Velame do campo	leaves	tea	anytime
Rhamnaceae	Zizyphus joazeiro	Juazeiro	buds	tea: 3 chunks of salt	anytime

1.4 SWOLLEN ABDOMEN

Plant nomenclature			Forms of use		
Scientific		*Folk*			
Family	*Species*	*Port./Kariri*	*Parts*	*Preparation*	*Dosage/ Condition*
Sapotaceae	Brumelia sertorum	Quixabeira	inner wood	tea	n times daily

2. INTESTINES (*intistino*): conditions are:

DIARRHOEA (*intistino solto*) – involves frequent bowel movements, loose stools, different causations, also known as '*abaixar muito*' (to squat a lot). *Causes*: (A.) Internal 'heat' (*quentura por dentro*), (B.) stomach problems, (C.) tootache, (D.) dysentery, and (E.) paediatric.

Plant nomenclature			Forms of use		
Scientific		Folk			
Family	Species	Port./Kariri	Parts	Preparation	Dosage/ Condition
Burseraceae	Bursera leptophlocos	Emburana de caboclo, de espinho	bark	infusion in cold water	sips n times daily (A.)
Selaginellaceae	Selaginella convulata	Girico	whole	infusion in hot water	sips n times daily (E.)
Asteraceae	Grangea prostrata	Macela	flowers	infusion in cold water	sips n times daily (B.)
Scrophulariaceae	Mollugo verticellata	Vassourinha de botão	roots	tea, mix with Ipeca	many times daily (C.)
Anacardiaceae	Spondias lutea	Cajazeira	bark	tea	3 times daily (D.)

2.2 CONSTIPATION (*Intistino preso, constipação*) – involves rare bowel movements, with hard stools (*Caga duro*), different causes: (A.) intestinal 'cold,' (B.) stomach problems, (C.) children's illnesses, (D.) sore throat (as a result rather than a cause). Most medicines are laxatives (*purgantes*) that may also be used for influenza, sore throats, fevers, associated with constipation.

Plant nomenclature				Forms of use	
Scientific		*Folk*			
Family	*Species*	*Port./Kariri*	*Parts*	*Preparation*	*Dosage/ Condition*
Convolvulaceae	Ipomoea altissima	Batata de purga	roots	infusion in cold water	1 cup daily (A.)
	Convolvulus operculatus	Jalapinha	tuber	milky extract	with diet no meat + manioc (A.)
Cyperaceae	Kyllinga odorata	Capim Santo	leaves	tea, no sugar	1 cup in morning (B.)
Aristolochiaceae	Aristolochia odore	Jarrinha	roots	tea	n times
Cactaceae	Cereus sp.	Mandacuru (*)	stem	skin off soak in water	sip once in a while
Caesalpinaceae	Tamarindus indica	Tamarineira	leaves	3 buds in tea	n times (D.)
Violaceae	Hybanthus Ipecacuanha	Ipeca, Papaconha	roots	tea + sugar	1 spoon, 3 × daily (C.)

(*) This succulent is used to quench thirst during droughts.

2.3 INTESTINAL HAEMORRHAGE (*sangue no intistino*): blood in stools (*fezes com sangue*) due to intestinal bleeding.

Plant nomenclature				Forms of Use	
Scientific		*Folk*			
Family	*Species*	*Port./Kariri*	*Parts*	*Preparation*	*Dosage/ Condition*
Amaranthaceae	Amaranthus hybridus	Bredo de espinho	roots	infusion	1 cup daily

2.4 HAEMORRHOIDS (*emorroida*)

Plant nomenclature			Forms of use		
Scientific		Folk			
Family	Species	Port./Kariri	Parts	Preparation	Dosage/ Condition
Scrophulariaceae	Mollugo verticellata	Vassourinha de botão	roots	tea	n times daily

2.5 INTESTINAL PROBLEMS IN GENERAL: (A.) Worms (*vermes*): antihelmintic.

Plant nomenclature			Forms of use		
Scientific		Folk			
Family	Species	Port./Kariri	Parts	Preparation	Dosage/ Condition
Caryophilliaceae	Dianthus caryophyllus	Cravo	flowers leaves	tea and strain	1 warm cup once
Chenopodiaceae	Chenopodium ambrosiodes	Santa-Maria, Mastruz	leaves	tea	(A.)
Cucurbitaceae	Cucurbita sp.	Girmum de caboclo, abobora	seeds	ground, in milk	1 cup for 3 days (A.)
Fabaceae	Dalbergia sp.	Flor de catingueira	flowers	tea of 3	n times

3. FEMALE PROBLEMS
3.1 MENSTRUATION (*REGRA, DESMANTELO*):
MENSTRUAL HAEMORRHAGE (*emorragia*): excessive bleeding, associated with 'thick blood' and 'internal heat,' or a miscarriage, accompanied by cramps.

Plant nomenclature			Forms of use		
Scientific		*Folk*			
Family	*Species*	*Port./Kariri*	*Parts*	*Preparation*	*Dosage/ Condition*
Lamiaceae	Rosmarinus officinalis	Alecrim de vaqueiro	leaves	soaked in water	3 days afterward
	Lavandula spica	Alfazema, Lavanda	whole plant	sitting baths/ infusion	during menses
Malvaceae	Hibiscus sp.	Algodão preto Endjui	roots	tea	for afterbirth
Anacardiaceae	Schinus sp.	Aroeira	bark	bath 'joins the flesh'	1 a day: 1st cycle afterbirth
Fabaceae	Torrensia acreana	Imburana de cheiro	bark	tea	n times
Solanaceae	Brunfelsia hopeana	Manacá/ To-atchuá	bark	soak in 'wine'	n times
Caesalpinaceae	Caesalpinia ferrea	Pau-ferro/ Akran to-tuá	bark	soak in 'wine'	n times
Verbenaceae	Lippia oregannides	Pissarra	leaves	tea	1 cup on the hour, $\frac{1}{2}$ cup 20 min. later

AMENORRHEA (*desmantelada/desregrada*): weak or no menstrual flow, mostly due to 'weak' or 'thin blood,' could also be pregnancy.

Plant nomenclature			Forms of use		
Scientific		Folk			
Family	Species	Port./Kariri	Parts	Preparation	Dosage/Condition
Caesalpinaceae	Cassia fistula	Canafista, canafistula	pods	soak in water, drain & add sugar	n times
Selaginellaceae	Selaginella convulata	Girico	whole	tea mixed with (*) 'tucuman'	n times until it starts
Fabaceae	Tephrosia sp.	Marizeira	bark	tea	3 times daily
Violaceae	Hybanthus ipecacuanha	Papaconha	roots	tea	n times
Euphorbiaceae	Phyllantus niruri	Quebra-pedra	roots	tea	n times

(*) 'tucuman' is the black charcoal that impregnates the kitchen wall above the wood stove.

MENSTRUAL PROBLEMS in general: (*quentura por dentro*)

Plant nomenclature			Forms of use		
Scientific		Folk			
Family	Species	port./Kariri	Parts	Preparation	Dosage/Condition
Asteraceae	Artemisia absinthium	Losna	leaves	tea, drain, mix with 'wine'	sip many times
Nyctaginaceae	Boerhavia diffusa	Pega-pinto	roots	soak overnight in water	3 baths in river before drinking

3.2 VAGINAL PROBLEMS (*vagina irritada*): (A.) discharge, (B.) itching.

Plant nomenclature				Forms of use	
Scientific		*Folk*			
Family	*Species*	*Port./Kariri*	*Parts*	*Preparation*	*Dosage/ Condition*
Asteraceae	Acanthos- permum hispidum	Federação, Dois irmãos	leaves flowers	sitting bath	once daily, (B.)
Convolvulaceae	Ipomoea altissima	Batata de purga	roots	soaked in water for laxative	1 spoon daily, (A.)

3.3 FERTILITY AND CHILDBIRTH

ABORTION (*aborto*): (A.) to arrest an abortion, whether spontaneous or induced, or a uterine haemorrhage, (B.) to induce an abortion, when menses stopped and pregnancy is sure.

Plant nomenclature				Forms of use	
Scientific		*Folk*			
Family	*Species*	*Port./Kariri*	*Parts*	*Preparation*	*Dosage/ Condition*
Anacardiaceae	Anacardium occidentalis	Caju	nut	ground, soaked in warm water	1 cup frequently (A.)
Caryophilliaceae	Diantus caryophyllus	Cravo	flower	boil in water, drain	1 warm cup (A.)
Chenopodiaceae	Chenopodium ambrosioides	Mastruz/ Prekuá	leaves	tea with sugar	many times (B.)
Cucurbitaceae	Momordica charantia	Melão de São Caetano	leaves	tea	(B.)
/	/	Embú/Oboé	bark	soak in water, drained	prevents abortion
Lamiaceae	Mentha sp.	Segurelha, Hortela da folha miúda	leaves juice	crush 6 extract	many cups (B.)

INFERTILITY (*frio na matriz*): medicines to cure female infertility, spoken of as 'cold in the uterus.'

Plant nomenclature			Forms of use		
Scientific		*Folk*			
Family	*Species*	*Port./Kariri*	*Parts*	*Preparation*	*Dosage/ Condition*
Chenopodiaceae	Chenopodium ambrosiodes	Mastruz/ Prekuá	leaves	tea without sugar	many times

CONTRACEPTIVE (*evitar filho*): 'to avoid children.'

Plant nomenclature			Forms of use		
Scientific		*Folk*			
Family	*Species*	*Port./Kariri*	*Parts*	*Preparation*	*Dosage/ Contition*
Rubiaceae	Genipa americana	Genipapo Kassatinga	leaves	5 leaves boiled with water	1 cup before sex
/	/	Kassatinga	leaves	bath with Genipapo leaves	12 baths: 3 Weds. 3 Thurs. 3 Friday 3 Saturday

CHILDBIRTH (*parto*): medicines used: (A): during labour, to recover strength, (B.) to help with expulsion of placenta, (C.) to stop a haemorrhage, (D.) afterwards, to suture the perinium ('*juntar as carnes*') usually one month after delivery.

Plant nomenclature			Forms of use		
Scientific		*Folk*			
Family	*Species*	*Port./Kariri*	*Parts*	*Preparation*	*Dosage/ Condition*
Cucurbitaceae	Citrullus vulgaris	Melancia/ Behedzí	seeds	tea	drink n times (A.)
	Cucurbita sp.	Girimum de caboclo	seeds	crush, make a mush	massage on belly (B./C.)
Malvaceae	Sida cordifolis	Malva-branca	leaves	bath	1 month after (D.)
Anacardiaceae	Schinus sp.	Aroeira	bark	bath	right after

3.4 MENOPAUSE: woman is '*quente por dentro*': 'hot inside' and needs to 'cool down' ('*ficar fria*').

Plant nomenclature			Forms of use		
Scientific		Folk			
Family	Species	Port./Kariri	Parts	Preparation	Dosage/ Condition
Nyctaginaceae	Boerhavia diffusa	Pega-pinto	roots	powder soaked in wine	as needed

4. ASTHMA (*asma*): best known as '*cansaço*' (tiredness), whenever it is not only difficult to breathe, but there is buzzing in the chest.

Plant nomenclature			Forms of use		
Scientific		Folk			
Family	Species	Port./Kariri	Parts	Preparation	Dosage/ Condition
Rubiaceae	Rondeletia sp.	Anjeriqueira, veludo	fruit	tea	many times
Caryophylliaceae	Diantus caryophyllus	cravo roxo	flower	infusion in cold water	sip once in a while
Lamiaceae	Mentha piperita	Hortelã da folha miúda	leaves	tea	
Boraginaceae	Cordia curassavica	Pau-cachorro Moleque duro	yellow inner bark	toast, make a lambedor	3 to 4 times daily
Lamiaceae	Mentha sp.	Segurelha, H. folha grande	leaves	'mel'	1 spoon n times
Solanaceae	Datura fausterosa	Trombeta, trombetinha	leaves	cigarette	regularly

5. COLDS: (A.) (*resfriadu*) when there is no fever, but symptoms are headache, general indisposition, sneezing, catarrh, runny nose, and is caused by a change in weather, the house being 'draughty' or the person is in the water for too long. (B.) (*Greepe*) involves fever, besides the other symptoms and is caused by having 'thin blood,' (slightly the same thing as being malnourished).

Plant nomenclature			Forms of use		
Scientific		Folk			
Family	Species	Port./Kariri	Parts	Preparation	Dosage/ Condition
Asteraceae	Bacharis macrodonta/ calvenses	Alecrim de vaqueiro, mato	leaves	tea	greepe
Lamiaceae	Rosmarinus officinalis	Alecrim de caco/sodô- akraô	leaves, stems, roots	tea, but separate leaves	greepe
	Ocymum incanescens	Alfavaca-de- vaqueiro	leaves, roots	infusion	greepe
Mimosaceae	Piptadenia macrocarpa	Angico-do- campo	bark	infusion	with chest spasms
/	/	Bonomi	bark	powder, toast for bath	1 bath daily
Verbenaceae	Lantana micrantha	Chumbinho/ Kamará	flowers	tea	3 cups for colds
	Lantana canescans	Cedreira/Totu- shuá	leaves	tea	3 cups for colds
Lamiaceae	Melissa officinalis	Cedreira/Totu- shuá	leaves	tea	3 cups for colds
	Leonotia nepethifolis	Cordão de frade, rabo de gato	leaves	squash, drain juice	1 cup in the morning, and at night
Fabaceae	Rhyncosia sp.	feijão brabo/ Guinhí	leaves	tea	greepe
Liliaceae	Smilax japicanga	Japicanga	roots, leaves	pounded to make a tonic	1 spoonful to prevent colds
Solanaceae	Solanum paniculatum	Jurubeba	fruit	raw	colds and fevers
Rhamnaceae	Zizyphus joazeiro (*)	Juazeiro	bark	powder, soak in water (*)	1 cup in the morning if coughing

Capparida-ceae	Cleome gynandra	Mussambê	flower, leaves	bath	1 daily for colds
Caesalpi-naceae	Caesalpinia ferrea	Pau-ferro/ Akranto-tuá	bark	scrape, soak in water: lambedor	tonic to prevent colds & thin blood
Rubiaceae	Bathysa australis	Quina-quina/ Manussí	bark	bark for tea, add wood if fever	colds and fevers
Crassula	Kalanchoe brailiensis	Saião	leaves	crush for juice, mix raw egg	cold
Lamiaceae	Hyptis pectinata	Sambacaitá	leaves	mix with roots of Mussambé: mel	n spoons for colds

6. THROAT: problems with the throat (*garganta*) include: (A.) sore throat (*dor de garganta*), (B.) hoarseness (*roquidão*), (C.) cough (*tossi*), and (D.) whooping cough (*crupi*).

Plant nomenclature				Forms of use	
Scientific		*Folk*			
Family	*Species*	*Port./Kariri*	*Parts*	*Preparation*	*Dosage/ Condition*
Mimosaceae	Piptadenia macrocarpa	Angico-do-campo	bark	infusion	for (B.)
Liliaceae	Allium sp.	cebola braba	bulb	cut in 4, take $\frac{1}{4}$, add sugar	children's *crupe*
Solanaceae	Solanum paniculatum	jurubeba	fruit	raw	for (A.)
Rhamnaceae	Ziziphus joazeiro	Juazeiro	bark	powder, soak, etc (*)	for (B./C.) 1 cup in the morning

(*) The Juazeiro tree is considered a 'strong and powerful' tree, also 'sacred' for the Fulnio. A medicine made of it has to be ritually correct: the powder of the bark is soaked in water, then the water is whipped, when it foams ('*espumar*'), the foam is scooped away, then whipped again, so that 9 foams are taken off. Afterwards, the liquid is put on the house's roof at night to '*serenar*' (exposed to the night's air) and taken the next morning.

7. CHEST (*peitu*): (A.) pneumonia, (B.) bronchitis, (C.) tuberculosis, (D.) congestion, and (E.) 'weak chest' or 'weak lungs' (*peitu fraco*).

Plant nomenclature			Forms of use		
Scientific		*Folk*			
Family	*Species*	*Port./Kariri*	*Parts*	*Preparation*	*Dosage/ Condition*
Mimosaceae	Piptadenia sp.	Angico	bark	soak in cold water	(A.)
	Piptadenia macrocarpa	Angico-do-campo	bark	infusion	(B.)
/	/	Brandão/ aleftu	roots	soaked in 'wine'	(D.)
/	/	Camarão	leaves bark	infusion, add sugar/honey	(D.)
Caesalpi-naceae	Cassia fistula	Canafista	pea pods	mashed and ground	eat for (E.)
Leguminosae	Parkinsonia aculeata	Espinheiro turco/Akran	pea pods	ground, toast make like coffee	drink regularly for (A.)
Solanaceae	Solanum paniculatum	Jurubeba	roots	crush, soak in water, add sugar, boil, bury for 3 days in pot	3 spoons daily for any lung condition
			fruit	crush, soak in water, add sugar, boil	tuber-culosis
Chenopodi-aceae	Chenopodium ambrosiodes	Mastruz Prekuá	leaves	crush, extract juice, add to milk	"
Violaceae	Hybanthus ipecacuanha	Papaconha 'mansa'	roots leaves	tea	any lung condition
Rubiaceae	Bathysa australis	Quina-quina/ Manussí	wood	syrup	regularly for (C.)

8. FEVER (*febri*): a condition in which the temperature of the outside of the body is above normal, having many causes. When the cause is specifically known, the medication is registered in the appropriate section, like a fever due to teething or a cold. However, a fever that appears suddenly and whose cause is not yet known will be treated by the following medicines:

Plant nomenclature				Forms of use	
Scientific		*Folk*			
Family	*Species*	*Port./Kariri*	*Parts*	*Preparation*	*Dosage/ Condition*
Lamiaceae	Rosmarinus officinalis	Alecrim de caco	leaves	tea	
	Rosmarinus officinalis	Alecrim de caco	stems + roots	boil for a longer time	
Acanthaceae	Ruellia hypercoides	Alecrim de verão/Aflô	flowers, leaves	secret use	secret
Lamiaceae	Ocymum incanescens	Alfavaca-vaqueiro	roots, leaves	infusion	
	Ocymum minimum	Manjericão	leaves flowers	warm bath	once daily
	Leonotis nepethifolis	Cordão de frade, rabo gato	leaves	squash raw leaves, drain juice	twice: in the morning and at night
Malvaceae	Hibiscus sp.	Algodão preto	leaves	infusion	
Cyperaceae	Kyllinga odorata	Capim-santo, cheiro	leaves	unsweetened tea	
Zingiberaceae	Enealmia brasiliensis	Colonia, levante	leaves	tea	
Fabaceae	Rhyncosia sp.	Feijão brabo Guinhí	leaves	squashed, boiled for tea	
Selaginel-laceae	Selaginela convulata	Girico	whole herb	dry & soak in water, tea	children's fever
Pedaliaceae	Sesamum indicum	Gergelim brabo/Kossaí	leaves	tea	5 leaves for adults, 3 for children
Asteraceae	Grangea prostrata	Macela	flowers	tea or infusion	drink it bitter
Solanaceae	Brunfelsia hopeana	Manacá/Tô-atchuá	bark	soak in wine garrafada	
Cactaceae	Cereus sp.	Mandacaru	stems	tea	

Leguminosae	Senna uniflora S. obtusifolia	Matapasto	leaves	3 leaves with Mandacaru for a tea	perspiration after tea
Cucurbitaceae	Citrullus vulgaris	Melancia/ Behedzí	seeds	tea	
Boraginaceae	Cordia curassavica	Pau-cachorro, Moleque-duro	bark wood	lambedor: scrape them, toast, add sugar, boil	3 to 4 times daily
Rubiaceae	Bathysa australis	Quina-quina	wood	tea	
Sapotaceae	Brumelia sertorum	Quixabeira	wood	tea	
Zygophyl-laceae	Kallstremia sp.	Sena	leaves	tea with honey	perspiration

9. WEAKNESS (*fraqueza*): resulting from 'internal heat', and 'hot blood' being thus necessary 'to cool the blood's heat' (*enfriar o calor no sangue*) that can cause diabetes and diarrhoea.

Plant nomenclature				Forms of use	
Scientific		*Folk*			
Family	*Species*	*Port./Kariri*	*Parts*	*Preparation*	*Dosage/ Condition*
Bruseraceae	Brusera leptophlocus	Emburana de caboclo	bark	soak in wine for 3 days	3 times daily for 3 days
Convolvu-laceae	Convolvulus operculatus	Jalapinha	tuber	milky extract	with diet: no meat, no manioc

10. HEART(*coração*): heart conditions in general, also including: (A.) heart failure and (B.) 'to give power to the heart' ('*valorar o coração*) which is the medicine for heart attacks.

Plant nomenclature			Forms of use		
Scientific		*Folk*			
Family	*Species*	*Port./Kariri*	*Parts*	*Preparation*	*Dosage/ Condition*
Solanaceae	Physalis angulata	Camapum	fruit	eaten raw	'courage'
Caryophi- laceae	Dianthus caryophyllus	Cravo branco	flower	infusion in water	sip water regularly
Leguminosae	Parkinsonia aculeata	Espinheiro turco/Akran	beans	grind and toast to make coffee	drink often
Violaceae	Hybanthus ipecacuanha	Papaconha 'braba'	leaves	tea	
Aristolo- chiaceae	Aristolochia gigantea	Papo de peru	roots	tea	

Glossary

Agreste – a semi-arid geographic zone of Northeast Brazil, located between the seashore and the interior's *caatinga*, characterized by scant vegetation and rocky soil.

Akra-un – sentence spoken by the Kariri that supposedly means 'I am going', when the shaman calls the people to go to the *Ouricuri* rituals.

Aldeia – village, the social unit established by the conquering Portuguese in the colonization period, now mostly known as a village where indigenous peoples live.

Alheia – alien.

Amansar – to domesticate.

Andar – to walk.

Andança – walking around.

Antipatia – disliking someone.

Aruanda – African city that still belongs to Black culture's point of reference.

Avô – grandfather.

Autussê – magical plant for the Kariri.

Ayahuasca – entheogenic beverage, used by native peoples of the Amazon region with the purpose of 'realizing the divine within'.

Axé – pronounced 'ashë', this is a word of African origin, signifying the power that resides within an object or person, a principle of divine origin that ideally has to be 'built up' in order to function.

Badzé – the ancient name for the spirit of the tobacco plant, considered to be the Father figure of a divine trinity; perhaps the word '*pajé*' comes from it.

Bambu – generic name for plants from the Graminae family, mainly the species *Bambusa arundinacea*.

Bandeira – a military expedition organized by Southerners during colonial times in Brazil, destined to enslave Indians and to discover mines of precious stones and gold, they usually departed from the state of São Paulo.

Bandeirantes – the individuals who were participants of a Bandeira.

Bizamu, Bizamye – one of the spiritual beings, or 'enchantments', that presided over the rituals of the ancestors of the native peoples who now form the Kariri; one of the 'three enchantments'.

Branco – White, a term for 'White people', that can have a derogatory connotation.

Brincadeira – playfulness, games, in the context here it means when a dance or a ritual is not being taken seriously, and in a religious way, but as for having fun.

Bruxa, bruxo – pronounced as 'brusha/o,' meaning witch.

Bruxaria – the 'x' prounced with the sound of 'sh', meaning witchcraft.

Caá – from the Tupi language, it means leaf.

Caatinga – region and type of woods natural to the Brazilian Northeastern interior, made up of trees that lose their leaves during the long dry season, rich in Cactaceae and Bromeliaceae.

Cabaça – originated from the African language of Kimbundo, it is the fruit of the *cabaceira*, a plant belonging to the Curcubitaceae family.

Cabeça seca – 'dried head', a derogatory term used by the Kariri-Shoko that means the White people.

Caboclo – descendants from indigenous populations, also serving to designate the inhabitants of the Amazon region, whether they are Indians or not.

Caçando – hunting.

Cacique – the usual title for headman in Brazilian indigenous groups, in fact given by the white colonizers.

Caiçara – farm at the river São Francisco, it used to belong to the Shoko tribe at the beginning of the century, to whom it has just been returned in 1995.

Caminhante – a walker, a person who 'walks' in their dreams, as if enchanted.

Candomblé – religious cult of African derivation, celebrated during colonial times by Black slaves secretly, now a major popular cult in Brazil.

Capanga, capangueiro – armed men who are hired by landowners to be a type of bodyguard and henchmen, also meaning followers who are protectors, as in 'capangueiro of *Jurema*'.

Capitania – political unit of land that was given to nobles by the Portuguese crown during the establishing of the Portuguese colony in Brazil.

Capitão – the nobleman who received a 'capitania', thereafter any powerful landowner, also a title for a military position.

Capuchinho – a religious order of the Catholic Church, known as such because its priests and monks wear a hood – 'capucho' – over their heads.

Carnaval – the Brazilian masquerade festival, of pagan origin, that takes place before Lent, related to other festivities known as Mardi Gras.

Casa – house, home, property, dwelling.

Casa do Indio - FUNAI maintains several Indian Houses in key cities of Brazil, like Brasília, Rio de Janeiro and São Paulo. Such places serve as a sort of 'half-way-house' and recovery place for the infirm, as a hostel for Indians in the city but also as a 'dumping ground' for Indians who really have no way to support themselves in the traditional economy, such as the retarded, the paraplegic and those with terminal diseases.

Catimbó, Catimbau – religious practices that used witchcraft, known as 'black magic' and related to the lower forms of Spiritism as a cult.

Ceocozes – a Brazilian native tribe, possibly ancestors to the modern Shoko.

Chefe de Posto – chief of a FUNAI station, the federal employee responsible for the well-being and protection of indigenous villages under federal jurisdiction in Brazil.

Ciencia – science.

CIMI – stands for Conselho Missionário Indigenista (Missionary Indigenist Council), a modern Catholic mission that takes action in indigenous affairs.

Colégio – a city of Alagoas, at the river São Francisco, also meaning school.

Coité – a bowl made of the hard shell of a fruit also known as coité.

Coivara – word of Tupi origin, designates the wood pile used to set a plot of wood afire and ready for the planting. It also designates the practice of preparing the land for planting by setting fire to a bound area.

Cuia – a bowl usually made of a coconut shell.

Encantado – a spiritual being, an 'enchanted' person or entity.

Encanto/encantamento – enchantment, the result of an action by a spiritual being with powers to bewitch or to interfere in the natural world.

Espinhela caída – a folk illness, or injury, that has to be cured by a folk healer who massages the patient's shoulders and back, straightening up the spine.

Feira – a market place, usually out in the open in the middle of a street, it also refers to salary and to the food one bought.

Festa – feast, party.

Filha/o – daughter, son.

Floresta – forest, woods.

Folha – leaf.

Força – strength, power.

Galega – the original term indicates a person born in Galícia, in the Iberian Península, but in the Northeast of Brazil it means a blond or very light-skinned person.

Hortelã da folha miúda – a plant belonging to the mint family, perhaps *Mentha piperina Linn.*

Iate – the language spoken by some of the Northeastern tribes, supposedly the language of the Kariri-Shoko as well.

Indio – Indian, a term applied by Columbus to mean the inhabitants of the territories in the so-called New World.

Jaciobá – in Tupi it means 'mirror of the moon', an indigenous village at the edge of the São Francisco river in the 19th century.

Junta das Missoes – Union of Missions, an institution of the Catholic Church in charge of all the missions in the so-called New World.

Juremado – to have been affected by the Jurema wine, thus becoming a 'child of Jurema'.

Lagoa – lagoon, lake, wet-rice field.

Legítimo – legitimate.

Lei – law.

Lei indígena – indigenous law.

Lei da Terra – Law of the Land, a law that regulated land ownership in the Brazilian territory.

Lírio – lily.

Loucura – craziness.

Manusi – the Kariri-Shoko say it means 'wind' but it is also the name of a plant.

Mata – woods, forest.

Mata do agreste – woods of the dry lands known as 'agreste'.

Mateiro – person who is very familiar with the woods and who gathers botanical species, whether for food or medicine.

Médico – medical doctor, a folk healer as well.

Medicina – medicine.

Meia – one half, it is a type of land tenancy in which the tenants – *meeiros* – plant and harvest the fields, giving half of the harvest to the land owner.

Mesa – table, it also a religious practice during which a healer performs magical healing through divinations and incantations directed to the icons set at a table or altar.

Mestiço – a person of 'mixed blood', whose parents are of different racial types.

Muinane – an indigenous tribe in Colombia.

Mulato – a person descended from Black and White parents.

Nordeste – Northeast.

Nordestino – Northeastern, a person born in the Northeast.

Niteroi – a hamlet in the state of Sergipe, at the margin of the São Francisco river, right across from Pão-de-Açúcar in Alagoas. There is a major city in the state of Rio de Janeiro with the same name.

Ouricuri – a palm tree (*Cocos coronata* Linn.), the religious ceremony that is still performed nowadays by the Kariri-Shoko.

Olho grande, olho mau – evil eye, a bad influence a person can cast over another for either desiring something from the other or simply wishing him or her bad luck.

Pão-de-Açúcar – a city in the state of Alagoas, at the edge of the São Francisco river, where the Shoko go for their commercial dealings.

Padre – priest.

Paciencia – patience.

Pajé – shaman, indigenous priest and healer.

Palmares – a village founded by run-away Black slaves in the 19th century.

Paricá – a snuff prepared from the resin of several species of Virola, family of Myristicaceae, widely used by some Amazonian tribes.

Passarinho – little bird.

Pau-ferro – a large tree, *Cesalpinian ferrea* Linn., from which a beverage can be made from the bark, rich in iron (*ferro*).

Pé-de-pau – trees in general.

Poditan, Poditão, Politão – one of the main deities of local native tribes' pantheon, mainly the Kariri.

Posse – the piece of arable land that a tenant (*posseiro*) rents and in return pays a contracted part of the harvest, usually half of the land production.

Quetalique – in indigenous language it means 'let us go'.

Quilombo – the socially organized agglomeration of run-away Black slaves in the colonial times.

Rainha do terreiro – the woman who presided over the secret ceremonies of the Indians.

Redução – reduction, the place where Indians were brought to in order to be 'pacified' and evangelized by Catholic missionaries.

Remédio – remedy, prescription medicine.

Reza – prayer, the healing procedure performed by a *rezadeira*, a woman healer.

Segredo – secret.

Sementeira – the model farm that the Kariri-Shoko invaded to claim as their land, a place where seeds are allowed to grow before being transplanted to the fields.

Senhor/senhora – sir/madam, Mr/Mrs, also the formal way to address an older person instead of the more familiar, informal *você* (you).

Sergipe – a state of Northeast Brazil.

Sergipano – a person born in the state of Sergipe.

Sertão – the interior, the remote rural areas.

Sertanejo – the person who inhabits the *sertão*, with a rather characteristic way of life, a moody, quiet person.

Sonsé – the main deity of the Kariri-Shoko.

Tarrafa, tarrafo – a handmade fishnet.

Toré – the traditional songs, accompanied by dance, of the Northeastern native peoples.

Trabalho – work, also the healing work.

Tribo – tribe.

Tronco – trunk, also refers to the ancestors and to a clan.

Tupã – one of the many nature deities of past indigenous tribes, that the missionaries popularized as being God for the Indians.

Tupi – one of the main languages and linguistic groups of native Brazilians.

Tupinambá – a Brazilian tribe, a spiritual entity belonging to the religious folklore of spiritualist cults.

Umbanda – a religious cult, of African origin, that has been mixed with elements of Catholic beliefs.

Umbandista – a person who follows the beliefs and the traditions of Umbanda.

Zona da Mata – vegetation that characterizes the semi-arid region known as *Agreste*, a transition zone between the seashore and the northern tropical forests.

Bibliography

Aamodt, A.M. (1978) 'The Care Component in a Health and Healing System' in E. Bauwens (ed.), *The Anthropology of Health*, C.V. Mosby, St. Louis, pp. 37–45.

Adam, L. (1897) *Materieux pour servir a l'etablissement d'une grammaire comparée des dialects de la famille Kariri*, J. Maisonneuve, Paris.

Alcorn, J.B. (1984) *Huastec Mayan Ethnobotany*, Austin: University of Texas Press.

Anderson, E. (1967) *Plants, Man and Life* Berkeley: University of California Press.

Antunes, C. (1973) *Wakona-Kariri-Xucuru: Aspectos Socio-Antropológicos*, Imprensa Universitária, Maceió.

Artaud, A. (1976) *The Peyote Dance*, New York: Farrar, Straus & Giroux.

Attias, I.L. (1979) *Medicina Tradicional y Espiritismo*, México: INAR.

Ayensu, E.S. (1981) 'A Worldwide Role for the Healing Powers of Plants, *Smithsonian*, Vol. 12, 8, pp. 86–97.

Bandeira, M.L. (1972) *Os Kariris de Mirandela: um Grupo Indígena Integrado*, Bahia: Universidade Federal da Bahia, Salvador.

Barth, F. (ed.) (1969) *Ethnic Groups and Boundaries: the Social Organization of Culture Differences*, Boston: Little Brown.

Barthes, R. (1964) *Elementos de Semiologia*, São Paulo: Cultrix.

Bartolomé, M.A. and Robinson, S.S. (1984) 'Indigenismo, dialética y conciencia étnica,' *Los Indios y la Antropologia en América Latina*, Junqueira, C. (ed.), Argentina: Busequeda-Yuchan, Buenos Aires.

Basson, K.H. & Selby, H.A. (ed.), (1976) *Meaning in Anthropology*, Albuquerque: University of New Mexico Press.

Bastide, R. (1955) 'O segredo das hervas', *Anhembi*, São Paulo, Vol. 18, pp. 333–4.

Bastide, R. (1971) *As Religiões Africanas no Brasil* 2 vols., São Paulo: Livraria Pioneira Editora.

Bauwens, E. (1978) *The Anthropology of Health*, St. Louis: C.V. Mosby.

Berlin, B. (1992) *Ethnobiological Classification: Principles of Categorization of Plants and Animals in Traditional Societies*, Princeton: Princeton University Press.

Berlin, B., Breedlove, D.E., and Raven, P.H. (1974) *The Principles of Tzeltal Plant Classification*, New York: Academic Press.

Bernardi, B. (1980) 'An anthropological approach: the problem of plants in traditional medicine,' *Journal of Ethnopharmacology*, vol. 2, pp. 95–98.

Bourdieu, P. (1993) *Outline of a Theory of Practice*, Cambridge: Cambridge University Press.

Branner, J.C. (1973) 'Os Carijós de Águas Bellas,' *Revista do Instituto Histórico e Geográfico do Brasil*, Rio de Janeiro, Vol. 94, 148, pp. 363–5.

Brow, J. (1981) 'Class Formation and Ideological Practice: a Case from Sri Lanka,' *Journal of Asian Studies*, Vol. 4, pp. 703–718.

Bryce-Laporte, R.S. (1970) 'Crisis, Contraculture and Religion among Indians in the Panama Canal Zone,' *Afro-American Anthropology*, Witten, N.E. and Szwed, J.F. (ed.), New York: The Free Press.

Castañeda, C. (1968) *The Teachings of Don Juan: A Yaqui Way of Knowledge*, New York: Ballantine.

Chagnon, N. (1968) *Yanomami: the Fierce People*, New York: Holt, Rinehart & Winston.

Cleaver, H. (1979) *Reading Capital Politically*, Austin, Texas: University of Texas Press.

Conceição, M. (1982) *As Plantas Medicinais no Ano 2000*, São Paulo: Tao Editora.

Croom Jr., E.M. (1983) 'Documenting and Evaluating Herbal Remedies,' *Economic Botany*, Vol. 37, no 1, pp. 133–157.

Cruz, G.L. (1982) *Dicionário das Plantas Úteis do Brasil*, Rio de Janeiro: Civilização Brasileira.

da Mota, C.N. (1987) 'As Jurema told us: Kariri-Shoko and Shoko Mode of Utilization of Medicinal Plants in the Context of Modern Northeast Brazil,' Michigan: Ph.D. Dissertation, University Microfilms, Ann Arbor.

da Mota, C.N. (1990) 'Jurema and Ayahuasca: Dreams to Live By,' *Ethnobiology: Implications and Applications*, Posey, D.A. and Overall, W. (es.), Museu Paraense Emílio Goeldi, Belém, Pará, Vol. 2, Part F, pp. 181–190.

da Mota, C.N. and de Barros, J.F.P. (1990) 'Jurema: Black-indigenous Drama and Representations,' *Ethnobiology: Implications and Applications*, Posey, D.A. and Overall, W. (eds.), Museu Paraense Emílio Goeldi, Belém, Pará, Vol. 2, Part F, 1990, pp. 171–180.

Dantas, B.G. (1973) *Missão Indígena no Geru*, Centro de Educação e Ciências Humanas, Universidade Federal de Sergipe, Aracaju, Sergipe.

Dantas, B. and Dallari, D. (1980) *Terra dos Indios Xocó*. São Paulo: Comissão Pró-India.

de Almeida, H. (1979) 'Confederação dos Cariris ou Guerra dos Bárbaros,' *Revista Instituo Histórico e Geográfico Brasileiro*, Rio de Janeiro, 316.

de Barros, J.F.P. and da Mota, C.N. (1995) 'Espaço e tempo: o sagrado e o profano nos candomblés Keto e entre os índios Kariri-Shoko,' *América Latina e Caribe: Desafios do Século XXI*, Lemos, M.T.T.B. and de Barros, J.F.P.. (orgs.), PROEAL, Rio de Janeiro: Unversidade do Estado do Rio de Janeiro, pp. 71–90.

de Oliveira, R.C. (1983) *Enigmas e soluções: exercícios de etnologia e de crítica*. Rio de Janeiro: Tempo Brasileiro.

dos Santos, J.E. (1976) *Os Nagô e a Morte*, Petrópolis: Vozes.

Douglas, M.T. (1966) *Purity and Danger: an Analysis of Concepts of Pollution and Taboo*. New York: Praeger.

Eliade, M. (1964) *Shamanism: archaic techniques of ecstasy*. New Jersey: Princeton University Press, Princeton.

Eliade, M. (1973) *Lo sagrado y lo profano*. Madrid: Ediciones Guadarrma.

Elisabetsky, E. (1986) 'Etnofarmacologia de algumas tribos brasileiras.' *Suma Etnológica Brasileira: Etnobiologia*, Ribeiro, D. and Ribeiro, B.G. (ed.), Vol. 1, FINEP/ Vozes, Rio de Janeiro, pp. 135–146.

Estrada, A. (1981) *Maria Sabina, her Life and Chants*. Santa Barbara, California: Ross-Erikson.

Fabian, J. (1981) *Time and the Other: how Anthropology Makes its Object*. New York: Columbia University Press.

Farnsworth, N.R. and Morris, R.W. (1976) 'Higher plants: the sleeping giant of drug development.' *American Journal of Pharmacy*.

Faulhaber, P. (1987) *O navio encantado: etnia e alianças em Tefé*. Belém, Pará: Museu Paraense Emilio Goeldi.

Ferrari, A.T. (1957) *Os Kariri: crepúsculo de um povo sem história* São Paulo: Sociologia 3, São Paulo.

Figueiredo, A. (1981) *Enforcados: o Indio em Sergipe*. Rio de Janeiro: Paz e Terra.

Foley, D. and Mota, C. (1977) *From Peones to Políticos: ethnic relations in a South Texas town, 1900–1977*. Austin, Texas: University of Texas Press.

Ford, R.I. (ed.) *The nature and status of ethnobotany*. Museum of Anthropology, University of Michigan, Ann Arbor, Vol. 67.

Forsberg, F.R. (1960) 'Plant Collecting as an Anthropological Field Method.' *Separata, El Palácio*, México.

Fry, P. and Vogt, C. (1985) 'Os mestres da "língua secreta" e o paradoxo do segredo revelado.' *Boletim do Museu Nacional*, Rio de Janeiro, Vol. 51.

Fry, P. and Gnerre, M. (1981) 'Mafambura e Caxapura: na encruzilhada da identidade.' *Dados*, Vol. 24, No 3, Rio de Janeiro, pp. 373–389.

Furst, P.T. (ed.) (1972) *Flesh of the Gods: the Ritual use of Hallucinogens*. New York, Praeger.

Furst, P.T. (1980) *Alucinógenos y Cultura*. México: Fondo de Cultura Economica.

Galvão, E. (1955) *Santos e Visagens: um estudo da vida religiosa em Itá, Amazonas*. São Paulo: Cia. Editora Nacional.

Garcia, R. (1922) 'O grupo Cariri.' *Dicionário Histórico, Geográfico e Etnográfico do Brasil.* Vol. 1, Rio de Janeiro, Brasil, pp. 262–266.

Geertz, C. (1976) 'From the Native's Point of View.' *Meaning in Anthropology.* Basso, K. and Selby, H. (ed.) Albuquerque, New Mexico: University of New Mexico Press.

Geertz, C. (1978) *A Interpretação das Culturas.* Rio de Janeiro, Brasil: Zahar.

Gonzalez, N.S. (1967) 'Health Behavior in Cross-Cultural Perspective: A Guatemalan example', *Human Organization,* Vol. 25, New Haven, Connecticut.

Gramsci, A. (1978) *Selections from political writings (1921–1926): with additional texts by other Italian Communist leaders.* London: Lawrence and Wishart.

Grieve, M. (1982) *A Modern Herbal,* 2 Vols. New York: Dover.

Grimm, W.C. (1968) *Recognizing Flowering Wild Plants.* Harrisburg, Pennsylvania: Stackpole Books.

Grossinger, R. (1982) *Planet Medicine: from Stone Age shamanism to post-industrial healing.* London: Shambhala.

Grunewald, R. (1995) Personal communication, Rio de Janeiro.

Harner, M. (1974) 'The Sound of Rushing Water.' *Native South Americans: ethnology of the least known continent,* Lyon, P. (ed.) Boston, Massachusetts: Little Brown & Co.

Harner, M. (1980) *The Way of the Shaman: a Guide to Power and Healing.* San Francisco, California: Harper & Row.

Harner, M.J. (ed.) (1973) *Hallucinogen and Shamanism.* New York: Oxford University Press.

Harner, M.J. (1989) *Shamanic Pathways.* San Francisco, California: New Dimensions Foundation.

Heath, D.B. (ed.) (1974) *Contemporary Cultures and Societies of Latin America.* New York: Random House.

Hemming, J. (1978) *Red Gold: the Conquest of Brazilian Indians.* Southampton, England: The Camelot Press.

Hill, A.F. (1952) *Economic Botany: a Textbook of Useful Plants and Plant Products.* New York: McGraw-Hill.

Hohenthal Jr., W.D. (1960) 'As tribos indígenas do médio e baixo São Francisco.' *Revista do Museu Paulista,* n.n., XII, pp. 37–71.

Holland, W.R. (1963) 'Mexican-American Medical Beliefs: Science or Magic?' *Arizona Medicine,* May, pp. 89–102.

Hopper, J.H. (ed.) (1967) *Indians of Brazil in the Twentieth Century.* Washington D.C.: Institute for Cross-Cultural Research.

Jones, D.E. (1972) *Sanapia: Comanche medicine woman.* New York: Holt, Rinehart & Winston.

Junqueira, C. and Carvalho, E.A. (eds.) *Los Indios y la Antropologia en America Latina.* Buenos Aires, Argentina: Buesqueda-Yuchan.

Kensinger, K.M. (1974) 'Cashinahua Medicine and Medicine Men.' *Native South Americans: Ethnology of the Least Known Continent.* Lyons, P. (ed.) Boston: Little, Brown, pp. 283–8.

Kertzer, D.I. (1988) *Ritual, Politics and Power.* New Haven, London: Yale University Press.

Kleinman, A. (ed.) (1976) *Medicine in Chinese cultures: comparative studies of health care in Chinese and other societies.* Washington, D.C.: U.S. Government Printing Office.

Kleinman, A. (1980) *Patients and Healers in the Context of Culture: an Exploration of the Borderland Between Anthropology, Medicine and Psychiatry.* Los Angeles, California: University of California Press.

Laclau, E. (1977) *Politics and Ideology in Marxist Theory: Capitalism, Facism and Populism.* London: Verson.

Lainetti, R. and de Brito, N.R.S. (1974) *A cura pelas ervas e plantas medicinais.* Rio de Janeiro, Brasil: Edições de Ouro.

Lamb, F.B. (1974) *Wizard of the Upper Amazon.* Boston, MA: Houghton Mifflin.

Lamb, F.B. (1985) *Rio Tigre and Beyond: the Amazon Jungle Medicine of Manuel Cordoba*. Berkeley, California: North Atlantic Books.

Lambo, J.O. (1977) 'The impact of colonialism on African cultural heritage with special reference to the practice of herbalism in Nigeria.' in P. Singer (ed.) *Traditional Healing*. Owerii, New York, London: Conch Magazine.

Langdon, E.J. (1989) 'Shamanism as the History of Anthropology.' *Shamanism: past and present*. Hoppal, M. and von Sadovsky, O. (ed.) Los Angeles-Budapest: Fullerton, pp. 53–68.

Levi-Strauss, C. (1950) 'The Use of Wild Plants in Tropical South America.' *Handbook of South American Indians*, Steward, J.H. (ed.), Vol. 6, U.S. Government Printing Office, pp. 465–485.

Levi-Strauss, C. (1969) *The Raw and the Cooked*. New York: Harper.

Levi-Strauss, C. (1979) *Myth and Meaning*. New York: Schocken Books.

Lewis, W.H. and Elvin-Lewis, M.P.F. (1977) *Medical Botany: plants affecting man's health*. New York: John Wiley and Sons.

Lyons, P.J. (1974) ed. *Native South Americans*. Boston: Little, Brown.

Mamiani, L.V. (1983) *Arte de grammática da língua Brasílica da Naçam Kiriri*. Rio de Janeiro: Biblioteca Nacional.

Marx, K. (1955) *Capital, edited by F. Engels*. Chicago: Encyclopedia Britannica.

Marx, K. and Engels, F. (1973) *The German Ideology*. New York: International Publishers.

Mata, V.C. (1989) *A Semente da Terra: Identidade e Conquista Territorial por um Grupo Indígena Integrado*. Rio de Janeiro: Museu Nacional, Programa de Pós-Graduação em Antropologia Social.

Matta, R. (1981) *Relativizando: uma introdução a Antropologia Social*. Petrópolis, Rio de Janeiro: Vozes.

Maxwell, N. (1961) *Witch Doctor's Apprentice*. Cambridge and Boston: The Riverside Press.

Meader, R.E. (1978) 'Indios do Nordeste: levantamento sobre os remanescentes tribais do Nordeste Brasileiro' In *Série Linguística*. Brasília, D.F.: Summer Institute of Linguistics.

Mors, W.B. and Rizzini, C.T. (1966) *Useful plants of Brazil*. San Francisco: Holden-Day.

Murdock, G.P. (1980) *Theories of Illness: a World Survey*. Pittsburg: University of Pittsburg Press.

Myerhoff, B. (1978) 'Aging and the aged in other cultures: an anthropological perspective'. Bauwens ed. *The Anthropology of Health*, pp. 151–176.

Naranjo, P. (1983) *Ayahuasca: Etnomedicina y Mitologia*. Quito: Ediciones Libri Mundi.

Negri, A. (1984) *Marx beyond Marx: lessons on the Grundisse*. Boston: Bergin and Garvey Publications.

O'Keefe, D.L. (1982) *Stolen lightning: the social theory of magic*. New York: Vintage Books.

Ott, J. (1994) *Ayahuasca Analogues: Pangaean Entheogens*. Kennewick, WA: Natural Products Co.

Pinto, E. (1935) *Os indigenas do Nordeste*. São Paulo: Biblioteca Pedagógica Brasileira, Brasiliana, Serie V, Vol. XLIV.

Pinto, E. (1956) *Etnologia Brasileira: Fulniô, os últimos Tapuias*. São Paulo: Editora Nacional.

Ribeiro, D. (1977) *Os Indios e a civilização: a integração das populações indígenas no Brasil moderno*. Petrópolis: Vozes.

Royce, A.P. (1982) *Ethnic Identity*. Bloomington, Indiana: Indiana University Press.

Sahlins, M.D. (1968) *Tribesmen*. Englewood Cliffs: Prentice-Hall.

Sangirardi Jr. (1983) *O Indio e as plantas alucinógenas*. Rio de Janeiro: Alhambra.

Saussure, F. (1973) *Curso de Linguística Geral*. São Paulo: Cultrix.

Schultes, R.E. (1960) 'Native Narcotics of the New World.' *The Pharmaceutical Sciences*, Third Lecture Series, Austin: University of Texas, College of Pharmacy, pp. 142–167.

Schultes, R.E. (1963) 'Hallucinogenic Plants of the New World.' *The Harvard Review*, pp. 18–32.

Schultes, R.E. (1976) *Hallucinogenic Plants*. New York: Golden Press.

Schultes, R.E. and Hoffman, A. (1973) *The Botany and Chemistry of Hallucinogens*. Springfield, Illinois: Charles C. Thomas.

Schultes, R.E. and Hoffman, A. (1987) *Plants of the Gods: Origins of Hallucinogenic Use*. New York: Alfred Van Der Marck Editions.

Scott, C.S. (1978) 'Health and healing practices among five ethnic groups in Miami, Florida'. *The Anthropology of Health*. Bauwens (ed.), pp. 61–70.

Singer, P. (ed.) (1977) *Traditional Healing: New Science or New Colonialism?* Conch Magazine, Owerii: New York, London.

Siqueira, B. (1978) *Os Cariris do Nordeste*. Livraria Ed. Cátedra, Rio de Janeiro.

Siskind, J. (1973) *To Hunt in the Morning*. New York: Oxford University Press.

Smith E.C. (ed.) (1973) *Man and his Foods: Studies in Ethnobotany of Nutrition: Contemporary, Primitive and Pre-historic Non-European Diets*, 11th International Botanical Congress, University of Alabama Press.

Snow, L.F. 'The religious component in Southern Folk Medicine'. In Singer (ed.), *Traditional Healing*, pp. 26–51.

Sofowora, A. (1982) *Medical Plants and Traditional Medicine in Africa*. New York: John Wiley.

Spicer, E.H. (1971) 'Persisting cultural systems', *Science* 174, pp. 795–800.

Steiger, Brad (1974) *Medicine Power: the American Indian's Revival of its Spiritual Heritage and its Relevance for Modern Man*. Doubleday, Garden City.

Taussing, M.T. (1980) *The Devil and Commodity Fetishism in South America*. Chapel Hill: University of North Carolina Press.

Taylor, P.E. (1981) *Border Healing Woman*. Austin: University of Texas Press.

Trotter, R.T. and Chavira, J.A. (1981) *Curanderismo: Mexican-American Folk Healing*. Athens: University of Georgia Press.

Trupp, F. (1981) *The Last Indians: South America's cultural heritage*. Austria: Perlinger.

Turnbull, C. (1961) *The Forest People: A Study of the Pygmies of the Congo*. New York: Touchstone.

Turner, V. (1969) *The Ritual Process: Structure and Anti-structure*. Chicago: Aldine.

Turner, V. (1967) *The Forest of Symbols: Aspects of Ndembu Ritual*. Ithaca, New York: Cornell University Press.

Turner, V. (1989) *The Forest of Symbols: aspects of Ndembu Ritual*. Ithaca, New York: Cornell University Press.

Urban, G. (1981) 'The semiotics of tabooed food: the Shokleng case'. *Social Science Information*, SAGE 20, 3, London and Beverly Hills. pp. 475–507

Urban, G. (1985) 'Developments in the situation of Brazilian tribal populations from 1976 to 1982'. *Latin American Research Review*, Vol. 20, 1, pp. 7–25.

Urban, G. and Hendrics, J.W. (1983) 'Signal functions of masking in Amerindian Brazil'. *Semiotica*, 47.

Van der Zee, B. (1982) *Green Pharmacy: A History of Herbal Medicine*. New York: Viking Press.

Wagley, C. (1952) *Race and Class in rural Brazil*. Paris: UNESCO.

Wagley, C. (1977) *Welcome of Tears: the Tapirape Indians of Central Brazil*. New York: Oxford University Press.

Wasson, R.G. (1972) *The Wondrous Mushroom*. New York: McGraw-Hill.

Weil, A. (1972) *The Natural Mind: a new way of looking at drugs and the higher consciousness*. Boston: Houghton Mifflin.

Weil, A. and Rosen, W. (1983) *From Chocolate to Morphine: understanding mind active drugs*. Boston: Houghton Mifflin.

Weinstein, M. (1981) *Positive Magic: occult self help*. Con., B.C., Canada & Custer, Wa: Pheonix Pub.

Westermeyer, J. (1977) 'Collaboration with traditional healers: new colonialism and new

Science'. In Singer (ed.), *Traditional Healing*, Owerii, New York, London: Conch Magazine, pp. 108–122.

Whiting, A.F. (1939) 'Ethnobotany of the Hopi' *Museum of North Arizona*. Bulletin 15, Flagstaff.

Whorf, B. (1956) *Language, thought and reality: selected writings of Benjamin Lee Whorf*. Institute of Technology, Wiley, Chapman and Hall.

Williams, C.H. (1977) 'Utilization of persisting cultural values of Mexican-Americans by Western practioners'. In Singer (ed.), *Traditional Healing*, pp. 108–122.

Williams, R. (1978) *Marxism and Literature*. Oxford: Oxford University Press.

Wittkower, E.D. and Weidman (1967) 'Magic, witchcraft and sorcery in relation to mental health and mental disorder'. In Petrilowitsch, N. and Flegel, H. (eds.), *Social Psychiatry*. Top Problems in Psychiatric Neurology 8, pp. 169–84.

Wyman, L.C. and Harris, S.K. (1941) 'Navajo Indian Medical Ethnobotany'. *University of New Mexico Bulletin*, Vol. 3, 5.

Yanovsky, E. (1936) 'Food plants of the North American Indians'. *USDA*, 237, Washington D.C.: Miscellaneous Publications.

Encyclopedias

Enciclopédia dos Municipios Brasileiros. Instituto Brasileiro de Geografia e Estatística, 1956.

Handbook of South American Indians, 1950.

Newspapers

Boletim Comissão Pró-Índio, São Paulo.

O Globa, Rio de Janeiro.

Correio de Propriá, Propriá, Sergipe.

A Defesa, Propriá, Sergipe.

Jornal de Sergipe.

Gazeta de Sergipe.

O Estado de São Paulo.

Tribuna da Imprensa, Rio de Janeiro.